ABC of Behaviour Change Theories

Susan Michie

Robert West

Rona Campbell

Jamie Brown

Heather Gainforth

Silverback Publishing

Copyright © Susan Michie, Rona Campbell, Jamie Brown, Robert West and Heather Gainforth 2014

The rights of Professor Susan Michie, Professor Rona Campbell, Professor Robert West, Dr Jamie Brown and Dr Heather Gainforth to be identified as the authors of this work have been asserted in accordance with the Copyright, Designs and Patents Act 1988.

This edition first published in Great Britain in 2014 by Silverback Publishing

All rights reserved. Apart from any use permitted under UK copyright law, this publication may only be reproduced, stored or transmitted, in any form, or by any means, with prior permission in writing of the publishers or, in the case of reprographic production, in accordance with the terms of licences issued by the Copyright Licensing Agency.

A CIP catalogue record for this book is available from the British Library.

Trade Paperback ISBN: 978-1-912141-01-2

Every effort has been made to fulfil requirements with regard to reproducing copyright material.

Cover artwork courtesy of paniklondon.com

The author and publisher will be glad to rectify any omissions at the earliest opportunity.

www.silverbackpublishing.org

Endorsements

This book provides an extensive and encyclopaedic compendium of theories of behaviour change - and is a wonderful resource for students, scientists and practitioners working to encourage and evaluate behaviour change strategies. The analysis and illustration of relationships among theories is a unique feature that should serve readers especially well. Michie and colleagues have indeed created a book that will serve as both a primer and a reference for understanding the many available conceptual frameworks, their key constructs and applications.
Professor Karen Glanz, George A. Weiss University Professor, University of Pennsylvania

This book and website will be an important resource for people working to improve public health in any setting. It will help us all to think through the programmes and policies we are trying to develop, implement or change. It will also help to break down the disciplinary boundaries that often get in the way of applied research and practice. I hope that many others will contribute through the website so that the resource can be deepened and widened as theory and evidence develop.
Sally Wyke, Deputy Director, Institute of Health and Wellbeing, University of Glasgow

To capitalize on the potential that theories of behaviour change offer for the design and implementation of interventions to promote health, resources are needed that facilitate engagement between theory and practice. This book addresses this critical need and will prove to be a valuable, accessible resource for information about a wide-range of social and behavioural theories and will enable all of us to use these theories in a more thoughtful manner.
Alex Rothman, Department of Psychology University of Minnesota

This book will greatly assist researchers and practitioners interested in behaviour change to navigate their way in the Babel of theories that have developed to describe very similar underlying approaches to changing behaviour in different disciplines that seek to change behaviour in different areas of application. It will be invaluable to researchers and practitioners who are looking for a more rational way of designing and explaining their approaches to changing behaviour.
Professor Wayne Hall, Director, Centre for Youth Substance Abuse Research, The University of Queensland

The authors have done the formidable task of systematically identifying and describing 83 theories explaining how human behaviour is changed. Together these theories offer a more complete picture than is typically achieved by those embracing the preferred theories of any one discipline, profession or practice - and certainly more complete than the implicit theories of those who claim not to use any theory in accounting for behaviour. This impressive book will facilitate the integration of theory and evidence in a cumulative science of behaviour change.
Professor Marie Johnston, Institute of Applied Health Sciences, University of Aberdeen

Implementation of innovation in healthcare and public health settings usually involves changing behaviours of citizens, patients, professionals, managers and policy makers. There is increasing interest in the application of behavioural theory to understanding determinants of behaviour and planning behaviour change interventions. However, non-behavioural scientists are often daunted by the sheer number of psychological theories that commonly have overlapping constructs. This compendium's structured summaries of current behavioural theory (and their inter-relationships) provides a comprehensive overview of current behavioural theories

and will be a major resource for anyone interested in developing theory informed implementation programs.
Professor Jeremy Grimshaw, Director, Cochrane Canada

Acknowledgements

This work was funded by the Medical Research Council through its Population Health Science Research Collaboration. Robert West's salary is funded by Cancer Research UK.

We are grateful to our advisory group for developing the literature search strategy and definitions of key terms and assisting in theory identification: Robert Aunger, Mary Barker, Mick Bloor, Heather Brown, Richard Cookson, Cyrus Cooper, Peter Craig, Paul Dieppe, Anna Dixon, Rachel Gooberman-Hill, Simon Griffin, Graham Hart, Kate Hunt, Susan Jebb, Marie Johnston, Mike Kelly, Steve Morris, Mark Petticrew, Paschal Sheeran, Mark Suhreke, Ivo Vlaev, Daniel Wight, Daniel Zizzo. We are also grateful for the advice on the search strategy that we received from Alison Weightman and Mala Mann at the Support Unit for Research Evidence (SURE), Cardiff University.

We would also like to thank the following researchers who have worked on the project: Rachel Davis, Zoe Hildon, Lorna Hobbs and Kate Sheals.

Thanks also go to the following who assisted with preparation of content for the book: Louise Atkins, Heather Brown, Sarah Dowling, Claire Garnett, Araf Khaled, Samantha Lawes, Sara Mathieu, David Morris, Victoria Nelson, Emma Norris, Pandora Pound, Helena Rubinstein, Christopher Russell and Caroline Wood.

Foreword

During the course of working at the interface of policy, politics, politicians and academic research, as I have done for a good part of my professional life, there has been a recurrent theme; that is the periodic discovery that human behaviour is really important and that all sorts of policy goals could be achieved if only governments could get the public to change their behaviour. Many spheres of life have fallen under the gaze of politicians and policy makers in this regard, including things like recycling, driving, willingness to donate our organs after our death, and our ability to fill in government forms properly.

In health and welfare, the centrality of human behaviour to the causes of the diseases which put a huge burden on the health service such as Type 2 diabetes, cardiovascular disease and obesity is indeed obvious. Whether we smoke, drink alcohol to excess, take exercise, and overeat drive the epidemics of these 'non-communicable' diseases (with non-communicable meaning not communicated by physical means although they are communicated by social and psychological means). It is a relatively simple step to assume that if only government could get people to change their smoking, eating, drinking and exercise habits, then all would be well. However, as many a politician has discovered, it turns out to be far from easy to bring about those changes on the scale that would make a difference to demand on the health service.

Our biggest success in this regard has been with smoking and we have seen what was once a very common habit in the adult population reduced considerably with huge health gains. However, the successes with smoking did not take place overnight and certainly not immediately after the truly lethal nature of the habit was discovered. It took the best part of 60 years in the UK to get to a largely smoke-free public environment. Sadly while we have seen a fall in the numbers of deaths from smoking-related disease, we are now in the position where many of these gains are being offset by deaths caused by obesity-related illness.

One of the problems has been a failure to take behaviour change seriously as a scientific topic. I have observed several common errors down the years committed by politicians, policy makers and indeed many doctors on the subject of behaviour change. First is the assumption that it's all common sense; that we know how to change behaviour and do not need to waste resources proving the obvious. Wrong! Common sense has led us repeatedly to ineffective interventions delivered at great cost in terms of money, resources and lost opportunities. Second there is a widespread assumption that knowledge and information drive behaviour and if we could only produce the right information, because people know more, they will behave differently. Wrong! Of course information and knowledge, and also beliefs and values are important factors in people's behaviour; but they are not the only ones, not least because the immediate environment, habit and emotion all play a crucial role in determining our actions.

The fact is that behaviour change needs to be studied as a science. There are tried and tested scientific principles, there is evidence and there is theory. In short, if you want to bring about behaviour change it is essential to go beyond common sense.

That is why this compendium is so important. It provides a very accessible account of theories of behaviour change. It presents them in a way that will allow users to understand the linkages and connections between the theories, which will deepen our understanding of where and how they might be applied. The volume is the result of a very important research project which sought to map the terrain of theories of behaviour change from the broad sweep of social and behavioural scientific disciplines. It is extensive but not necessarily comprehensive; the associated website allows readers to amend and add to the collection of 83 theories. This is a very important resource for anyone charged with bringing about health-related behaviour change.

For policy makers and those involved in the policy process where the goal is changes in individual or population behaviour, this book should be compulsory reading.
Professor Mike Kelly, Director of the Centre for Public Health, The National Institute for Health and Care Excellence

Contents

Acknowledgements 6

Foreword 7

Chapter 1: Behaviour Change Theories and their Uses 17
    Public health and behaviour change 17
    Behaviour change and behavioural science 20
    What is theory? 22
    Complexity, public health and why theory is useful 25
    Use of theory for intervention design 28
    Previous attempts to characterise theories of behaviour change 29
    The need for a compendium of behaviour change theories 30
    How to use this book 32

Chapter 2: Identifying and characterising behaviour change theories 35
    Identification of Theories 35
    Theory Sources 38
    Theory Descriptions 39
    Interconnectedness of Theories 40
        Identification of contributing theories 40
        Inclusion criteria 41
        Inter-coder agreement 41
        Network analysis 41

Chapter 3: General observations about behaviour change theories 43
    Theories identified 43
    Frequency of use 43
    Interconnectedness of Theory 43

Chapter 4: Descriptions of Behaviour Change Theories 49

1. Action Theory Model of Consumption (Bagozzi)..........51
2. Affective Events Theory (Weiss & Cropanzano)..........55
3. Aids Risk Reduction Model (Catania et al.)..........57
4. Behavioural-Ecological Model of Adolescent Aids Prevention (Hovell et al.)..........63
5. CEOS Theory (Borland)..........71
6. Change Theory (Lewin)..........79
7. Classical Conditioning (Pavlov)..........81
8. COM-B System (Michie et al.)..........85
9. Consumption as Social Practices (Spaargaren & Van Vliet)..........89
10. Containment Theory (Reckless)..........93
11. Control Theory (Carver & Scheier)..........95
12. Differential Association Theory (Sutherland)..........101
13. Diffusion of Innovations (Rogers)..........105
14. Ecological Model for Preventing Type 2 Diabetes in Minority Youth (Burnet et al.)..........113
15. Extended Information Processing Model (Flay et al.)..........117
16. Extended Parallel Processing Model (Witte)..........121
17. Feedback Intervention Theory (Kluger & DeNisi)..........125
18. Focus Theory of Normative Conduct (Cialdini et al.)..........133
19. General Theory of Crime (Gottfredson & Hirschi)..........137
20. General Theory of Deviant Behaviour (Kaplan)..........139
21. Goal Directed Theory (Bagozzi)..........143
22. Goal-Framing Theory (Lindenberg & Steg)..........147
23. Goal Setting Theory (Locke & Latham)..........149
24. Health Action Process Approach (Schwarzer)..........153
25. Health Behaviour Goal Model (Maes & Gebhardt)..........159
26. Health Behaviour Internalisation Model (Bellg)..........165
27. Health Belief Model (Rosenstock)..........171

28. Health Promotion Model (Pender et al.) 177

29. I-Change Model (De Vries et al.) 183

30. Information-Motivation-Behavioural Skills Model (Fisher & Fisher) 187

31. Information-Motivation-Behavioural Skills Model of Adherence (Fisher et al.) 193

32. Integrated Theoretical Model for Alcohol and Other Drug Abuse Prevention (Gonzalez) 199

33. Integrated Theory of Drinking Behaviour (Wagenaar & Perry) 203

34. Integrated Theory of Health Behaviour Change (Ryan) 207

35. Integrative Model of Behavioural Prediction (Fishbein) 211

36. Integrative Model of Factors Influencing Smoking Behaviours (Flay et al.) 215

37. Integrative Model of Health Attitude and Behaviour Change (Flay) 219

38. Integrative Model of Factors Influencing Smoking And Attitude And Health Behaviour Change (Flay et al.) 223

39. Model of Pro-Environmental Behaviour (Kollmuss & Agyeman) 229

40. Motivation-Opportunities-Abilities Model (Ölander & Thøgersen) 233

41. Needs-Opportunities-Abilities Model (Gatersleben & Vlek) 237

42. Norm Activation Theory (Schwartz) 243

43. Operant Learning Theory (Skinner) 249

44. Precaution Adoption Process Model (Weinstein & Sandman) 255

45. Pressure System Model (Katz) 259

46. PRIME Theory (West) 263

47. Problem Behaviour Theory (Jessor) 273

48. Prospect Theory (Kahneman & Tversky) 281

49. Protection Motivation Theory (Rogers) 287

50. Prototype Willingness Model (Gerrard et al.) 291

51. Rational Addiction Model (Becker & Murphy) 295

52. Reflective Impulsive Model (Strack & Deutsch) 301

53. Regulatory Fit Theory (Higgins) 309

54. Relapse Prevention Model (Marlatt & Gordon) 313

55. Risk as Feelings Theory (Lowenstein et al.) 317

56. Self-Determination Theory (Deci & Ryan) 321

57. Self-Efficacy Theory (Bandura) 329

58. Self-Regulation Theory (Kanfer & Gaelick) 335

59. Six Staged Model of Communication Effects (Vaughan & Everett) 339

60. Social Action Theory (Ewart) 343

61. Social Action Theory (Weber) 351

62. Social Change Theory (Thompson & Kinne) 355

63. Social Cognitive Theory (Bandura) 359

64. Social Consensus Model of Health Education (Romer & Hornik) 363

65. Social Development Model (Hawkins & Weis) 367

66. Social Ecological Model of Behaviour Change (Panter-Brick et al.) 371

67. Social Ecological Model of Walking (Alfonzo) 375

68. Social Identity Theory (Tajfel & Turner) 379

69. Social Influence Model of Consumer Participation (Dholakia et al.) 383

70. Social Learning Theory (Miller & Dollard) 389

71. Social Norms Theory (Perkins & Berkowitz) 395

72. Systems Model of Health Behaviour Change (Kersell & Milsum) 399

73. Technology Acceptance Model 1, 2 & 3 (Davis; Venkatesh & Davis; Venkatesh & Bala) 405

74. Temporal Self-Regulation Theory (Hall & Fong) 411

75. Terror Management Theory (Greenberg et al.) 415

76. Terror Management Health Model (Goldenberg & Arndt) 419

77. Theory of Interpersonal Behaviour (Triandis) 423

78. Theory of Normative Social Behaviour (Rimal & Real) 429

79. Theory of Planned Behaviour (Ajzen) 433

80. Theory of Triadic Influence (Flay & Petraitis) 437

81. Transcontextual Model of Motivation (Hagger et al.) 441

82. Transtheoretical Model of Behaviour Change (Prochaska & DiClemente) 445

83. Value Belief Norm Theory (Stern et al.) 453

Chapter 5 Use of theory for intervention development: looking to the future 457

    Current state of theories 457

        Insights from the theories 457

        Reporting of theories 461

        Theory overlap 462

        Focus on current behaviour rather than generating behaviour change 463

        Theory modifications 463

        Connectedness of theories 464

    Limitations of the current review 464

    The way forward 466

        Updating the compendium using the website 466

        Applying quality criteria 466

        Developing a system for theory modification and replacement 466

        Guidelines on reporting of theories 467

        From theory to intervention 473

        Theory testing and application 474

    Final observations 476

References 479

About the authors 495

ABC OF BEHAVIOUR CHANGE THEORIES

Chapter 1: Behaviour Change Theories and their Uses

"He who loves practice without theory is like the sailor who boards ship without a rudder and compass and never knows where he may cast."
(Leonardo Da Vinci, 1452-1519)

This book aims to facilitate the task of reviewing and selecting relevant theories to inform the design of behaviour change interventions and policies. The main goal is to provide an accessible source of potentially useful theories from a range of disciplines beyond those usually considered. It also provides an opportunity to analyse broad issues around the use of theory in the design of behaviour change interventions and examine areas where there is scope for improvement.

This chapter begins by considering the role of behaviour change in public health before focusing on the questions of what is 'theory', why theory is useful and how theory has been used. Finally, it describes the rationale for writing this compendium.

Public health and behaviour change

The factors contributing to the global disease burden shifted substantially in the 20th century. Where once communicable diseases among children were the scourge of humanity, now non-communicable diseases in adults have the greatest impact on premature mortality and morbidity (Lim et al., 2012). Reducing the disease burden in the 21st century will require changes at the population level in tobacco smoking, alcohol use, physical activity and diet. Such changes could lead to substantial improvements in life expectancy and quality of life.

At the same time infectious diseases have not been conquered and may well see resurgence with the advent of anti-biotic resistant strains. Behaviour change is clearly required to prevent the spread of such diseases, whether it be in uptake of immunisation or behaviours that limit transmission.

In addition to behaviours involved in primary prevention of disease, there are two other sets of behaviour that are important for promoting population health. The first set involves behaviours that limit the progression and effects of long-term conditions and illness, such as adhering to medication and other advice, and seeking health care appropriately – often referred to as secondary and tertiary prevention (Sabaté, 2003).

The second set involves behaviours that deliver health and social care (Michie, van Stralen, & West, 2011; Michie & West, 2013). This requires a wide range of people, including health professionals, community workers, and policy makers to design and deliver interventions in line with evidence (Grol & Grimshaw, 1999; Grol & Wensing, 2004; Michie et al., 2005). Failure to translate research findings into clinical practice is common, with studies finding 30-40% of patients not receiving treatments of proven effectiveness and 20–25% patients receiving care that is not needed or potentially harmful (Grol, 2001; Schuster, McGlynn, & Brook, 1998).

Achieving behaviour change is not straightforward. It requires the development and implementation of interventions that are affordable, practicable, effective, acceptable, safe and equitable (see the APEASE framework, Michie, Atkins, & West, 2014). Unfortunately investment in preventive and behavioural science has been very small relative to the scale of this opportunity for improving population health (Marteau, Dieppe, Foy, Kinmonth, & Schneiderman, 2006). Despite the lack of resources, many behaviour change interventions have been found to be effective at individual, community and population levels (Abraham, Kelly, West, & Michie, 2009; Albarracin et al., 2005; Michie & West, 2013; National Institute for Health and Care Excellence, 2007, 2014; Nigg, Allegrante, & Ory, 2002). Moreover, interventions and policies that effect even small changes in relevant health behaviours can lead to substantial improvements in public health (Ezzati et al., 2002; Mokdad, Marks, Stroup, & Gerberding, 2004; National Institute for Health and Care Excellence, 2007, 2014; Solomon & Kington, 2002). For example, every percentage point decrease in smoking prevalence in the UK can be expected to prevent some 3,000 premature deaths per year (West & Shahab, 2009).

Interventions have been successfully applied to a wide variety of health behaviours (Susan Michie, 2008). The most well-documented are those aimed at behavioural risk factors such as smoking (Hartmann-Boyce, Stead, Cahill, & Lancaster, 2013), excessive alcohol consumption (Kaner et al., 2009), sedentary lifestyles and poor diet (World Health Organisation, 2009). Other relevant health behaviours to have been successfully targeted include protective behaviours, such as health screening (Sabatino et al., 2012); behaviours to cope with chronic and acute illness, such as medication adherence (Cutrona et al., 2010); and health professional behaviours to improve the quality of healthcare (Grimshaw et al., 2004), such as hand hygiene compliance (Fuller et al., 2012; Pfoh, Dy, & Engineer, 2013). However, it is also the case that there are many examples of interventions aimed at these various behaviours that have proved ineffective (for example, Coleman, 2010; Summerbell et al., 2005).

Behaviour change and behavioural science

Understanding the nature of a behaviour and the part played by the context in which it occurs is important to developing interventions that are more likely to prove effective in changing that behaviour (House of Lords Science and Technology Select Committee, 2011; Michie et al., 2011; Michie & West, 2013).

Altering the incidence of any particular behaviour requires a change in at least one of capability, motivation or opportunity to engage in the activity (Michie, Atkins, et al., 2014; Michie et al., 2011). Capability refers to the psychological and physical abilities to perform a behaviour, and includes knowledge and skills; motivation involves all the processes that energise and direct behaviour, including not just goals, plans and beliefs but also 'automatic' processes involving emotions, habits and impulses; and opportunity involves all factors that are external to an individual that may influence engagement with an activity, ranging from the physical environments in which people spend time to the social and cultural milieu that dictates how we perceive and think about particular activities. To maximise the potential benefit of behaviour change interventions, it is important for designers to understand how these factors of capability, motivation and opportunity vary as a function of particular behaviours, target populations and contexts (Glanz & Bishop, 2010; Michie & Abraham, 2004; Michie et al., 2011; Noar & Zimmerman, 2005).

There is growing recognition that attempts to change behaviour should draw on theories of behaviour and behaviour change. In the United Kingdom, the Medical Research Council recommends beginning the development of any complex intervention by identifying relevant theories to advance an understanding of the likely process of change before conducting any exploratory piloting and formal testing (Campbell et al., 2000; N. C. Campbell et al.,

2007; Craig et al., 2008). The guidance and supporting documents have been cited more than 2500 times to date (Campbell et al., 2000; Craig et al., 2008).

However, there is also a legitimate question as to how far explicit use of theory promotes the design of effective behaviour change interventions. In fact, interventions that have purportedly been informed by theory have not necessarily been found to be more effective than those that have not. Some reviews have found a positive association (Albada, Ausems, Bensing, & van Dulmen, 2009; Albarracin et al., 2005; Glanz & Bishop, 2010; Noar, Benac, & Harris, 2007; Swann, Bowe, Kosmin, & McCormick, 2003; Taylor, Conner, & Lawton, 2011), but others have found no association, or, even a negative association (Gardner, Wardle, Poston, & Croker, 2011; Roe, Hunt, Bradshaw, & Rayner, 1997; Stephenson, Imrie, & Sutton, 2000). Some reviews have reported a mixture depending on the measure of effectiveness (Ammerman, Lindquist, Lohr, & Hersey, 2002; Bhattarai et al., 2013; Kim, Stanton, Li, Dickersin, & Galbraith, 1997).

One factor that may contribute to this mixed picture is the way the theory has been used. It is clearly very different for a theory to be used as a stepping off point for ideas versus being used in a systematic manner to develop intervention content. Unfortunately, it has been found that the reported use of theory in intervention design is generally inadequate. In an attempt to improve, the reporting of use of theory in intervention design, a 19-item 'Theory Coding Scheme' has been developed (Michie & Prestwich, 2010). The scheme assesses whether theory was mentioned, how theory was used in intervention development, whether theory had an indirect influence on an intervention, how theory was used to explain intervention effects on outcomes and the implications for future theory development.

Another crucial factor is the choice of appropriate theory. For example, if a behaviour is fundamentally under influence of habitual or emotional factors then a theory that focuses exclusively on beliefs and reflective thought processes may not be appropriate when informing intervention design.

Before considering the use of theory in the design of interventions and policies in more detail, it is helpful to consider what we mean by 'theory' and what makes for a good theory.

What is theory?

The term 'theory' can be defined in many different ways. At its core it is a coherent description of a process that is arrived at by a process of inference, provides an explanation for observed phenomena and generates predictions (West & Brown, 2013). In the context of behaviour change, theories seek to explain why, when and how a behaviour does or does not occur, and the important sources of influence to be targeted in order to alter the behaviour. They should reflect an integration of the knowledge accumulated about the relevant mechanisms of action and moderators of change.

Much scientific endeavour does not constitute theory because it consists of disparate observations or descriptions rather than explanation. This does not necessarily make that knowledge or description unimportant but it is not a theory.

An expert multidisciplinary group that oversaw some of the work reported in this book (see Chapter 2) agreed nine criteria by which to assess the quality of theory in a series of consensus exercises:

1. Clarity of constructs: 'Has the case been made for the independence of constructs from each other?'

2. Clarity of relationships between constructs: 'Are the

relationships between constructs clearly specified?'

3. Measurability: 'Is an explicit methodology for measuring the constructs given?'

4. Testability: 'Has the theory been specified in such a way that it can be tested?'

5. Being explanatory: 'Has the theory been used to explain/account for a set of observations? (statistically or logically);

6. Describing causality: 'Has the theory been used to describe mechanisms of change?'

7. Achieving parsimony: 'Has the case for parsimony been made?'

8. Generalizability: 'Have generalisations been investigated across behaviours, populations and contexts?'

9. Having an evidence base: 'Is there empirical support for the propositions?'

Good theories, as described above, begin with a parsimonious, coherent explanation of phenomena and generate predictions that can be compared against observation. However, science is fundamentally about discovery and progress, and theories always need to be developed and refined. There are different approaches to theory development (Carlile & Christensen, 2004; Dixon-Woods, Bosk, Aveling, Goeschel, & Pronovost, 2011; Head, 2013; Lipsey, 2004) but a common theme is to ask searching questions of the existing body of theory. It has been noted (West & Brown, 2013) that important among these are:

- Is it contradicted by consistent observations?

- Does it fail to encompass important relevant observations?

- Does it have more elements than are needed?
- Is it misleading?

The answers to these questions provide a starting point for modifying theory. The aim is for theories to evolve to become closer to the truth, and to be more useful explanations as more observations are collected and understanding matures.

The process of theory development could be much more systematic and rigorous. Theories are rarely tested in a way that would allow them to be falsified, and even when they come up against conflicting evidence, they are often not modified or rejected (Gigerenzer, 2010; Meehl, 1978). In addition, theory proponents typically start with an incomplete analysis of what is already in the literature and how existing theories are interrelated.

It has been argued by some that a theory does not need to produce predictions that can be tested so long as it generates new concepts that suggest where to look and provide a general frame of reference (Blumer, 1986). This 'sensitising' role of theory can be useful but only to the extent that the ideas generated allow a greater understanding of the phenomena concerned and ultimately that must be determined by a correspondence with data arising from systematic observation. Otherwise, there is little to prevent theories being proposed despite conflicting with observed data leaving no rational basis for systematic refinement or improvement. Informal explanations, unfalsifiable statements and ideas are important but they are not scientific theories (Popper, 1959).

Other functions that a theory may fulfil beyond sensitisation include the provision of a common language that aids communication between groups and disciplines. Theory can improve the efficiency of the research process by helping people to address questions methodically and to accumulate incremental knowledge systematically. A new theory may also provide an impetus to co-ordinate and focus research efforts using a common approach. Again, these functions are all valuable but are not intrinsic to theory and may be met by other scientific tools such as taxonomies, ontologies and research agendas. A theory must provide an explanation for observed phenomena and generate potentially falsifiable predictions.

Complexity, public health and why theory is useful

Complexity abounds in the field of behaviour change. Theories can provide a way of addressing this. One source of complexity is that interventions aimed at changing behaviour typically consist of many interrelated components such that is never possible to identify a single key 'active ingredient' (Campbell et al., 2000). Even when an experiment compares the presence or absence of a single identifiable component, this effect will almost certainly be contingent on other components that are present in both the intervention and comparison conditions. A good example is the provision of nicotine replacement therapy for smoking cessation where active placebo differences appear to depend on whether at least some level of advice and support is provided (Kotz, Brown, & West, 2014).

Another source of complexity is the sheer diversity of targets for behavioural interventions. Public health improvement covers a very broad field of operation ranging from psychological interventions to influence the human mind and behaviour, through family and community interventions to change collective social behaviour, to policy, investment, environmental and legislative interventions aimed at societal level change.

Further sources of complexity involve: the number of behaviours required by those delivering or receiving the intervention; the number of groups or organisational levels targeted by the intervention; the number and variability of outcomes; and the degree of flexibility or tailoring of the intervention required (Craig et al., 2008).

In public health the relationship between the intervention and outcome is also often complex. This can be because the outcome may not occur at the same operational level as the intervention (Kelly et al., 2010). For example, setting a minimum price for a unit of alcohol would aim to change individual alcohol purchasing decisions whereas educational interventions on the harms of excessive alcohol consumption could produce outcomes at the population level by changing social and cultural norms.

Complexity may also arise from the long causal chain between intervention and outcome (Kelly et al., 2010). For example, a complex set of psychological, social, cultural and economic relationships and processes are involved between midwives giving prenatal advice on a healthy diet and parents making and sustaining changes to family meals so that they contain more fresh fruits and vegetables and less fat and sugar such that children achieve a healthy body mass index. Conceptual maps and logic models have evolved as a way of delineating such relationships and processes and disentangling some of the complexity (R. Campbell & Bonell, in press), and, it is suggested, these can be particularly useful if they have overarching theoretical frameworks which acknowledge both individual and population level processes (Kelly et al., 2010). Complexity also arises in relation to the implementation of interventions, in terms of fidelity of delivery, target population and context (Bonell, Fletcher, Morton, Lorenc, & Moore, 2012; Weiss, 1995).

As noted earlier, explicit use of theory is not a guarantee of designing an effective intervention. However, there are good reasons for believing that when done well it is important in advancing science and can lead to more effective interventions.

First, a theory can provide a framework in which the designer of an intervention can consider and identify what needs to change for behaviour to change, in terms of capability, opportunities or motivational processes (Michie et al., 2011). These need not be the current antecedents of a behaviour. Antecedents usefully reveal *possible* causal determinants of change that an intervention can be designed to target (Hardeman et al., 2005; Michie & Abraham, 2004; Michie, Johnston, Francis, Hardeman, & Eccles, 2008; Michie & Prestwich, 2010). However, particular factors may not be currently related to a behaviour; this may be due to a lack of variance, or may be because potential levers of change are not naturally occurring.

It is therefore important to canvas the full range of potential levers for change. The use of theory promotes a systematic approach to this process and reflection about the causal nature of particular relationships, which is important given the myriad of influences that may be incidentally, rather than causally, associated with any given behaviour. Subsequent to producing a plausible list of levers for changing behaviour, appropriate behaviour change techniques (BCTs) can be selected and/or refined and tailored (Michie et al., 2008; Michie & Prestwich, 2010; Rothman, 2004).

Secondly, theorising about the mechanisms of action promotes the assessment of appropriate mediators. Researchers are subsequently able to determine whether an intervention influenced the hypothesised mediator, and whether the mediator had an effect on the behaviour. Progress in the refinement of interventions is much quicker if an investigator is able to distinguish between the failure of an intervention for two quite different reasons: i) the intervention did not affect the mediator hypothesised to be important; ii) the intervention successfully affected a hypothesised mediator but the mediator turned out not to influence the behaviour concerned (Michie & Abraham, 2004; Rothman, 2004, 2009). Theory can advance understanding of what works and why. Consequently, the process of adapting and refining particular interventions for different contexts, populations, and behaviours is made more efficient (Michie et al., 2008).

Designing an intervention on the basis of a behaviour change theory also allows the outcome of evaluations of the intervention to provide a test of that theory. Thus the results of intervention evaluations can in the right circumstances lead to the refinement of the relevant theory or theories, which in turn can facilitate the design and adaptation of new interventions drawing on that theory in future (Michie et al., 2008; Rothman, 2004).

Use of theory for intervention design

Despite the points raised above, behaviour change interventions are often designed without reference to theory. A recent review estimated that approximately a third of empirical research articles published in health journals drew on theory (Painter, Borba, Hynes, Mays, & Glanz, 2008), while a review of implementation research estimated that only about 20% of studies employed theory (Davies, Walker, & Grimshaw, 2010).

While a review of 190 physical activity and dietary interventions found that half reported using theory during development (Prestwich et al., 2013), only a small proportion systematically applied theory rather than referred to it in a general way as having informed the intervention (Michie & Prestwich, 2010; Painter et al., 2008; Prestwich et al., 2013; Webb, Joseph, Yardley, & Michie, 2010). It is reasonable to expect that application of theory would involve reporting how the theory was used in the design of the intervention, with an explicit explanation of how theory constructs led to the selection of specific features of the intervention and/or tailoring of these to specific populations or contexts, and a discussion of the relationship between the results and theory (Michie & Prestwich, 2010; Webb et al., 2010).

Previous attempts to characterise theories of behaviour change

There is a plethora of theories relevant to behaviour change. It has been noted that most of these address a small subset of the relevant constructs and there is considerable overlap between them (West & Brown, 2013). For example, the Theory of Planned Behaviour (Ajzen, 1991) draws attention to some important influences on behaviour (intentions, attitudes, perceived control and perceived norms) and in some circumstances can predict behaviour quite well (Armitage & Conner, 2001), but it does not include important factors that play often play important role in behaviour such as self-control and momentary emotional reactions (Sheeran, Gollwitzer, & Bargh, 2013).

Most of the widely used theories used to predict or explain health-related behaviours focus on beliefs rather than emotions or habit: in a review of theory-based articles published between 1986 and 1988 in two major health education journals, the three most frequently cited theories were Social Learning Theory, the Theory of Reasoned Action, and the Health Belief Model (Glanz, Rimer, & Viswanath, 2008). In a review of theory use covering a sample of research published between 2000 and 2005 in ten leading health journals, the most often used theories were the Transtheoretical Model/Stages of Change, Social Cognitive Theory, and the Health Belief Model

(Painter et al., 2008), while a more recent meta-analysis identified that Social Cognitive Theory and the Transtheoretical Model were the two most widely used theories for developing physical activity and dietary interventions (Prestwich et al., 2013).

Another review of theories in the field found that the most widely-used theories also focus on intra-individual, and sometimes interpersonal, rather than broader social and environmental factors (Glanz & Bishop, 2010). As a result interventions have tended to target intra-individual factors, relating to motivation and, to a small extent, capability, whereas, at least until recently social and environmental variables relating to the opportunity for the behaviour to occur have been relatively neglected.

The need for a compendium of behaviour change theories

Although there is broad agreement that theory should inform intervention development, for example in the MRC's guidance for developing and evaluating complex interventions (Craig et al., 2008), there is little guidance on how to choose an appropriate theory for a particular purpose (Michie et al., 2005), and the result is that selection is often based on personal preference or fashion (Bandura, 1998). This could be why for the past few decades a small number of theories have dominated the literature (Painter et al., 2008). The potential benefit of using theory is severely limited by relying on a restricted set of theories rather than considering the range available theories and identifying which is particularly applicable to the behaviour concerned within a specific environment and population.

Apart from the issue of narrowness of focus, there is an issue of overlap of constructs across theories and with each other (Michie et al., 2005). For example, in a narrative review of the construct of 'control', Skinner identified more than 100 conceptualisations

(Skinner, 1996). Intervention designers and researchers face a challenging task when selecting from this myriad of overlapping theories, using a variety of terms for similar constructs.

The Theoretical Domains Framework (TDF) was developed as a response to the difficulty of selecting between many overlapping theories (Michie et al., 2005). The framework was produced by a team of psychologists and health service researchers and aimed to make theory more accessible to intervention designers from a range of disciplines. Relevant theories were identified, integrated and broken down into key theoretical domains. The framework originally assimilated 128 explanatory constructs from 33 theories of behaviour change and has since been refined to 84 component constructs across 14 domains during a further 3-step validation process (Cane, O'Connor, & Michie, 2012).

The TDF has been widely used to understand a range of different health behaviours across many contexts in order to facilitate the design of interventions informed by a theoretical understanding of the problem (Francis, O'Connor, & Curran, 2012). For example, fruit and vegetable intake in the general population (Guillaumie, Godin, & Vezina-Im, 2010); provision of smoking cessation advice by dental healthcare providers (Amemori, Michie, Korhonen, Murtomaa, & Kinnunen, 2011); hand hygiene among healthcare professionals (Dyson, Lawton, Jackson, & Cheater, 2010); management of lower back pain by physiotherapists (McKenzie et al., 2010); and prevention of childhood obesity (Taylor et al., 2013).

Another useful resource for identifying theoretical constructs is the US National Institute of Health's Grid Enabled Measures web-based database, 'GEM' (Moser et al., 2011; Rabin et al., 2012). The database was first developed with the primary aims of promoting the use of standardised and theoretically-based measures and facilitating the sharing of harmonised data resulting from the use of such standardised measures (Moser et al., 2011). The database has since been expanded to include 312 definitions of a range of theoretical constructs identified by expert opinion and crowd-sourcing (US National Institutes of Health, 2014).

Apart from the TDF and the GEM database, a number of useful compendia have been produced of theories in the field, most notably ones by Glanz and colleagues (Glanz, Rimer, & Viswanath, 2008; Nutbeam, 2004) in the field of health promotion and Conner and Norman in the field of health psychology (Conner & Norman, 2005). However, we lack an up-to-date compendium that brings together theories from across key disciplines.

Thus the main aim of this compendium was to identify and summarise theories of behaviour change, drawn from a range of disciplines relevant to designing interventions to improve health. We also sought to characterise the explicitly reported interconnectedness of theories included in this compendium. Finally, we wanted to draw lessons from the exercise as to how we might do a better job in the future of developing and using theory in this area.

How to use this book

The summaries of theories in this book can be read as one would read any review. But they can also be used in a more instrumental way for intervention design. This can be done by identifying the behaviour change issue and scanning the summaries of theories to identify those that might be relevant. This will be assisted by the brief summaries, the list of constructs and the network diagrams showing linked theories.

We would recommend also using the companion volume, 'The Behaviour Change Wheel: A Guide to Designing Interventions' (Michie, Atkins, et al., 2014). That book provides a step by step guide to intervention design in which one starts with a 'behavioural diagnosis' to establish which out of capability, opportunity and/or motivation would provide suitable targets for interventions. It then links these with broad intervention functions and specific behaviour change techniques. The current compendium provides a way of mapping this analysis to theories which can create a coherent narrative linking the intervention functions and behaviour change techniques together so that they work synergistically.

To facilitate the use of this compendium, we have created a website that will allow electronic searching of theories by author, title and component construct (**www.behaviourchangetheories.com**). Thus, it will be possible to identify all the theories that share a particular construct, or two or three etc. constructs.

The website also provides a facility for readers to provide feedback on the book in relation to:

- additional theories that meet our criteria but have not been included

- empirical data relating to the application or evaluation of the theory

- amendments to the current theory description, with supporting evidence

- add to or amend information for the network analyses.

These will be collated and incorporated into future editions of the compendium.

see **www.behaviourchangetheories.com**

Chapter 2: Identifying and characterising behaviour change theories

This chapter outlines the process by which the theories presented in this book were identified, and summarised, and the method used to describe connections between them. A literature review overseen by a multidisciplinary group of experts, including psychologists, sociologists, anthropologists and economists was accompanied by a network analysis to identify reported connections between theories. For a fuller description of the methods used to identify and characterise the theories, see Davis, Campbell, Hildon et al, 2014). It is recommended that this book be read in conjunction with that paper.

Identification of Theories

Expert advisory group. An expert advisory group was convened which consisted of five psychologists, four sociologists, three anthropologists, five economists, four health service researchers, two epidemiologists and one policy researcher. They developed consensus definitions of the key terms, 'behaviour' and 'theory' which was necessary for deciding which theories to include in the review. The group also agreed the databases and search terms to represent the disciplines involved.

Forming definitions. Potentially relevant definitions from peer-reviewed journals, reports and books were submitted by the advisory group and a shortlist agreed. To synthesise these to form an agreed definition, a two-round Delphi-like process involving the authors and members of the advisory group was conducted.

The consensus definition of theory was

> *"a set of concepts and/or statements with specification of how phenomena relate to each other. Theory provides an organising description of a system that accounts for what is known, and explains and predicts phenomena"*

and the definition of behaviour was

> *"anything a person does in response to internal or external events. Actions may be overt (motor or verbal) and directly measurable or, covert (activities not viewable but involving voluntary muscles) and indirectly measurable; behaviours are physical events that occur in the body and are controlled by the brain".*

Identification of theories. Theories of behaviour and behaviour change were identified in an initial scoping search of the literature, using both generic and discipline-specific terms relating to behaviour/behaviour change theory, and through consultation with the advisory group. Theories generated from these two sources informed the strategy for the subsequent systematic literature search.

Six databases were searched for articles published between 1st Jan 1960 - 11th September 2012 (PsycINFO, Econlit, Cochrane Database of Systematic reviews, International Bibliography of Social Sciences, EMBASE and MEDLINE), with the final search being conducted on 11th September 2012. The search strategy included four sets of search terms: those relating to behaviour change theory (e.g. behaviour change theory, behaviour change model), those relating to specific behaviour theories (e.g. affective events theory, theory of planned behaviour), those relating to behaviour change more generally (e.g. behaviour change, population change) and those relating to disciplines combined with the term 'behaviour change' (e.g. economics AND behaviour change, psychology AND behaviour change).

Forward and backward citation searches were then performed and hand searches were also made of key behavioural science journals (e.g. Annals of Behavioural Medicine, Health Psychology, Implementation Science, Social Science and Medicine). Further theories were identified through expert consultation and web searches for documents published by organisations with a known interest in behaviour change: the National Institute of Health's Behaviour Change Consortium, the National Institute for Health and Clinical Excellence (NICE), the Evidence for Policy and Practice Information and Co-ordinating Centre (EPPI-Centre), the Government Social Research Unit, the House of Lords Science and Technology Select Committee Report on Behaviour Change, and National Institute of Health Research's Health Technology Assessment (all based in the UK except the first, which is based in the US).

Inclusion criteria. Theories were included if they considered behaviour either as an outcome or as part of the process leading to the outcome and met the agreed definitions of 'theory' and 'behaviour'. Theories that *only* considered behaviour at the group level (e.g. organisational behaviour) were excluded.

Theories that focused on emotions, drives or cognitions and did not explicitly address behaviour were excluded because of the difficulty of knowing where to draw the line, given the potential for any of these to influence behaviour and ending up with a compendium of all theories of psychology, sociology, anthropology and economics.

We recognised that this would result in a number of what might be surprising omissions. Most notably, it would mean omitting key theories of decision making such as Subjective Expected Utility Theory, Multi-Attribute Utility Theory and other important choice theories. This omission is something we will return to in the discussion.

The focus on specific theories meant that we did not include broader theoretical approaches of which specific theories would be examples. This was in contrast to, for example, the compendium of addiction theories compiled by West and Brown (2013) which drew on 'theories' as many levels of specificity. Conceptual frameworks that are developed to guide the design, implementation or evaluation of interventions and the Theoretical Domains Framework were also excluded, as these are not specific theories of behaviour or behaviour change. Within these constraints, a high level of agreement was observed for decisions on inclusion in relation to both the theories and the articles included in the review (> 90%).

Theory Sources

Once theories had been identified, every effort was made to find the relevant primary theory sources (i.e. the publications in which the original theories were described by the theory developers). In cases where this was not possible, or not clear which article should be considered as the primary theory source, a theory source was selected that was authored by the theory developer(s) and provided a good description of the theory. If a theory was presented in a large book or volume, a chapter that provided a comprehensive summary of the theory was selected. For theories that had been refined or expanded over time by the original developer(s), efforts were made to identify both the primary source of the theory and any publications reporting refinements or expansions.

We recognised that there would inevitably be some omissions and misrepresentations in the theory descriptions. That is one reason why we set up the website associated with the book: so that proponents of theories or others who believed that a theory could be more accurately described could comment and we could take that into account in updates.

Theory Descriptions

Theory descriptions are presented in four sections: a construct list, a brief summary, a full description, and a list of explicitly mentioned contributing theories from this compendium.

Construct lists. To promote a systematic approach to identifying constructs, a definition of the term 'construct' was agreed:

> *'A construct in a theory is a component of that model or theory. It is a representation of an object, event, state of affairs, feature of one of these or relationship between two or more of them, derived from observation and inference'.*

Where theory constructs contained one or more sub-constructs (e.g. 'social norms' comprising 'others' beliefs' and 'motivation to comply'), this was reflected by listing the constructs hierarchically.

Brief summaries. Brief summaries of each theory (usually around 3-5 lines, but more in the case of integrative theories) were written, outlining the aims and the core propositions of each theory.

Descriptions. We tried to keep the description as close to the theoretical descriptions in the primary theory sources as possible. The theory descriptions therefore vary in length, clarity and detail, reflecting the original theory description.

Where theories have been expanded or refined over time, these changes were explained and incorporated into the descriptions. To ensure that information was extracted from primary theory sources consistently and reliably, all descriptions were checked by a second researcher who was not involved in the original writing process. Any disagreements about content or construct extraction were discussed between researchers until a consensus was reached.

Interconnectedness of Theories

As a first attempt to examine the interconnectedness of theories within the compendium, an approach called 'network analysis' was used. This provides a set of theories, tools and methods for describing, exploring and understanding the structural and relational aspects of members of a set (e.g. the theories within this book). By examining the theories that appear to have contributed to each theory within this book, the links and patterns among theories within the compendium could be identified.

Identification of contributing theories

Three pairs of coders were each randomly assigned to read and extract network data from primary theory sources. For each primary theory source, coders independently identified the names of theories within the compendium named by theory authors as contributing to the development of the theory concerned.

Using a data extraction chart, coders also provided the page number of the primary theory source where the author stated the theory contributed to development, provided comments about any additional contributing theories not included in this compendium, and recorded challenges or concerns encountered when assessing the primary theory source. To ensure coders' decisions could be reviewed by the lead researcher, coders were asked to annotate the original primary theory source documents with comments indicating why they chose to include or exclude a contributing theory.

Inclusion criteria

To avoid unwarranted inference by coders and ensure replicability, strict inclusion criteria were established. For a theory to be named as a contributing theory, the primary theory source had to *clearly* and *explicitly* state that a particular theory within the compendium informed the development of the theory or a construct. If a theory was merely mentioned or critiqued in the review of the theoretical literature or in a comparison of theories, this was not included as a contributing theory. We recognised that this would probably underestimate the connectivity between theories but we judged that this would be preferable to a process that could not be replicated.

Inter-coder agreement

Inter-coder agreement between coding pairs was assessed using the adjusted Kappa statistic (i.e. PABAK). PABAK was used rather than percentage agreement or Cohen's Kappa statistic because of its adjustment for 1) coders sharing bias in the use of categories and 2) high prevalence of negative agreement (i.e. when both coders agree on non-contributing theories). Across the coding pairs, agreement was high with a mean adjusted Kappa statistic of 0.99. All differences were easily resolved through discussion.

Network analysis

The network analysis was performed using UCINET v6. Network- and individual theory-level measures were calculated to describe individual theory and network attributes. Network diagrams, known as 'sociograms', were generated using NETDRAW software. In each network diagram, the nodes represent theories, and arrows represent connections between the theories. Arrow heads indicate the direction of contribution. Thus a connection between one theory and another is a directional link indicating that the theory at the tip of the arrow was influenced by the one at the base.

Chapter 3: General observations about behaviour change theories

Theories identified

A total of 83 theories of behaviour and behaviour change were identified, of which 59 were found directly from the review articles. The remaining 24 theories were identified by the advisory group and/or through abstracts of the articles retrieved in the literature search.

Frequency of use

Just four theories accounted for 174 (63%) of articles found: the Transtheoretical Model of Change (TTM) (n=91; 33%), the Theory of Planned Behaviour (TPB) (n=36; 13%), Social Cognitive Theory (SCT) (n=29; 11%), and the Information-Motivation-Behavioural-Skills Model (IMB) (n=18; 7%). A further four theories accounted for an additional 32 (12%) of the included articles: the Health Belief Model (HBM) (n=9; 3%), Self Determination Theory (SDT) (n=9; 3%), Health Action Process Approach (HAPA) (n=8; 3%), and Social Learning Theory (SLT) (n=6; 2%) (Social Learning Theory is a precursor of Social Cognitive Theory). The remaining theories (n= 70) were found fewer than six times each in the literature that met our inclusion criteria, with most only being applied once or twice.

Interconnectedness of Theory

The network analysis identified 122 connections or ties between the 83 theories within the compendium. Figure 3.1 presents a network diagram of connections between theories within this book.

ABC OF BEHAVIOUR CHANGE THEORIES

Figure 3.1 Network diagram depicting connections between the theories in this compendium

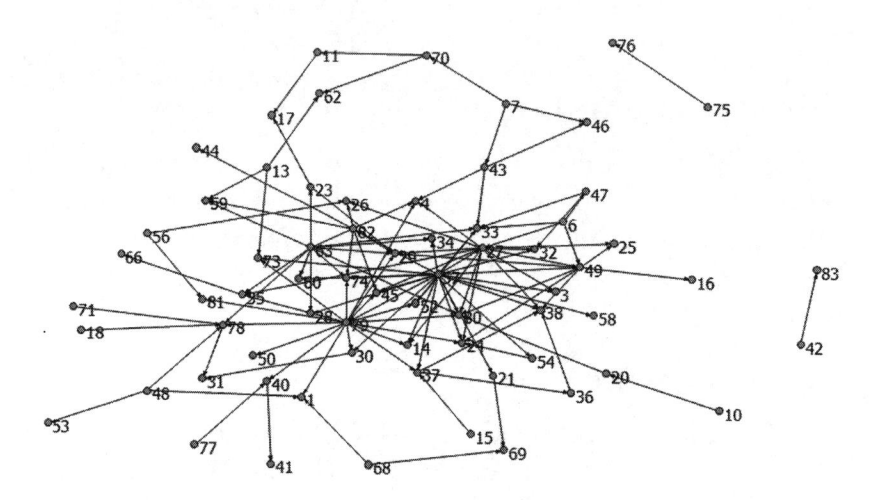

NOTE: Theories 2, 5, 8, 9, 12, 19, 22, 39, 51, 55, 61, 64, 65, 67 and 72 are not connected to any other theory within this book, therefore these theories are not depicted in the diagram.

This network had a 'density' of 1.8%, meaning less than 2% of all the possible connections within the network were present (Hanneman & Riddle, 2005; Valente, 2010). Although we lack a comparison group, these data suggest that the network density is very low (Valente, 2010).

Figure 3.2 presents a network diagram that is identical to Figure 3.1 except that the size of the nodes corresponds to the centrality associated with each theory in the compendium (i.e. larger nodes are more central in the sense that they have more connections).

ABC OF BEHAVIOUR CHANGE THEORIES

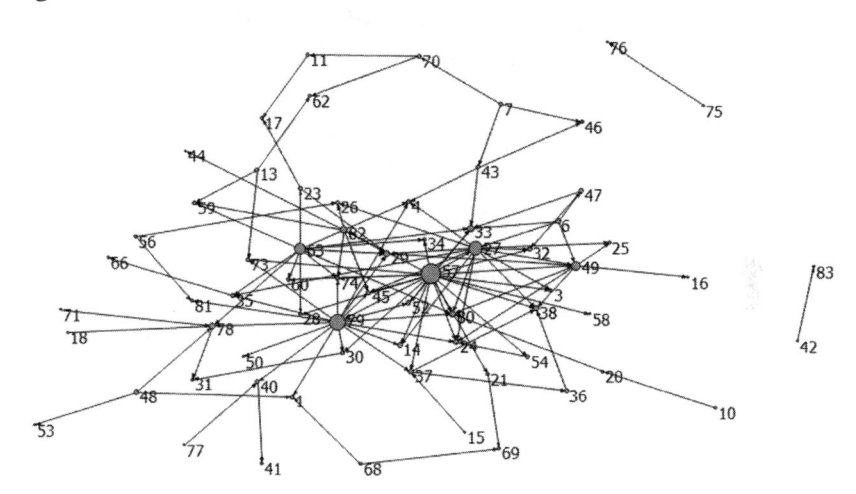

Figure 3.2 Centrality of theories within the network

NOTE: Theories 2, 5, 8, 9, 12, 19, 22, 39, 51, 55, 61, 64, 65, 67 and 72 are not connected to any other theory within this book, therefore these theories are not depicted in the diagram.

To identify central behaviour change theories, degree centrality was assessed. This measure assesses the number of links to (in-degree) and from (out-degree) a theory and is calculated without reference to the overall structure of the network. This measure is directional; in-degree centrally measures the number of theories that contributed to an individual theory whereas out-degree centrality measures how many theories an individual theory contributed to (see Table 3.1).

Table 3.1 Degree Centrality Scores

	Mean Score	Standard Deviation	Minimum Score	Maximum Score
Out-Degree	1.47	3.69	0	23
In-Degree	1.47	1.61	0	6

The range of out-degree scores was wide but on average theories contributed to one or two theories within the compendium (Table 3.1). While 60% of theories did not contribute to any theory in this book, seven theories had an out-degree score of greater than or equal to four indicating that they contributed to the development of ≥4 theories (Table 3.1). In ascending order these theories included:

6. Change Theory contributed to four theories

49. Protection Motivation Theory contributed to six theories

82. Transtheoretical Model of Behaviour Change contributed to six theories

63. Social Cognitive Theory contributed to 12 theories

27. Health Belief Model contributed to 13 theories

79. Theory of Planned Behaviour contributed to 17 theories

57. Self-Efficacy Theory contributed to 23 theories

On average theories were informed by one or two theories within the compendium (Table 3.1). While 36% of theories did not name any theories within this book contributing to their development, eight theories had an in-degree score of ≥4 indicating that at least four theories contributed to its development. In ascending order these theories included:

4. Behavioural-Ecological Model of Adolescent AIDS Prevention was influenced by four theories

45. Pressure System Model was influenced by four theories.

74. Temporal Self-Regulation Theory was influenced by four theories

24. Health Action Process Approach was influenced by five theories

78. Theory of Normative Social Behaviour was influenced by five theories

29. I-Change Model was influenced by six theories

33. Integrated Theory of Drinking Behaviour was influenced by six theories

80. Theory of Triadic Influence was influenced by six theories

Chapter 4: Descriptions of Behaviour Change Theories

This chapter constitutes the main part of this book and provides an alphabetical list of the behaviour change theories identified. In each case the name of the theory and its principal proponent is given, followed by a list of constructs identified as forming part of the theory. This is followed by a brief summary of the theory, then a more detailed description and finally a list of theories in the compendium that were explicitly stated as having informed it. This list is accompanied by a network diagram depicting the interconnections between the theory and its contributing theories.

We have done our best to characterise the theories accurately but it is inevitable that interpretations will have had to be made and in the case of some theories, it will not have been possible to describe every facet of the theory. Readers are therefore strongly advised to go to the primary theory source for more information.

1. Action Theory Model of Consumption (Bagozzi)

Constructs

- Goal intention
- Desirability and feasibility of goals
- Anticipated emotions
- Attitudes
- Normative beliefs
- Subjective norm
- Motivation to comply
- Beliefs and evaluations
- Somatic marker processes
- Desire
- Social identity processes
- Perceived behavioural control
- Moral imperatives
- Implementation intention
- Trying
- Performance of goal-directed behaviours
- Situational forces
- Feedback
- Goal attainment or failure
- Frequency of past behaviour
- Recency of past behaviour

Brief Summary

The Action Theory Model of Consumption is a micro model of consumption that aims to explain the processes involved in purchasing an item or a service. The theory takes into account not only rational cognitive processes, but also the influence of habitual, non-conscious, emotional and social processes.

Description

According to the Action Theory Model of Consumption, the decision to pursue a particular goal (i.e. a **goal intention**) is made after assessing the **desirability and feasibility** of various possible goals. The goal may be to purchase and own an object as an end in itself, or to purchase something as a means of attaining further goals (e.g. an exercise bike in order to lose weight). Potential consumers imagine how they will feel if they make or do not make the purchase. These **anticipated emotions** are seen as key motivators for moving towards the goal (if the emotion is positive) or withdrawing from it (if the emotion is negative). Potential consumers hold a personal **attitude** towards the product or service, and an internalised sense of important others' **normative beliefs** about the product and whether or not it should be purchased. Purchasing decisions are influenced by this felt **subjective norm**, i.e. by the potential consumer's **motivation to comply** with the expectations of these significant others. Both attitudes and subjective norms are proposed to be a function of a person's **beliefs and evaluations** about/of the characteristics of a product or service. In addition, 'subconscious' activities termed '**somatic marker processes**' (i.e. biases arising from previous emotional experiences associated with consuming) influence all conscious reasoning - and all of the above processes - and serve to improve decision-making.

The factors involved in deciding whether or not to buy something are mediated by the role of **desire**, which is the catalyst for action. In addition, **social identity processes** (i.e. the ways in which people process information based on an awareness of their place in a group, their emotional attachment to the group and the value they place on being a member of that group), **perceived behavioural control** (i.e. a person's beliefs about their ability to carry out a behaviour, and about the possible outcomes of that behaviour) and **moral imperatives** are proposed to influence behaviour through the mediating role of desire.

Implementation intentions (relating to behaviours that are thought to promote goal attainment) follow on from desire. These can be defined as encompassing commitments to act, memory processes and execution rules (e.g. I intend to do [X] in [Y] situation). The realisation of intentions begins with **trying** to consume, when a combination of cognitive, emotional and physical processes occur (in sequence, in parallel, or interactively) that move a person towards achieving their goal. The end-point of the theory is the **performance of goal-directed behaviours**, which should lead to goal attainment. However, situational forces within the environment may either facilitate or prevent goal attainment.

People receive **feedback** via satisfaction, dissatisfaction and other affective, interpretive and intellectual responses to **goal attainment or failure**. Feedback in turn influences beliefs and evaluations, subjective norms, attitudes etc. and thus influences any future decision-making. The **frequency of past behaviour** and **recency of past behaviour** also have a positive influence upon future behaviour.

A diagram of the Action Theory Model of Consumption can be found on p.105 of Bagozzi (2000)[1].

---

[1] We would have liked to reproduce all relevant theory diagrams in this book but could not because of the high cost set by publishers.

Contributing Theories:

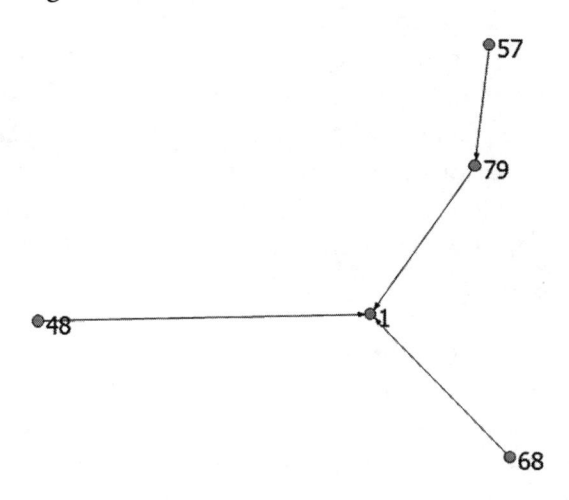

As indicated in the network diagram, the following theories included within this book were identified as contributing to the development of the Action Theory Model of Consumption:

48. Prospect Theory

68. Social Identity Theory

79. Theory of Planned Behaviour

Taken from:

Bagozzi, R.P. (2000). The Poverty of Economic Explanations of consumption and an Action Theory Alternative. *Managerial and Decision Economics*, 21, 95-109.

2. Affective Events Theory (Weiss & Cropanzano)

Constructs

- Affective reactions
- Work events
- Dispositions
- Work environmental features
- Work attitudes
- Judgment driven behaviours
- Affect driven behaviours

Brief Summary

Affective Events Theory aims to explain how affective experiences (i.e. those relating to moods, emotions and attitudes) affect job satisfaction and performance. It focuses on the structure, causes and consequences of affective experiences at work and explores their direct effects on attitudes and behaviours.

Description

Affective Events Theory focuses upon **affective reactions**; specifically the structure, causes and consequences of such reactions at work. Affective reactions fluctuate over time and these fluctuations can be attributed to internal causes (e.g. affective **dispositions**) and external causes (e.g. affect-relevant events). Externally, **work events**, as opposed to the work environment, directly influence affective reactions. **Work environmental features** have an indirect effect on affective reactions by influencing the actual or perceived likelihood of work events occurring. Internally, **affective reactions** are directly influenced by a person's **dispositions** (fluctuations in mood). Dispositions can also affect the influence of work events on affective reactions.

Affective reactions lead to both attitudinal and behavioural outcomes. Affective reactions directly influence **work attitudes** which are also directly and indirectly influenced by work environment features. Whilst features of the work environment are seen to directly influence the 'cognitive judgement' component of work attitudes, work environment features also influence work attitudes indirectly through its influence on affective reactions.

In addition to work attitudes, affective reactions also influence two categories of behaviour: '**affect driven behaviours**' and '**judgement driven behaviours**'. Affect driven behaviours are directly influenced by affective reactions and are a consequence of processes such as coping or mood-management, or the effect of affect upon cognitive processing or judgement bias. Alternatively, judgement-driven behaviours are indirectly influenced by affective reactions through work attitudes. Judgement-drive behaviours are seen as the consequences of decision-making processes which incorporate a person's evaluations of his or her job.

A diagram of Affective Events Theory can be found on p.12 of Weiss & Cropanzano (1996).

Contributing Theories:

None of the theories included within this book were identified as contributing to the development of Affective Events Theory.

Taken from:

Weiss, H. M. & Cropanzano, R. (1996). Affective events theory: A theoretical discussion of the structure, causes, and consequences of affective experiences at work. *Research in Organisational Behaviour*, 18, 1-74.

3. Aids Risk Reduction Model (Catania et al.)

Constructs

- Problem perception
    - Knowledge
    - Perceived susceptibility to HIV
    - Beliefs about the undesirability of AIDS
- Commitment to change
    - Response efficacy
    - Enjoyment values
    - Self-efficacy
- Taking action
    - Information-seeking
        - Health education
    - Help-seeking
        - Global self-esteem
        - Prior related experiences
        - Prior success or failure
        - Perceived importance of problem
        - Resources
    - Enacting solutions
        - Partner engagement
        - Communication skills
- Social networks
- Social norms
- Aversive emotional states
- External motivators

Brief Summary

The AIDS risk reduction model is a model that aims to explain and, facilitate study of, HIV-protective behaviours. The model conceptualises the behaviour change process in three stages (labelling, commitment and enactment) and outlines social, psychological and emotional factors that influence progress through these stages.

Description

The AIDS Risk Reduction Model proposes that the process of adopting HIV-protective behaviours occurs in 3 stages. Stage 1 (**labelling**) involves labelling sexual behaviours as high risk for HIV infection. Stage 2 (**commitment**) involves making a **commitment to change** by reducing their high risk behaviours and increasing their low risk behaviours. Stage 3 (**enactment**) involves finding and carrying out strategies to achieve this goal. Progression through the stages is dependent on achieving goals in previous stages. However, movement through the stages is not unidirectional. For instance, failed behaviour change attempts may lead to a loss of commitment or to 're-labelling' behaviours as unproblematic.

Stage 1: Labelling

Three factors are influential in the labelling of sexual behaviours as problematic or risky (**problem perception**). First, **knowledge** of the risk factors for HIV transmission is essential for personal risk to be assessed accurately. Knowledge is also necessary for development of the second factor: **perceived susceptibility to HIV** infection. People who do not believe that they are at risk of HIV infection are unlikely to engage in behaviour change attempts. The third factor is '**beliefs about the undesirability of AIDS**'. If these three factors exist then a person will label their sexual behaviour as problematic. **Social norms** and **social networks** are also influential during this process. For instance, social networks may influence knowledge of risk factors, whilst social norms could influence labelling through the disapproval of high risk behaviours.

Stage 2: Commitment

This commitment stage involves a complex decision-making process that bridges the acknowledgement of problematic or risky behaviour and actual behaviour change. Commitment to change is influenced by whether perceived benefits of change outweigh the perceived costs. This assessment involves perceptions of **response efficacy** (i.e. whether reducing high-risk sexual behaviours and increasing low-risk behaviours is effective in reducing HIV-risk) and **enjoyment values** (i.e. whether protective behaviours such as condom use are seen as more or less enjoyable than high-risk behaviours such as unprotected sex).

If response efficacy beliefs and enjoyment values for HIV-protective behaviours are high, the likelihood of commitment is greater. In addition, greater levels of **self-efficacy** (i.e. a person's perceptions of their ability to perform the protective behaviours) facilitate commitment. Knowledge may also influence this process, with the likelihood of commitment being higher if a person is knowledgeable about the health benefits of protective behaviours and/or ways of increasing the enjoyableness of protective behaviours. Social networks and social norms that build self-efficacy (e.g. observation of another's successful behaviour change) and reinforce beliefs about benefits outweighing costs are also influential in the commitment process.

Stage 3: Enactment

Once a person commits to behaviour change, they begin **taking action** to achieve the goal. This process involves three phase: **information-seeking, help-seeking** and **enacting solutions**. These three phases may occur concurrently, and some phases may be skipped.

During the information-seeking phase, people gather ideas and opinions regarding ways to change high-risk sexual behaviours. **Health education** is important in this phase, specifically education that provides information on the best types of help and how to access them.

During the help-seeking phase, people decide whether to choose self-help, formal help, professional help or any combination of the three. Social norms may be influential in this process, as cultural norms might stigmatise less self-reliant forms of help-seeking (i.e. professional help). Other factors also affect the help-seeking process by influencing beliefs about the effectiveness of help or help-seeking choices. These include **global self-esteem, prior related experiences** of problems or solutions, the size of a person's social network, **prior success or failure** in attempts to solve the problem, **perceived importance of the problem** (compared to other on-going problems) and the **resources** required to obtain help.

During the final stage of 'enactment', efforts to change risk-related sexual behaviours are made. The success of these efforts may be influenced by **partner engagement** (i.e. whether a person's sexual partner is also willing to change behaviour). Relatedly, **communication skills** facilitate enactment as successful communication may be necessary in persuading a reluctant partner to change sexual behaviours. For communication to be effective in determining behaviour change, at least one partner in a relationship must have progressed through prior stages in the model, and the chances of behaviour change are greatest when both have made this progression.

Movement through the Stages

In addition to variables within the three stages of the model, other internal and external factors can influence movement from stage to stage. **Aversive emotional states** (such as distress, fear and anxiety) influence movement by impacting on perceptions of seriousness of the problem, prompting help-seeking or influencing self-efficacy beliefs. **External motivators** such as public health education campaigns motivate movement through the stages by influencing perceptions of susceptibility to and severity of HIV infection. Other external factors such as support groups and social norms that promote risk-related behaviour change may also facilitate progression through the stages of the model.

A diagram of the AIDS Risk Reduction Model can be found on p.54 of Catania, Kegeles & Coates (1990).

Contributing Theories:

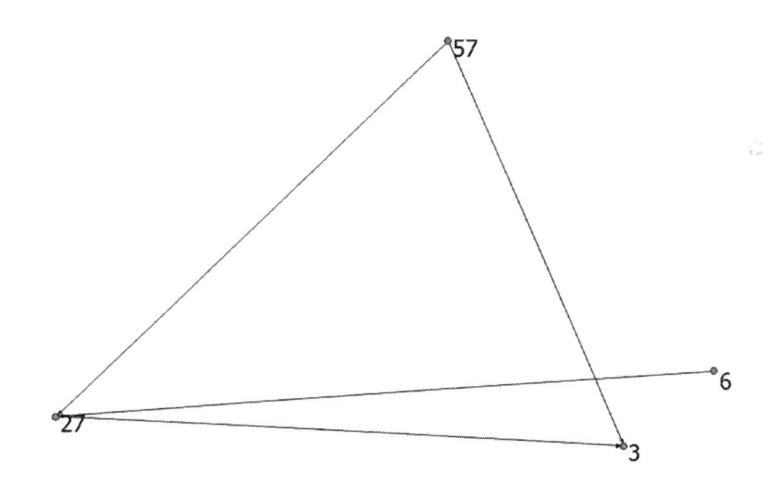

As outlined in the network diagram, the following theories included within this book were identified as contributing to the development of the AIDS Risk Reduction Model:

27. Health Belief Model

57. Self-Efficacy Theory

Taken from:

Catania, J.A., Kegeles, S.M., & Coates, T.J. (1990). Toward an Understanding of Risk Behaviour: An AIDS Risk Reduction Model (ARRM). *Health Education & Behaviour, 17,* 53-72.

4. Behavioural-Ecological Model of Adolescent Aids Prevention (Hovell et al.)

Constructs

- Background variables/antecedents
    o Genetics/biology
    o Past reinforcement/reinforcement history
    o Culture and gender roles
    o Socio-economic status
    o Family influences
    o School influences
    o Peer influences
    o Media models
    o Sexual partners
    o Assertiveness/social skills
    o Knowledge
    o Attitudes
    o Self-efficacy
    o Drug use/abuse
- Consequences:
    o Sexual pleasure
    o Partner's sexual pleasure
    o Communication with others
    o Hassles
    o Peer/social reactions
    o Physical outcomes
    o Family reactions
    o General community reactions
- Wider influences:
    o Dynamic systems
    o Multiple schedules
    o Meta-contingencies
    o Density of social reinforcement

Brief Summary

The Behavioural-Ecological model of Adolescent AIDS Prevention aims to guide effective strategies to change adolescent sexual risk behaviour. The model is based on an integration of learning theories within a socio-ecological model of behaviour, and proposes that experiences of reward and punishment for sexual behaviours play a central role in determining safe or unsafe sexual behaviours.

Description

The Behavioural-Ecological model of Adolescent AIDS Prevention proposes that experiences of reinforcement (i.e. reward) and punishment for sexual behaviours play a central role in determining safe or unsafe sex behaviours (i.e. condom use/non-use). The **antecedents** of these behaviours, and the rewarding/punitive **consequences** of them, are generated from a number of social institutions. Behavioural antecedents are arranged along a continuum of less influential ('background' and 'distal' variables) to more influential ('proximal') antecedents. Similarly, behavioural consequences are arranged along a continuum of 'proximal' to 'distal'. These consequences provide feedback and become antecedents of future behaviour. Behavioural consequences are the most powerful determinant of sexual risk behaviour.

Antecedents of Behaviour

There are a number of antecedents to sexual behaviour, which are outlined below.

- **Genetics and biology:** Influence a person's propensity to engage in (or be rewarded by) sexual behaviour. These are among the most distal influences and so do not exert a direct effect on sexual behaviour. Their influence is moderated by social context and social learning.

- **Reinforcement history:** One of the strongest influences on sexual behaviour. Past reinforcement for condom use or for risky sex practices raises the likelihood of condom use or risky sexual behaviour, respectively, in the future.

- **Culture and gender roles:** The general culture within which a person is raised exerts an influence on sexual behaviour as it provides 'rules' for behaviour and establishes the gender roles to be followed. Culture can provide reinforcing or punishing feedback, and exerts influences through multiple channels such as media, family and schools. Subcultures may also provide concurrent cultural influences of behaviour. Because sexual behaviour occurs in relative privacy, the role of culture in determining sexual behaviour is weak in comparison to the reinforcement obtained from sexual intercourse.

- **Socio-economic status:** Represents social experiences and social ecology, which influence behaviours. It influences sexual practices specifically through determining quality of education and community services, and the nature of peer groups associated with different levels of socio-economic status.

- **Family influences:** Family influences may determine sexual behaviour depending on the degree to which parents communicate about sexually sensitive issues, and express love. Parental relationships, divorce and dating may provide a model for social and sexual relationships, as might siblings' relationships. Parental rule-setting and/or positive reinforcement are also seen to play a potential role in determining sexual behaviour.

- **School influences:** Schools are seen to influence sexual behaviours primarily through the influence of peers, and through sex education. Education promotes educational aspirations or career goals, which may influence condom use (e.g. desire to avoid pregnancy, since pregnancy would present a barrier to such goals).

- **Peer influences:** Peers provide models of behaviour which are often imitated by a person. Peers may also shape sexual behaviour as a result of criticism or praise. This relationship is described as 'imprecise', due to the privacy in which sexual behaviour occurs.

- **Sexual partners:** Partners influence sexual behaviours in a number of ways: prompting, modelling and reinforcing certain sexual behaviours. Enjoyable experiences of sex are reinforcing, and thus promote further pursuit of sexual intercourse. Skills in communication with a potential sexual partner may dictate the likelihood of being able to engage in safe-sex behaviours (e.g. condom use).

- **Assertiveness and social skills:** These are very influential in facilitating the discussion of HIV risk, elicitation of sexual/drug use history and persuading a partner to use a condom. However, if reinforcement history does not support restraint from/postponement of sexual gratification, assertiveness skills may not be enough to dictate safe-sex behaviours.

- **Media models:** This is an antecedent to sexual behaviours, as the media provides models of sexual behaviour which may or may not promote condom use/safe sex.

- **Knowledge and attitudes:** These are not direct determinants of behaviour, but have influences on other motivational or context variables which may determine behaviour.

- **Self-efficacy:** This can be defined as a person's confidence in their ability to carry out a given behaviour. It is proposed to be a the most powerful attitudinal variable, which might arise from previous observation or reinforcement.

- **Drug use/abuse:** This is a potential determinant of risky sexual behaviour as the disinhibiting effects of drugs can compromise judgement. As risky sexual behaviour often co-occurs with drug use, alcohol consumption and cigarette smoking, a certain class of adolescents may be 'risk behaviour responsive'.

Consequences of Behaviour

These include **sexual pleasure, partner's sexual pleasure, communication with others, hassles** (e.g. minor discomfort), **peer/social reactions, physical outcomes** (e.g. pregnancy or disease), **general community reactions** and **family reactions**. Temporally, the more proximal a consequence is to the behaviour (e.g. condom use) the greater an influence it has. Similarly, the more temporally distal a consequence is from the behaviour, the weaker the influence on future behaviour. The combination of these consequences results in a balance of rewarding or punitive/aversive consequences, which defines a 'net' rewarding or punitive effect. This 'net' effect feeds back into the model as an antecedent, contributing to the reinforcement history.

Broader Ecological Influences

The constructs can be understood in the context of **wider influences**:

- **Dynamic systems:** Environmental antecedents are seen as ever-changing, and this change influences behaviour. Thus, to establish and maintain routine condom use, prompting and reinforcing variables must remain present. Factors that prompt or reinforce may change along with the environment.

- **Multiple schedules:** Complex behaviours can be maintained by complex multiple schedules (i.e. multiple reinforcers for multiple behaviours). Sexual intercourse is seen to be a powerfully reinforcing behaviour, whilst condom use is mildly aversive. Therefore, multiple schedules of reinforcement are required to reinforce condom use behaviours. This means all institutions (i.e. schools, family, peers) need to promote condom use: one is insufficient.

- **Meta-contingencies:** A whole culture or cultural norm either reinforces or punishes a behaviour. If the norm is to use condoms, it is hard to avoid punitive social consequences if one does not.

- **Density of social reinforcement:** The punishment for condom use can be counteracted by relatively weak social prompts and reinforcers *if* they are provided frequently, e.g. explicit social pressure to use condoms.

A diagram of the Behavioural-Ecological Model of Adolescent AIDS Prevention can be found on p.270 of Hovell, Hillman, Blumberg, Sipan, Atkins, Hofstetter & Myers (1994).

Contributing Theories:

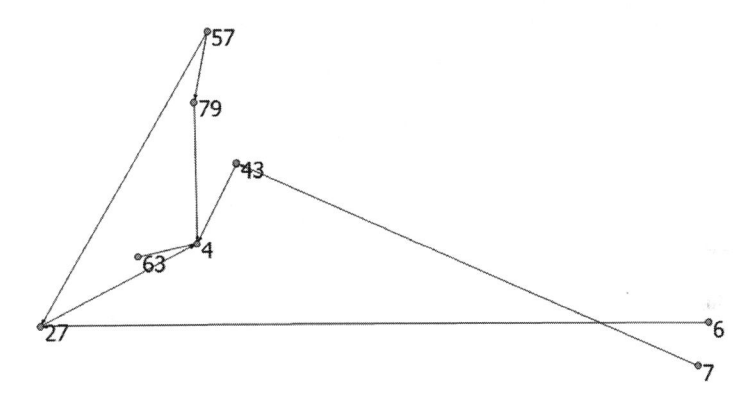

As outlined in the network diagram, the following theories included within this book were identified as contributing to the development of the Behavioural-Ecological Model of Adolescent AIDS Prevention:

27. Health Belief Model

43. Operant Learning Theory

63. Social Cognitive Theory

79. Theory of Planned Behaviour

Taken from:

Hovell, M. F., Hillman, E. R., Blumberg, E., Sipan, C., Atkins, C., Hofstetter, C. R., Myers, C. A. (1994). A behavioural-ecological model of adolescent sexual development: A template for AIDS prevention. *Journal of Sex Research*, 31, 267-281.

5. CEOS Theory (Borland)

Constructs
- Behaviours
    - o Hard to maintain
        - ☐ Hard to sustain
        - ☐ Hard to resist/reduce
    - o Easy to maintain
- Context
    - o The relatively stable environment
        - ☐ Physical
        - ☐ Social
            - • Laws and regulations
            - • Normative behaviours
        - ☐ Intellectual/Conceptual
    - o Cues/Stimuli
        - ☐ Approach
        - ☐ Avoid
        - ☐ Propositions
        - ☐ Reminders and prompts
        - ☐ Models
    - o Resources
        - ☐ Change agents
        - ☐ Tools
            - • Drugs
            - • Physical aids
            - • Conceptual aids
- Executive processes: Conceptual, top-down, limited capacity
    - o Frames
    - o Goals
    - o Values and beliefs
    - o Episodic memories
    - o Propositional knowledge
    - o Analysis and inference
    - o Scripts
        - ☐ Rules and plans
    - o Self-regulation
- Operational processes: Relational, bottom-up
    - o Inputs

- ☐ Attention
- ☐ Sensations
  - o Internal states
    - ☐ Arousal
    - ☐ Needs and drives
  - o Outputs
    - ☐ Action tendencies
    - ☐ Response Inhibition
    - ☐ Emotional expression
    - ☐ Action schemata
  - o Change mechanisms
    - ☐ Conditioning
    - ☐ Imitation
  - o Internal resources
    - ☐ Skills
    - ☐ Capacities
      - Physical and mental
      - Variation in population over time
    - ☐ Fatigue
- Systems
  - o Hierarchical
    - ☐ Inputs and outputs
    - ☐ Reference levels
    - ☐ Homeostasis
  - o Feedback
- Operational inputs to Executive Processes
  - o Perception
  - o Feelings
    - ☐ Negative affect
    - ☐ Positive affect
  - o Experienced needs/desires
  - o Urges/Impulse to act
  - o Associative memories
    - ☐ Images
- Change processes
  - o Goal identification
  - o Desirability (motivation to change)
    - ☐ Outcome expectancies (relatively stable)
    - ☐ Decisional balance (situational)

- [ ] Priority
- o Achievability
  - [ ] Perceived capacity (relatively stable)
  - [ ] Task difficulty (perceived)
  - [ ] Self-efficacy (situational)
- o Self-regulation
  - [ ] Action scripts (strategy)
  - [ ] Self-control
  - [ ] Commitment
  - [ ] Self re-orientation
  - [ ] Reflection /Evaluation
  - [ ] Vigilance
- o Changing the context
  - [ ] Policy and institutional change
  - [ ] Restructuring personal environments

Brief Summary

CEOS (standing for Context, Executive and Operational Systems) is a general theory of behaviour and behaviour change, specifically focusing on hard to maintain (HTM) behaviour. CEOS proposes a) an Executive System, ES that formulates and acts towards conceptually generated goals via scripts for action, and b) an Operational System (OS) that acts continuously to seek a homeostatic balance between environmental context and internal needs, and through which ES processes can only act to control behaviour when they generate sufficient affective force to counter that which is generated by the OS in response to the prevailing context. These processes of self-regulation involve self-control, strategic capacity, and capacity for self-reorientation (acting to recondition OS processes or by re-conceptualising the problem). The pursuit of a goal requires self-regulatory mechanisms to balance continual changes in the perceived desirability and achievability of the goal, modulated by two levels of feedback, one immediate and the other, a more reflective and conceptual evaluation.

Description

CEOS Theory is a model of **behaviour** that is designed to be consistent with knowledge about control systems and human capacities. It highlights the interaction between conscious and non-conscious influences on behaviour. The focus on **Hard to Maintain (HTM)** behaviours means it is designed to be an all-encompassing theory of behaviour change.

HTM behaviours are those where there is an imbalance between the assessed desirability of a **goal** of the **Executive System (ES)** and the extent to which relevant behaviours are generated by the bottom up **Operational System (OS)**. Behaviours desired by the ES but not supported by the OS are **hard to sustain**, while those not wanted by the ES, but strongly cued within the OS are **hard to reduce** or eliminate. Somewhat different challenges are involved in maintaining these two kinds of HTM behaviours.

The **context** that supports behaviour, understood from an executive perspective, has **relatively stable** aspects, critical for planning, resources available to facilitate action, and situational factors which act as cues for acting or reacting.

The OS is a bottom-up, hierarchical, relational system that continually acts to maintain or regain homeostatic balance in relation to its needs and the ever-changing environmental context. Each level of the hierarchy has flexible reference criteria as to whether information can lead to stimuli to generate actions and/or signals being passed up to the next highest level of the hierarchy for more integrated processing (including by the ES). OS processes are continually reactive to the context (environment) plus to influences from ES conceptualisations, resulting in continually changing patterns of action tendencies. More complex actions require higher-level processing, and thus take more time before action can be initiated. This delay for processing requires capacity for inhibition of any action tendencies before the final decision to act is made, which is critical for ES functioning.

The ES is an emergent property of the OS. The actions of the ES are grounded in conscious experience and operate to influence behaviour in pursuit of linguistically created goals. It is self-reflective and operates top-down. It can set itself goals and has the **self-regulatory capacity** to work to achieve them. It is informed about the world, the needs of its OS, and of emerging action tendencies via **perceptions, feelings, associative memories,** and **urges**. It organises aspects of the world through **stories**, which act to **frame** the way an issue is thought about and thus constrain the elaboration of **scripts** for action. The ES has capacity to directly inhibit action tendencies (self-control) to allow time for higher level processing. However, the ES cannot act independently of the OS; it needs to stimulate activity within the OS sufficient to generate goal-congruent action tendencies sufficient to compete with any incompatible tendencies arising from bottom-up processing within the OS.

Changes in the context can lead to different **conditioned actions** emerging, different **models** to imitate, new **tools** to facilitate actions, and/or change the framing or perspective from which the situation is analysed which can bring in new ways of thinking about the problem and consideration of new issues that are not physically present, and thus not automatically taken into account. HTM behaviours are ones that typically require active self-regulation on top of any useful changes in framing or in environmental conditions.

Concepts and ideas generated within the ES stimulate **associative networks**, but they need to evoke sufficient **affective force** if they are to activate **action tendencies**. Unlike OS reactions which are generated by relevant environmental cues, so are always there when the context for action is right, ES ideas which are inconsistent with OS tendencies are not automatically evoked. It requires active self-regulatory action to generate them. **Concrete concepts** activate OS processes more rapidly than relational terms. To maximise congruence between conceptual meaning and OS reactions, communications should be conceptually simple and avoid negations. **Temporal discounting** occurs in part because more distant events are harder to imagine and thus generate less affective force.

Feelings (emotions and urges) are signals to the ES as to states of the OS, while emotional expressions are signals to other beings. For the most part, **negative affect** signals OS-generated need for remedial action, while **positive affect** either signals the desirability of continuing/resuming an activity or its successful completion. Feelings, along with perception, ground ideas in the present reality (person in context), and under most conditions guide people to choose the ideas to implement that will be most likely to minimise risks and maximise benefits to both the self and the broader community. However, for HTM behaviours, aspects of this grounding lead people astray.

The central role of the ES is self-regulation. The key elements of self-regulation are self-control which involves the inhibition of action to provide time for alternative solutions to emerge or be developed; the development of plans or scripts for action, and re-orientation, which involves retraining the OS to respond differently to stimuli that evoke undesirable action tendencies. 'Scripts' refer to the range of conceptual **rules** and constraints a person brings to a task, and can include specific **plans** such as **implementation intentions**.

Beyond **goal-setting**, the main challenges of behaviour change are **initiating attempts** to change, **persisting** in the face of pressures to relapse and coming to accept the change as a desirable new way of living (i.e. integrating it with valued aspects of one's lifestyle). This requires **vigilance**, and the nature of this changes as this behaviour change is displaced as a priority action by other life goals.

HTM behaviours typically require a number of attempts to change over an extended period of time. Initially, goals are generated by some analysis of the **desirability** of the action with consideration of whether it is possible (**achievability**). Goals need to be able to be maintained over time, but their active contemplation only occurs when the relevant thoughts are evoked. On these occasions, attempts to change may occur where the **decisional balance** between three sets of factors point to action. First, **outcome expectancies**, the **priority** of the goal for action, and immediate concerns about losses (experienced discomfort) result in a decisional balance that action is or remains desirable. Second, perceptions of **task difficulty** in relation to capacity result in shifts in moment to moment **self-efficacy** as to the achievability of acting now. The third set of factors is having adequate self-regulatory capacity including a script for action and some form of **commitment** to act. As action progresses, immediate **feedback** and more reflective **evaluation** can alter the balance of forces, which if there are too many challenges can lead to temporarily abandoning the goal (**relapse**). A strong commitment (self-control) based in a script of temporary suffering, can be used to span short periods of perceived net loss.

Understanding change is about identifying the elements of the biopsychosocial determinants of HTM behaviours that are most central to facilitation of the desired change. For those predominantly conceptual or social in origin, environmental change and educational strategies are likely to be sufficient. However, where there is a bio-psychological element, facilitating change will require self-regulatory strategies as well, and where biological aspects hinder change, it may also require biological interventions. Failure to sustain attempts to change is evidence that the determinants of success are outside the framing of the script for action, sometimes manifest as incapacity to implement aspects of the action script. Some people will be unable to make changes that are relatively unproblematic for others. Low levels of other rewarding activities in life and psychological trauma are both factors that increase the difficulty in shifting from immediately attractive, but destructive, long-term behaviours, in part because they increase temporal discounting. Individual differences, whether innate or acquired, are a reality. Among those for whom change is more difficult, the use of external aids can make it easier, either in the short-term (e.g. use of quit smoking medications) to allow for adjustment of OS-processes; or longer term by providing attractive alternatives (e.g. low fat foods), thus obviating the need to accept such a large loss of value. The limits of human capacity to reshape behaviour through executive actions are unknown, so part of the job of behavioural scientists is to continually push these boundaries.

Contributing Theories:

None of the theories included within this book were identified as contributing to the development of CEOS Theory.

Taken from:

Borland, R. (2014). *Understanding Hard to Maintain Behaviour Change: A dual process approach.* Oxford, UK: Wiley Blackwell

6. Change Theory (Lewin)

Constructs
- Equilibrium
- Driving forces
- Restraining forces
- Group standard
    o Social habits
- Processes of change
    o Unfreezing
    o Movement
    o Freezing

Brief Summary

Change Theory describes a three-stage process of social change: 1) unfreezing, 2) movement and, 3) freezing. Change or lack of change occurs as a result of the balance between opposing driving and restraining forces.

Description

Change Theory proposes that to understand the conditions that will facilitate change, the conditions for 'no change' (**equilibrium**) must first be understood. Equilibrium occurs when the strength of '**driving forces**' (i.e. forces that promote change in the desired direction) is equal and opposite to the strength of '**restraining forces**' (i.e. forces that prevent change in the desired direction). The strength of these forces is presumed to vary, but equilibrium is maintained as long as they remain equal and opposite (i.e. if the strength of driving forces and restraining forces increase/decrease equally). Changes in levels of social conduct can thus occur in two ways: through driving forces being increased or through restraining forces being decreased.

The application of a force may not always be sufficient to achieve change. In the case of '**social habits**' (i.e. recurrent, established patterns of social attitudes and behaviours) there may be an inner resistance to change and an additional force is needed to 'break the habit' in order for change to be achieved. Social habits are a function of the relationship between individual people and the **group standard** (i.e. the values, beliefs, norms and behaviours shared by the group). Individual change perceived as deviating too greatly from group standards may be resisted as this could lead to ridicule or ostracism, resulting in these resistant 'social habits'. For resistance to change to be overcome, either reductions in the strength of the value of a group standard or reductions in a person's perceptions of the strength of this value must occur.

The process of permanent change involves three **processes of change: 'unfreezing'** of the present level, **'movement'** to a new level of social conduct and **'freezing'** at the new level. Unfreezing involves overcoming resistance to group standards, and may not always be a necessary stage. Movement is facilitated by changes to driving or restraining forces, and results in the establishment of a new equilibrium at the desired level. Freezing at the new level is necessary for change to be maintained, and may be facilitated by group decision-making and organisational changes.

Contributing Theories:

None of the theories included within this book were identified as contributing to the development of Change Theory.

Taken from:

Lewin, K. (1952). *Field Theory in Social Science*. London, UK: Tavistock Publications.

Supplemented by:

Lewin, K. (1958). Group Decision and Social Change. In E.E. Maccoby, T.M. Newcomb & E.L. Hartley (Eds.) *Readings in social psychology* (pp.197-211). New York, USA: Hartley, Holt, Rinehart and Winston.

7. Classical Conditioning (Pavlov)

Constructs
- Unconditioned stimuli
- Unconditioned reflexes
- Neutral stimuli
- Conditioned stimuli
- Conditioned reflexes
- Time relation
- Health and normality
- Alertness
- Properties of the neutral stimulus
- Properties of the unconditioned stimulus

Brief Summary

According to Pavlov's original formulation, classical conditioning theory describes how innate responses to stimuli can become elicited by a previously 'irrelevant' stimulus, through a repeated process of presenting the irrelevant stimulus after the original stimulus. It also proposes factors that can influence this process.

Description

Classical conditioning theory describes how the environment can shape behaviour. It originally focused on how innate, natural responses to environmental stimuli can become learned responses, elicited by alternative stimuli. The theory describes five main concepts; **unconditioned stimuli, unconditioned reflexes, neutral stimuli, conditioned stimuli and conditioned reflexes.**

An 'unconditioned stimulus' is an environmental stimulus which holds a natural significance for a person or animal (e.g. sight or smell of food). An 'unconditioned reflex' is the natural response to the perception of this stimulus (e.g. salivation upon perception of food). Stimuli holding little significance and which therefore have no paired response are described as 'neutral stimuli'. If a neutral stimulus (e.g. the sound of a metronome) is presented repeatedly before an unconditioned stimulus (and never alone), it will begin to elicit the same behavioural response as the unconditioned stimulus (with no need for presentation of the unconditioned stimulus). For instance, repeated presentation of the sound of a metronome prior to the presentation of food will ultimately lead to salivation upon the presentation of the sound of the metronome, even when no food is introduced to the environment. When this stage is reached, the neutral stimulus (metronome) has become a 'conditioned stimulus', and the previously unconditioned response (salivation) has become a 'conditioned response': the neutral stimulus has become superimposed upon the unconditioned stimulus.

Factors Necessary for Establishing Conditioned Responses

For conditioning of stimuli and responses to be successful, certain criteria must be met. First, the **time relation** of the presentation of neutral and unconditioned stimuli is important - to become conditioned, the neutral stimulus must be presented first, as the properties of innate (unconditioned) reflexes are built in to signalled responding behaviour. Second, the nervous system must be in a state of **alertness**. If a person or animal is drowsy, a conditioned reflex will take significantly longer to establish and may not even occur. Third, the **health and normality** of a person's or animal's cerebral hemispheres determine how quickly conditioned reflexes can be established. Finally, the establishment of conditioned reflexes is determined by the **properties of the neutral stimulus** which is to become conditioned, and the **properties of the unconditioned stimulus** which has been selected. Stimuli which initially provoke indifference can readily become conditioned, whilst strong or unusual stimuli make the establishment of conditioned reflexes difficult or even impossible. In conditions where the unconditioned stimulus is quite weak, it is harder or impossible to transform a neutral stimulus into a conditioned stimulus even if it is very favourable. If conditioning does occur then responses are likely to be weak.

Contributing Theories:

None of the theories included within this book were identified as contributing to the development of Classical Conditioning.

Taken from:

Pavlov, I. P. (1927). *Conditioned Reflexes: An Investigation of the Physiological Activity of the Cerebral Cortex.* London: Oxford University Press.

8. COM-B System (Michie et al.)

Constructs

- Capability
    - o Physical
    - o Psychological
- Motivation
    - o Automatic
    - o Reflective
- Opportunity
    - o Physical
    - o Social
- Behaviour

Brief Summary

The COM-B model conceptualises behaviour as a part of system of interacting elements that also involves capability, opportunity and motivation. For any behaviour to occur at a given moment, there must be the capability and opportunity to engage in the behaviour, and the strength of motivation to engage in it must be greater than for any competing behaviours. Capability may be physical or psychological, opportunity may be social or physical and motivation may be 'reflective' or 'automatic'.

Description

In the COM-B system, **behaviour** at a given moment arises from a person's **capability, opportunity** and **motivation** and **opportunity** to enact it.

Capability is conceptualised as both the physical and psychological capacity of a person to perform the behaviour. **Physical** capability includes skill, strength and stamina. **Psychological** capability includes having the knowledge and skills to perform the behaviour, and the capacity to engage in the necessary thought processes such as comprehension and reasoning.

Motivation is the processes in the brain that energise and direct behaviour. This includes not only conscious decision making but also habitual processes, emotional responses or processes involving analytical decision-making. Motivation therefore includes **reflective** processes (involving evaluations and plans) and processes that are **automatic** (emotions and impulses that result from innate dispositions or associative learning).

Opportunity is defined as all the factors extrinsic to a person that either prompt the behaviour or allow enactment of the behaviour. This includes both the **physical opportunities** created by the environment (e.g. time, financial resources, access, and cues) and **social opportunities** created by the cultural environment.

Components can interact: for example, motivation can be influenced by both opportunity and capability, which can in turn influence behaviour. Behaviour can then have a feedback influence upon a person's opportunity, motivation and capability to perform the behaviour again.

COM-B can be used to design behaviour change interventions. Having determined the behaviour/s to be changed (the 'target behaviour/s'), intervention designers can use COM-B to identify which of the components need to change for behaviour to change.

The COM-B system proposes that all intra-physic and external factors are essential and thus no priority is placed on the individual, group or environmental perspective. It may not be necessary to target all the components of the system. To change a particular behaviour the focus may be more on addressing capabilities barriers, while for another a greater focus may need to be placed on motivation. For some behaviours it will be necessary to target all three components.

The COM-B Model

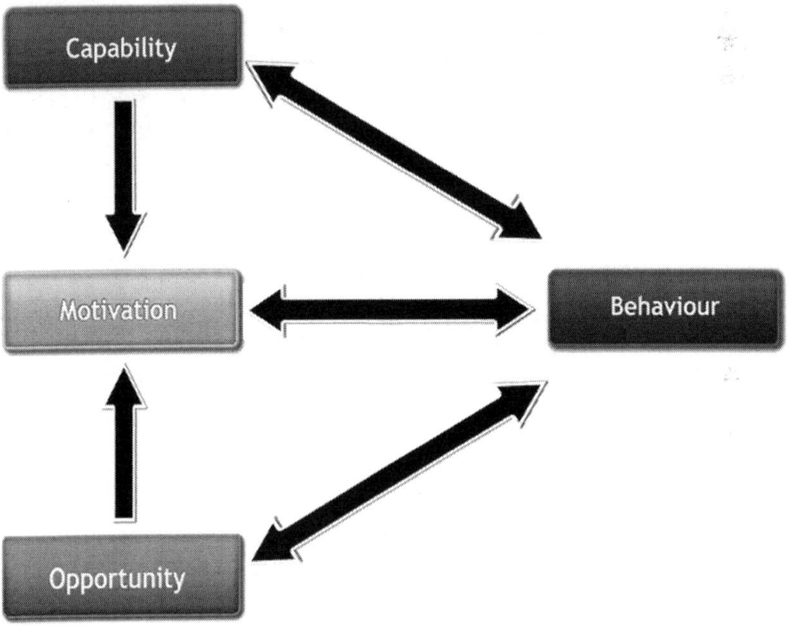

Source: Reproduced from Michie, S., van Stralen, M.M. & West, R. (2011). The behaviour change wheel: a new method for characterising and designing behaviour change interventions. *Implementation Science*, 6:42. Published by BioMed Central.

Contributing Theories:

None of the theories included within this book were identified as contributing to the development of the COM-B System.

Taken from:

Michie, S., van Stralen, M.M. & West, R. (2011). The behaviour change wheel: a new method for characterising and designing behaviour change interventions. *Implementation Science*, 6:42.

9. Consumption as Social Practices (Spaargaren & Van Vliet)

Constructs

- Social practices
- Lifestyle
- Discursive and practical consciousness
- Systems of provision
- Rules and resources
- Socio-technical innovations
- Domestic time-space structure
- Standards of comfort, cleanliness and convenience
- Consumption

Brief Summary

Consumption as Social Practices theory aims to explain consumer behaviour, focusing on pro-environmental domestic behaviour. It describes a mutual dependency between domestic consumers and external systems that provide domestic goods, where consumers are unable to engage in environmentally sustainable lifestyles unless external systems provide facilitative goods and take into account consumers' domestic practices.

Description

Consumption as Social Practices Theory aims to explain people's consumer behaviour in context (i.e. as they are situated in time and space and shared with other people), and refers to behaviours as **'social practices'**. The theory attempts to avoid divisions between the analysis of individual behaviour and of institutional behaviour by embedding social practices centrally between individual-level factors and institutional-level factors.

People's unique behaviours diverge into distinct social practices, and every person's unique set of social practices forms their **lifestyle**. Lifestyle is not defined solely as this set of social practices, but also as an expression of identity or who a person wants to be. From the institutional perspective, social practices are influenced by **rules and resources** (i.e. infrastructures such as sewage systems, domestic commodities, conventions). Their influence upon social practices is supported by the **systems of provision** (e.g. sewage systems, electricity grids, water systems) that underpin everyday life, as people can only make use of them of them if they are made available through systems of provision.

Socio-technical innovations are domestic goods or services that facilitate pro-environmental behaviour and can influence social practices and domestic **consumption**. People's consumption of these goods is influenced by the systems of provision that make them available, their **standards of comfort, cleanliness and convenience** (e.g. social standards about acceptable levels of hygiene, etc.) and their **domestic time-space structure**. The latter relates to the domestic tasks that a person has to do (e.g. cleaning, laundry, childcare) and how the amount of time they have to spend on them limits their personal availability (i.e. the amount of time they have available to engage in social activities). People are motivated to maximise their personal availability as this facilitates increases in their social status.

People with high levels of environmental awareness (termed **discursive and practical consciousness**) who aim to live more environmentally sustainable lifestyles are reliant upon external systems to provide the necessary goods or services that facilitate such a lifestyle. External systems of provision are, in turn, reliant upon consumers. For people's social practices and lifestyles to become more environmentally sustainable, external systems must provide goods that increase people's personal availability and are consistent with their lifestyles and standards of comfort, cleanliness and convenience.

A diagram of Consumption as Social Practices Theory can be found on p.71 of Spaargaren & Van Vliet (2000).

Contributing Theories:

None of the theories included within this book were identified as contributing to the development of Consumption as Social Practices.

Taken from:

Spaargaren, G. & Van Vliet, B. (2000). Lifestyles, Consumption and the Environment: the ecological modernisation of domestic consumption. *Environmental Politics*, 9(1), 50-76.

Supplemented by:

Spaargaren, G. (2000). Ecological Modernization Theory and Domestic Consumption. *Journal of Environmental Policy & Planning*, 2, 323-335.

10. Containment Theory (Reckless)

Constructs

- Inner containment
- Outer containment
- Environmental pressures
- Environmental pulls
- Inner pushes
- Regulation of normative behaviour
- Resistance to deviancy

Brief Summary

Containment Theory is a theory of deviant behaviour. It proposes that people are subject to both an inner control system and an outer control system, each of which regulates conduct and prevents deviant behaviour.

Description

Containment Theory proposes that there are two forces that regulate behaviour: **inner containment** and **outer containment**. 'Inner containment' relates to factors that are involved in regulation of the self, such as self-control, self-concept, ego strength, the ability to tolerate frustration and resist diversions, a high sense of responsibility and orientation towards goals, as well as the ability to find alternative sources of satisfaction and ways of releasing tension.

'Outer containment' refers to aspects of a person's social world that are able to hold that person within certain boundaries. These might include a consistent moral presence, the reinforcement of norms and goals, achievable social expectations, supervision, discipline, opportunities for activity, including tension-releasing activity (with limits and responsibilities set down) and a feeling of being accepted and of belonging.

Some of the factors encompassed by inner containment and outer containment may be more influential than others in their effects upon behaviour. Containment Theory explains both the **regulation of normative behaviour** and **resistance to deviancy**.

Inner containment and outer containment occupy a central position between the pulls and pushes of the inner and outer environments. External, **environmental pressures** towards deviancy include factors such as poverty and minority group status. **Environmental pulls** include attraction, temptation, advertising, propaganda, deviant subcultures and so on. **Inner pushes** include drives, motives, frustrations, disappointments and rebellions.

In cases where outer containment is weak, environmental pressures and pulls need to be handled by inner containment for deviancy to be resisted. Similarly, if inner containment is weak then inner pushes need to be handled by outer containment. Some very strong forces (e.g. compulsions) cannot be contained.

Contributing Theories:

None of the theories included within this book were identified as contributing to the development of Containment Theory.

Taken from:

Reckless, W. (1961). A New Theory of Delinquency and Crime. *Federal Probation Journal*, 25, 42-46

11. Control Theory (Carver & Scheier)

Constructs
- Input function (perception)
- Comparator
- Negative feedback loop
- Output function (behaviour)
- Impact on environment
- Disturbance
- Reference values
- Hierarchy of systems
    - o System concept
    - o Principle control
    - o Program control

Brief Summary

Control Theory is a theory of the processes underlying the regulation of human behaviour. It proposes that behaviour is regulated by a negative feedback loop, in which a person's perception of their current state is compared against a goal state. According to the theory, people strive to reduce perceived discrepancies between the two states by modifying their behaviour.

Description

Control Theory aims to provide a model of human functioning and behavioural regulation, explaining people's moment-to-moment actions, behaviour change and maintenance of physical health. The core component of the theory is a **negative feedback loop**, which functions to reduce or remove perceived discrepancies between current behaviour and a comparison value (such as a goal behaviour state).

A person perceives their current condition via an **input function**, and compares that perception against a particular standard through a mechanism termed a **comparator**. If the person perceives a difference between their current condition and the **reference value**, they attempt to reduce the discrepancy by performing a behaviour (termed the **output function**). Performance of the behaviour, in turn, has an **impact on the environment**, thus leading to changes in a person's perceptions of their current condition, and a new comparison with the reference value, and so on. Behaviour is governed by a closed loop of control which continuously functions to minimise discrepancies between a person's current situation and a particular standard of comparison.

There are two further influences on behaviour that are external to this closed loop. The first is **disturbance**, which refers to factors external to the system which affect a person's current condition. Disturbance does not affect the components of the model directly. However, it can modify perceptions entering the system via the input function and lead to increased or decreased discrepancy from the standard.

The second factor is the desired condition or comparison standard that is external to the closed loop, and is termed the reference value. The reference value arises from a **hierarchy of systems** of interconnected feedback loops. Each of these relates to superordinate (at the higher end of the hierarchy) or subordinate (at the lower end of the hierarchy) goals, where achievement of subordinate goals is a necessary for the attainment of superordinate goals. The reference values for each level of control are set by the level above, and at the highest level the reference value is derived from prior knowledge and experience.

Hierarchical Systems and Reference Values

The most superordinate system creates the reference value for the system at the next level down in the hierarchy, which in turn creates the reference values for next, and so on (i.e. the behavioural output of the superordinate system directs the standard set in the next level down). At the lowest level of the hierarchy behaviour outputs are simple and concrete (i.e. muscular movements), and at the higher levels behaviour outputs become more abstract, with the highest level being to live up to one's self-image (e.g. to be a responsible and thoughtful person). The reference value at this highest level of the hierarchical system is termed a **system concept**. This system concept generates general guiding principles for the regulation of behaviour, and thus the level directly below this is called **principle control**, and the associated behaviour output is adherence to the principles of one's self-image (e.g. to stick to one's commitments). At the next level down is **program control**, where the reference value is the general course of action needed to adhere to the principal. At levels further down, this 'general course of action' is broken down into even more concrete and specific acts, all the way to the specificity of muscle movements.

Behavioural regulation does not always involve every level of the hierarchy right up to system concepts, and people will often function at the level of program control. Thus, the level of the hierarchy that is functionally superordinate may vary over time, dependent upon the behavioural goals which a person is trying to achieve at the time. The reference value for the functionally superordinate goal is generated through a process in which the behavioural situation is categorised according to its observable characteristics and a person's prior knowledge about physical and social environments. This categorisation leads to a retrieval of behaviour-specifying information, which becomes the reference standard.

Control Theory: Negative Feedback Loop

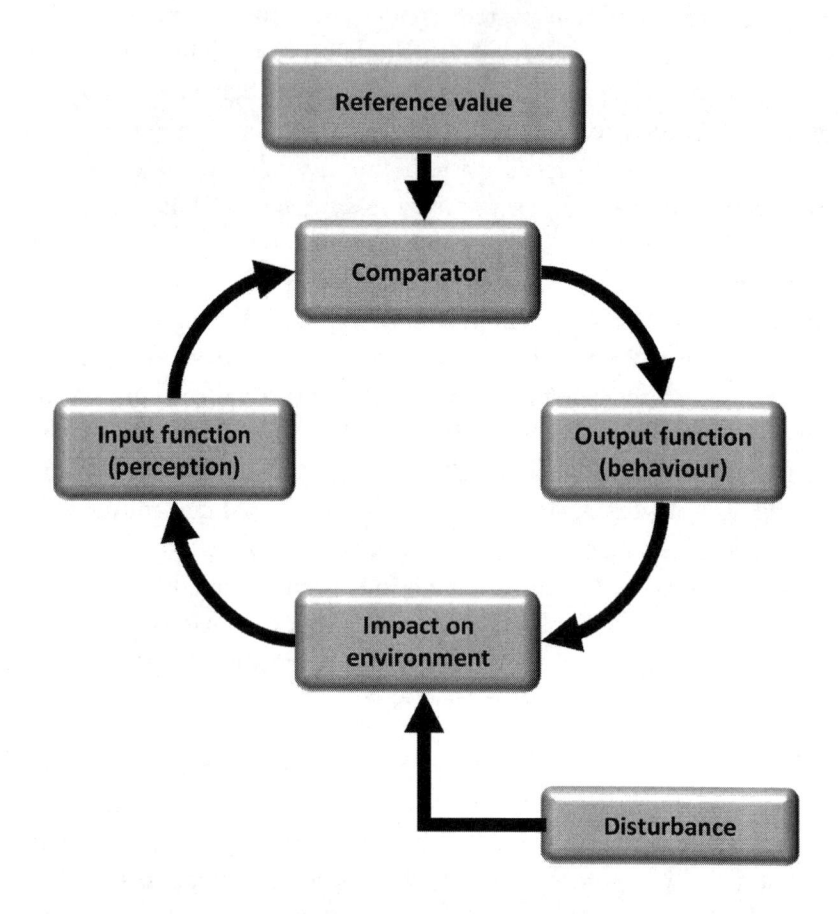

Source: Carver, C.S., & Scheier, M.F. (1982) Control theory: A Useful Conceptual Framework for Personality-Social, Clinical, and Health Psychology. *Psychological Bulletin*, 92, 111-135. Originally published by APA and reprinted here with permission.

Contributing Theories:

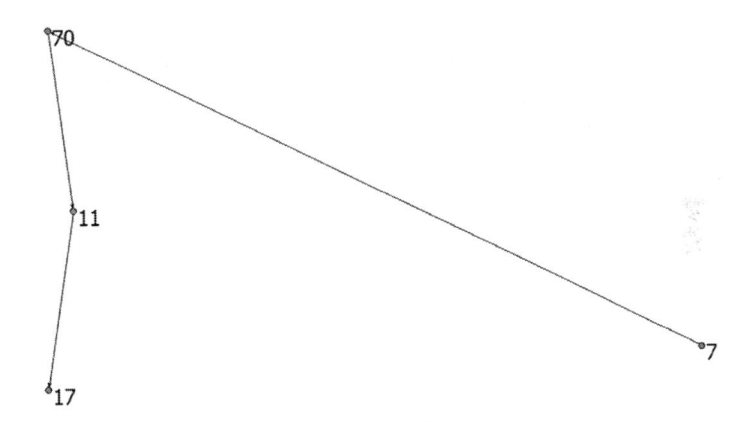

As outlined in the network diagram, the following theory included within this book was identified as contributing to the development of the Control Theory:

70. Social Learning Theory

Taken from:

Carver, C.S., & Scheier, M.F. (1982) Control theory: A Useful Conceptual Framework for Personality-Social, Clinical, and Health Psychology. *Psychological Bulletin*, 92, 111-135.

ABC OF BEHAVIOUR CHANGE THEORIES

12. Differential Association Theory (Sutherland)

Constructs

- Person-situation complex
- Learning
- Communication
- Intimate personal groups
- Techniques
- Motives, drives, rationalisations and attitudes
- Definitions of legal codes
- Differential association
    o Frequency
    o Duration
    o Priority
    o Intensity
- Needs and values
- Social organisation
- Criminal behaviour

Brief Summary

Differential Association Theory is a theory of criminal behaviour which proposes that people engage in criminal behaviour due to their life experiences, the presence of situations that facilitate criminal behaviour and the degree to which they associate with criminal and non-criminal individuals.

Description

Differential Association Theory aims to identify the antecedents of **criminal behaviour** and is based on the assumption that criminal behaviour (at the point at which the behaviour occurs) is the result of a **person-situation complex** (i.e. an interaction between a person's life experiences and a situation appropriate for criminal behaviour). The theory is composed of nine propositions:

1. Criminal behaviour arises through **learning**. Specifically, criminal behaviour cannot be inherited and cannot be invented by a person who has not learnt about crime.

2. The process of **communication** is central to the learning of criminal behaviour. Criminal behaviour is learned during interactions with other people through verbal and non-verbal communication.

3. The majority of learning in relation to criminal behaviour takes place within **intimate personal groups**. Less personal communication sources such as the media play little to no role in the development of criminal behaviour.

4. The process of learning criminal behaviour includes both learning **techniques** for enacting criminal behaviour and learning the direction of **motives, drives, rationalisations and attitudes**.

5. The direction of motives and drives is learned from **definitions of legal codes** within a group. Definitions can be unfavourable or favourable. For instance, some groups may view legal codes as something they should adhere to, whilst others might promote violation of legal codes.

6. Delinquency or criminal behaviour occurs as a consequence of exposure to unfavourable definitions of legal codes (i.e. those that favour the violation of legal codes) being greater than exposure to favourable definitions of legal codes (i.e. those that favour adherence to legal codes). This is the effect of **differential association**: people become criminal not only because of associations with criminal groups but also as a result

of isolation from non-criminal groups. Criminal and non-criminal associations are viewed as counteracting forces that determine criminality or non-criminality.

7. A person's differential associations with criminal or non-criminal behaviour vary in terms of **frequency, duration, priority** (e.g. associations may influence behaviour most strongly during childhood) and **intensity** (e.g. the prestige of criminal or non-criminal associations, the emotions associated with different associations).

8. The learning processes underlying the development of criminal behaviour are the same as those involved in any other type of learning; learning of criminal behaviour is not based solely on imitation.

9. Criminal behaviour is an expression of a person's **needs and values**, but is not caused by those needs and values. For instance, a criminal might steal because they need money, whereas a non-criminal might seek employment.

Social organisation (e.g. socioeconomic status, the neighbourhood in which someone lives) also plays a role in the development of criminal behaviour. Criminal behaviour can be seen as an expression of social organisation, as social organisation determines a person's associations.

Contributing Theories:

None of the theories included within this book were identified as contributing to the development of Differential Association Theory.

Taken from:

Sutherland, E.H. (1947). *Principles of Criminology* (4th Ed.). United States: J.B. Lippincott Company.

13. Diffusion of Innovations (Rogers)

Constructs

- Innovation
    - Technology
        - Hardware aspect
        - Software aspect
    - Uncertainty
    - Software information
    - Innovation-evaluation information
    - Innovation clusters
    - Relative advantage
    - Compatibility
    - Complexity
    - Trialability
    - Observability
    - Re-invention
- Communication channels
    - Mass media channels
    - Interpersonal channels
        - Near-peers
        - Modelling
    - Homophily
        - Localite channels
        - Cosmopolite channels
- Time
    - Innovation-decision process
        - Knowledge
        - Persuasion
        - Decision
        - Implementation
        - Confirmation
        - Adoption
        - Rejection
    - Innovativeness/adopter categories
        - Innovators
        - Early adopters

- ☐ Early majority
- ☐ Late majority
- ☐ Laggards
  - o Rate of adoption
- Social system
  - o Social structure
  - o Communication structure
  - o System norms
  - o Opinion leaders
    - ☐ Communication networks
  - o Change agents
    - ☐ Aides
  - o Innovation decisions
    - ☐ Optional innovation-decisions
    - ☐ Collective innovation-decisions
    - ☐ Authority innovation-decisions
    - ☐ Contingent innovation-decisions
  - o Consequences
    - ☐ Desirable versus undesirable
    - ☐ Direct versus indirect
    - ☐ Anticipated versus unanticipated

Brief Summary

Diffusion of Innovations Theory attempts to explain the process by which people or social groups adopt or reject a new idea, behaviour, or object. It specifies numerous mechanisms through which adoption or rejection is achieved, and factors that facilitate adoption.

Description

According to Diffusion of Innovations Theory, 'diffusion' is the process by which **innovations** are communicated in different ways, over **time**, to people within a **social system**. The theory conceptualises this process as having four main elements; **innovation, communication channels,** time and the social system.

Innovation

An innovation is defined as an idea, behaviour or object that is seen as new by a person or group that may adopt it. Technological innovations were the original focus of the theory, and are conceptualised as having two components: a **hardware aspect** (the physical tool that embodies the **technology** in a material sense) and a **software aspect** (the informational basis of the tool). Technology is defined as the mechanism that explains the cause and effect relationships involved in reducing the **uncertainty** of achieving a goal. Technological innovations elicit uncertainty in potential adopters of the technology (about the potential consequences of the technology). The information within the technology (**software information**) provides a means of reducing uncertainty, referred to as **innovation-evaluation information**.

Innovation clusters are multiple distinguishable elements of a technology or an innovation that are interrelated (e.g. paper recycling and glass recycling). As the boundary between one innovation and another is blurred, introducing innovation clusters rather than a single innovation may facilitate rapid **adoption**.

Characteristics of innovations may also influence how quickly innovations are adopted. First, the greater the perceived **relative advantage** of the new innovation over the idea that it supersedes, the faster it will be adopted. Second, the greater the perceived **compatibility** with the needs and values of adopters, the faster it will be adopted. Third, the greater the perceived **complexity** (perceived difficulty of understanding and usage) of the innovation, the more slowly it will be adopted. Fourth, the greater the **trialability** (the extent to which it can be experimented with temporarily) of the innovation, the faster is will be adopted. Fifth, the greater the **observability** (the degree to which results or outcomes are visible) of the innovation, the more quickly it will be adopted. Finally **re-invention** (the ability of an innovation to evolve to fit people's needs) affects adoption rates.

Communication Channels

Communication channels are the ways in which information about the innovation is passed from people or groups to others. The characteristics of this information exchange determine whether or not an innovation is passed from the source to the recipient. **Mass media channels** can transmit the message quickly, and from a source of a single person (or just a few people) to a large audience. However, **interpersonal channels** which involve face-to-face communication are more effective in promoting the adoption of innovations, especially if communication comes from **near-peers**. This is due to the influence of potential adopters **modelling** the behaviour of previous adopters.

Communication channels are particularly effective in facilitating adoption of innovations if communicators and potential adopters are **homophilious** (share the same attributes). If people differ on attributes, the communication of innovations is impaired. Later conceptualizations of the theory further articulate the concept of homophily by categorizing communication channels as either **localite** or **cosmopolite**. **Localite channels** link people to others within their social system whereas **cosmopolite channels** link people with sources outside their social system.

Time

Time is an important part of the diffusion process. To adopt an innovation, people undergo an **innovation-decision** process through which they pass from first being aware of the innovation before forming opinions on it and deciding whether to adopt it. This process occurs in five stages; **knowledge** (exposure to the innovation and understanding of the innovation), **persuasion** (the formation of a positive or negative opinion about the innovation, **decision** (choosing to adopt or reject the innovation), **implementation** (using the innovation) and **confirmation** (seeking reinforcement of an innovation decision). The information gained during confirmation may lead to reversal of the decision to adopt or reject.

The characteristics of potential adopters may also determine the length of time required for the diffusion of an innovation. Five **adopter categories** describe adopters' **innovativeness**. At the most innovative end, **innovators** are those who actively seek information about new ideas, have high exposure to mass media, large interpersonal networks and cope well with uncertainty. Progressing down the scale of **'innovativeness'**, people can be categorised as **early adopters, early majority, late majority** and **laggards**. Those in the latter categories (i.e. late majority and laggards) generally have opposite characteristics to innovators and have low social status.

Finally, time affects the **rate of adoption**, which refers to the relative speed that an innovation is adopted. Rate of adoption generally follows an 's' curve, with a few initial adopters followed by a rapid rate of adoption, which then slows again until it reaches its peak.

Social Systems

The social system can influence the rate of adoption, with new innovations being taken up at different rates in different systems. The **social structure** (the formal arrangement of social units within the system) decreases levels of uncertainty, whilst the **communication structure** (communication flows in an informal system determined by interpersonal networks) promotes communication between homophilious individuals, as people are most likely to talk to others similar to themselves.

System norms (established behaviour patterns for people within a social system) can be either a barrier or facilitator of adoption, as they define which behaviours are acceptable and provide a standard for people to follow. At the individual level, **opinion leaders** (characterised by technical ability, social accessibility and conformity to system norms) may provide a model for other people to follow in terms of adoption or **rejection**. The influence of opinion leaders spreads through **communication networks**. Some opinion leaders may be **change agents** – individuals who represent external groups and make efforts to influence **innovation decisions** in line with the desire of the external group. Change agents, however, are often experts in technology and therefore may not be homophilious to potential adopters, presenting a barrier to promoting the adoption of innovations. Change agents may use **aides** to influence potential adopters' decisions, as they are less expert, and thus the level of homophily is greater.

A social system can also influence diffusion through decisions to adopt or reject at different levels (e.g. individual decisions versus decisions by the entire system). There are four categories of these innovation decisions; **optional innovation-decisions** (decisions by a person independent of the system, which may still be influenced by system norms), **collective innovation-decisions**

(decisions made by consensus among the system) and **authority innovation-decisions** (decisions made by a few people who have power in the system). **Contingent innovation-decisions** may be made where **prior adoption of** an innovation is necessary to make an **innovation decision** (e.g. a worker may make an optional innovation-decision to use a computer *only* where the employing company has made a decision to purchase computers).

A social system is also influenced by the **consequences** of the adoption of innovations. Consequences are defined as the changes that occur to a person or a social system as the result of an innovation decision. There are three types of consequences; **desirable versus undesirable** (which depends of whether the innovation effects are functional or dysfunctional), **direct versus indirect** (which depends on whether changes occur because of an innovation, or as a second-order result of the consequences of the innovation) and **anticipated versus unanticipated** (which depends on whether the changes were intended).

A diagram representing the decision-making process in Diffusion of Innovations Theory can be found on p.159 of Rogers (2003).

Contributing Theories:

None of the theories included within this book were identified as contributing to the development of Diffusion of Innovations.

Taken from:

Rogers, E.M. (1983). *Diffusion of Innovations* (3rd Ed.). London: Collier Macmillan.

Supplemented by:

Rogers, E. M. (2003). *Diffusion of Innovations* (5th Ed.). New York: Free Press.

14. Ecological Model for Preventing Type 2 Diabetes in Minority Youth (Burnet et al.)

Constructs
- Cognitive factors
    - Outcome expectations
    - Self-efficacy
    - Incentive
    - Perceived susceptibility
    - Perceived severity
    - Perceived benefits
    - Perceived costs
- Community and environmental factors
    - Social/interpersonal influences
    - Social norms
    - Institutional factors
    - Community factors
    - Public policy
- Behavioural intention
- Behaviour

Brief Summary

The Ecological Model for Preventing Type 2 Diabetes in Minority Youth emphasises the need to target individual-level cognitive factors and environmental-level institutional and social factors when attempting to promote behaviour change.

Description

The Ecological Model for Preventing Type 2 Diabetes in Minority Youth is a framework for designing interventions to prevent Type 2 diabetes in high-risk youths from minority groups. It emphasises the importance of intrapersonal (cognitive) determinants as well as environmental influences on **behaviour** (e.g. individual behaviour change support alongside changes in **public policy**).

Cognitive factors that influence behaviour include knowledge, attitude and belief-related constructs from Social Learning Theory and the Health Belief Model. A number of determinants of type 2 diabetes-related behaviour are proposed:

- **Outcome expectations:** For behaviour change to occur, a person must hold the belief that their current behaviour will have negative impact upon their health, and that behaviour change would benefit their health in a way that they value.

- **Self-efficacy:** For behaviour change to occur, a person must believe that they are capable of making the behaviour change (i.e. have high self-efficacy).

- **Incentive:** For behaviour change to occur, the perceived consequences of behaviour change must be personally valued.

- **Perceived susceptibility:** A person's perceptions of their personal susceptibility to type 2 diabetes (i.e. beliefs about their likelihood of developing the disease if no behavioural changes are made).

- **Perceived severity:** A person's perceptions of the severity of the consequences/experience of type 2 diabetes.

- **Perceived benefits:** A person's beliefs about the benefits of a behaviour or behaviour change.

- **Perceived costs:** A person's beliefs about the costs of engaging in behaviour change. For behaviour change to occur, these should be outweighed by perceived benefits.

The **community and environmental factors** that influence behaviour are drawn from constructs from the Theory of Planned Behaviour and the Ecological Model, with an emphasis on the role of

social and interpersonal influences (e.g. family, peers) and **social norms** (e.g. perceptions of whether important others support the behaviour) in influencing dietary behaviour in children. Behaviour is determined by wider influences such as **institutional factors, community factors** and **public policy**.

Central Framework

The factors that make up these cognitive and environmental arms of influence come together to determine **behavioural intentions**, which are regarded as being the primary determinants of an attempt to perform behaviour. Self-efficacy is instrumental in facilitating the translation of behavioural intentions into actual behaviour.

A diagram representing the Ecological Model for Preventing Type 2 Diabetes in Minority Youth can be found on p.783 of Burnet, Plaut, Courtney & Chin (2002).

Contributing Theories:

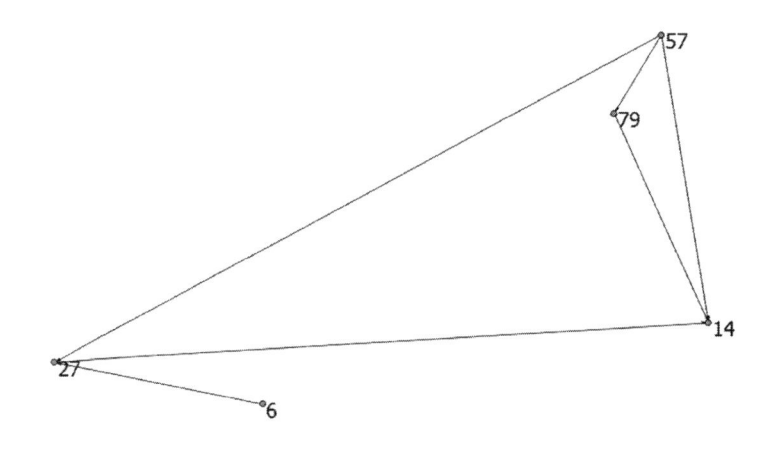

As outlined in the network diagram, the following theories included within this book were identified as contributing to the development of the Ecological Model for Preventing Type 2 Diabetes in Youth:

27. Health Belief Model

57. Self-efficacy Theory

79. Theory of Planned Behaviour

Taken from:

Burnet, D., Plaut, A., Courtney, R. & Chin, M.H. (2002). A Practical Model for Preventing Type 2 Diabetes in Minority Youth. *The Diabetes Educator*, 28(5), 779-795.

15. Extended Information Processing Model (Flay et al.)

Constructs
- Communication Factors
    o Source factors
    o Message factors
    o Channel factors
    o Receiver factors
    o Destination factors
- Intermediate factors
    o Presentation
    o Attention
    o Comprehension (and memory)
    o Acceptance/yielding (and retention)
- Outcomes
    o Exposure
    o Awareness
    o Knowledge
    o Memory
    o Opinion/belief
    o Retention
    o Attitude
    o Persistence
    o Intentions
    o Resistance
    o Behaviour
    o Maintenance

Brief Summary

The Extended Information Processing Model aims to provide an explanation of the processes underlying attitude and behaviour change resulting from mass media campaigns (e.g. public health campaigns). It proposes five communication factors relating to the source of the message, the message content and style, the channel used to transmit the message, the message audience, and the issues being targeted. It further proposes 12 steps in the process from exposure through retention to maintenance.

Description

The Extended Information Processing Model aims to explain the processes underlying **attitude** and behaviour change in response to mass media campaigns. Changes in attitudes and behaviour occur in twelve steps (**outcomes**), in response to up to five **communication factors** related to the media campaign. The occurrence of these outcomes is also dependent upon the presence of a number of **intermediate factors**.

The five communication factors are **source factors** (the attributes of the source of the message), **message factors** (the message content, structure and style), **channel factors** (the medium used to transmit the message and how it is used), **receiver factors** (characteristics of the message audience) and **destination factors** (the issue being targeted by the message, the component of general **attitude** being targeted, whether the target change is short or long, etc.).

The twelve outcomes are stochastic steps toward behaviour change (i.e. one causes the next, and so on). These steps are:

1. **Exposure** (to the message)

2. **Awareness** (of the message)

3. **Knowledge** (change in knowledge)

4. **Memory** (of the message content)

5. **Beliefs** (changes in beliefs)

6. **Retention** (of new beliefs)

7. **Attitude** (changes in attitude)

8. **Persistence** (retaining the attitude change)

9. **Intentions** (to engage in the wanted behaviour)

10. **Resistance** (of intentions to change)

11. **Behaviour** (acting on the basis of attitude/intention change)

12. **Maintenance** (maintaining behaviour changes)

Achievement of these outcomes is dependent on a number of intermediate factors. First, exposure to the message will only occur if the message is presented (**presentation**). Second, exposure will only lead to awareness if the message is attended to (**attention**). Third, awareness will only lead to changes in knowledge if the message is comprehended and remembered (**comprehension & memory**). Fourth, changes in knowledge will only lead to changes in beliefs and retention when the message content is accepted and retained (**acceptance/yielding & retention**). Changes in beliefs may or may not result in change in attitudes, intentions and behaviour.

The model acknowledges that the inclusion of factors not formally incorporated into the model such as behavioural skills, social support and various social-cognitive constructs are needed for a comprehensive model of behaviour change.

A diagram of the Extended Information Processing Model can be found on p.139 of Flay, DiTesco & Schlegel (1980).

Contributing Theories:

None of the theories included within this book were identified as contributing to the development of the Extended Information Processing Model.

Taken from:

Flay, B.P., DiTesco, D. & Schlegel, R.P. (1980). Mass Media in Health Promotion: An Analysis Using an Extended Information Processing Model. *Health Education Quarterly, 7(2),* 127-147.

16. Extended Parallel Processing Model (Witte)

Constructs
- Fear appeal
- Fear
- Perceived susceptibility
- Perceived severity
- Perceived efficacy
- Response efficacy
- Perceived self-efficacy
- Outcomes
- No response
- Danger control processes
    o   Protection motivation
    o   Adaptive changes
- Fear control processes
    o   Defensive motivation
    o   Maladaptive changes
- Individual differences
- Critical point

Brief Summary

The Extended Parallel Processing Model aims to explain the cognitive processes and behavioural outcomes that occur in response to fear appeals and to identify the factors that determine whether responses to a perceived threat will be adaptive or maladaptive.

Description

The Extended Parallel Process Model is a theoretical explanation of how people respond to fear appeals (i.e. messages which depict threats posed by an unwanted behaviour such as smoking in an attempt to persuade people to change their behaviour). Fear appeal messages are described as having four possible components;

susceptibility (the likelihood of being vulnerable to the threat), severity (the seriousness of the threat), self-efficacy (one's ability to take recommended protective action) and response efficacy (the likelihood that taking protective action will be effective).

Upon encountering a **fear appeal**, people first engage in appraisals of perceived threat (**perceived susceptibility** and **perceived severity**). If this results in a perception of low threat, then **no response** to the fear appeal occurs. However, if this results in perceptions of high or moderate threat, then fear is elicited. Upon elicitation of fear, people engage in a second appraisal process, comprising an evaluation of perceived efficacy (**perceived self-efficacy** and **perceived response efficacy**). A core proposition is that as a threat is perceived to be severe at the same time as perceived efficacy is high, a message is more likely to be accepted. However, when a threat is perceived to be severe at the same time as perceived efficacy is low, people may do the opposite of what the message is recommending.

Fear may also contribute to perceptions of threat in a feedback loop (i.e. high fear leads to increases in perceived threat), if it is cognitively appraised. If both perceived efficacy and perceived threat are both high, people are motivated to avoid the threat (**protection motivation**) by devising strategies to avert the threat (**adaptive changes**), defined as a '**danger control process**'. However, if perceived threat is high but perceived efficacy low, a '**fear control process**' will be initiated. In this case, the fear originally felt in response to the initial threat appraisal is magnified. People become motivated to cope with fear (**defensive motivation**) by using fear-reducing strategies (**maladaptive changes**) such as denial, dissonance or rejection of the message. **Individual differences** may influence appraisals of both threat and efficacy, as messages are appraised in the context of a person's prior experiences, personality characteristics and culture.

ABC OF BEHAVIOUR CHANGE THEORIES

A '**critical point**' exists at the juncture where perceptions of threat become greater than perceptions of efficacy. This critical point determines whether a person will engage in danger control processes or fear control processes. When perceptions of efficacy are greater than perceptions of threat, danger control is initiated. When perceptions of threat are greater than perceptions of efficacy, fear control processes are initiated. The two processes cannot co-occur (i.e. if danger control processes are initiated then fear control processes will not occur, and vice versa). Thus, perceptions of threat dictate the intensity of the reaction to a fear appeal, whilst perceptions of efficacy dictate the nature of the reaction (i.e. initiation of danger control or fear control processes).

A diagram of the Extended Parallel Process Model can be found on p.338 of Witte (1992).

Contributing Theories:

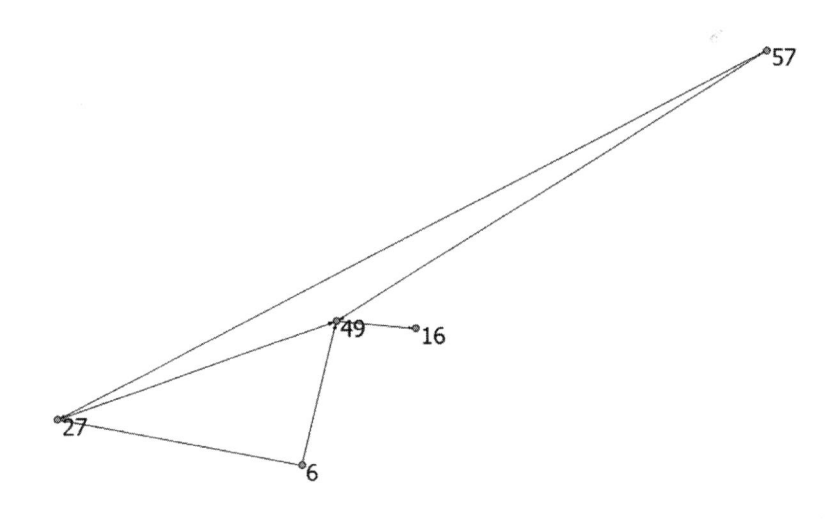

As outlined in the network diagram, the following theory included within this book was identified as contributing to the development of the Extended Parallel Processing Model:

49. Protection Motivation Theory

Taken from:

Witte, K. (1992). Putting the fear back in fear appeals: The extended parallel processing model. *Communication Monographs*, 59, 329-349.

17. Feedback Intervention Theory (Kluger & DeNisi)

Constructs

- Feedback intervention
- Standards
- Performance
- Feedback-standard discrepancies
- Negative feedback loops
- Feedback sign
- Strategies for eliminating the feedback-standard gap
    o Goal-setting
    o Abandoning the standard
    o Lowering the standard
    o Rejecting the feedback
- Locus of attention
- Hierarchy of negative feedback loops
    o Meta-task processes
        ▫ Resolving feedback-self discrepancies
            • Self-efficacy
            • Anxiety
            • Feedback intervention velocity
        ▫ Attention to the self
        ▫ Depletion of cognitive resources
        ▫ Affective processes
            • Pleasantness
            • Arousal
    o Task-motivation processes
    o Task-learning processes
        ▫ Hypotheses
- Feedback intervention-induced affect
- Feedback intervention cues
- Task characteristics
- Situational variables
    o Personality

Brief Summary

Feedback Intervention Theory explains how feedback on performance can influence behaviour and describes how the factors that determine whether feedback has a positive or negative influence on performance.

Description

Behaviour, or 'task **performance**', is regulated by the comparison of feedback on performance with goals or performance **standards**. Feedback interventions involve the provision of feedback on task performance in an effort to improve performance. Where there is a discrepancy between performance and the goal set (i.e. the standard) (**feedback-standard discrepancy**), people become motivated to remove the discrepancy. This is usually achieved by increasing the effort invested in a task. This system is referred to as a **negative feedback loop**. Discrepancies are evaluated and a '**feedback sign**' is created. The sign can be either positive (i.e. performance matches or exceeds standards) or negative (i.e. performance is not meeting standards). A negative feedback sign is more likely to prompt increased effort towards performing the task than a positive feedback sign. A positive feedback sign may mean that effort to perform the task reduces as task performance is perceived as exceeding standards.

There are four strategies to eliminate a negative feedback-standard discrepancy: **goal setting, abandoning the standard, lowering the standard** or **rejecting the feedback**.

There are a **hierarchy of negative feedback loops**. Loops at the top of the hierarchy refer to goals related to the 'self', whilst loops at the bottom relate to goals for physical action (e.g. turning on a tap). Loops that are higher in the hierarchy supervise the activity of lower loops, such that the output of a higher loop can be the change of goals in a lower loop. This hierarchy is split into three levels of linked processes: **meta-task processes** (relating to self-goals, and positioned at the top of the hierarchy), **task motivation processes** (related to the focal task) and **task learning processes** (relating to the details of the focal task, and positioned at the bottom of the hierarchy). Which one of these processes is used depends on where a person's attention is directed. The normal **locus of attention** is thought to exist at a moderate level of the hierarchy (i.e. task motivation processes). Feedback interventions are capable of determining which level the locus of attention is directed to.

Task Motivation Processes

Feedback interventions direct attention to task motivation processes through the value of the feedback sign and its effects on motivation to perform and reduce the feedback-standard discrepancy. Positive feedback signs may signal that task performance is an opportunity for self enhancement, leading to an increase in the performance standard and thus an improvement in performance. However, if efforts are not successful in removing a negative discrepancy, attention will be diverted to either task-learning processes or meta-task processes (see below). It is not clear which of these is most likely to be activated, but it is thought that they are interdependent and may influence each other's activity.

Task Learning Processes

Attention shifts to task learning processes when the feedback sign is negative. When additional effort is not successful in reducing the feedback-standard discrepancy a change to behaviour is necessary. Task learning processes may also be activated by certain cues in feedback intervention messages, specifically those that relate to components of the task that are not being performed to the expected standard. When learning process are activated, **hypotheses** (new, task component standards) are generated and tested for their success in improving performance. Activation of task learning processes does not always improve performance and may hinder it, as the resultant increase in attention to detail can disrupt automatic scripts for well-practiced tasks and decrease cognitive consistency.

Meta-Task Processes

Meta-task processes include aligning the focal task to higher-level goals (e.g. evaluation of the implications of task performance for the self), processes relating to non-focal tasks and increasing attention to the self and affect-related processes. Feedback interventions and the outputs of task processes can shift attention to meta-task processes and away from task learning or task motivation processes. This shift in attention involves four interdependent processes; **the mode of resolving feedback-self discrepancies, attention to the self, depletion of cognitive resources for task performance** and **affective processes**.

Mode of resolving feedback-self discrepancies. Discrepancies between feedback and self-related goals can be removed by making a resolve to continue working on the task in question. If meta-task processes recognise the relevance of task performance to the self, attention may be diverted back down the hierarchy to task motivation processes. However, the discrepancy can also be removed by diverting attention to tasks that would result in a positive self-view, or by lowering the standard for task motivational processes. The mode chosen is determined by **self-efficacy** (with higher self-efficacy leading to a lower likelihood of abandoning the task), **anxiety** levels (with higher anxiety leading to a higher likelihood of shifting attention to self-related goals) and the **feedback intervention velocity** (frequency of feedback intervention delivery). Frequent delivery of feedback interventions allows for better assessment of improvements in performance, with rapid improvement leading to adherence to the task and slow or absent improvement leading to task abandonment.

Attention to the self. Certain cues in feedback intervention messages can divert a person's attention to the self (e.g. normative feedback). Attention to the self can improve performance in dominant tasks or non-demanding tasks, but has a negative impact on non-dominant or cognitively demanding tasks. If attention is diverted to the self, this has an impact not only on the feedback intervention-related tasks but also on other, unrelated tasks.

Depletion of cognitive resources. Shifting attention away from the task and towards the self re-allocates and thus depletes cognitive resources for the task. This will have a negative impact on task performance unless the task is automated and poses little cognitive demand.

Affective processes. When attention is diverted to the self, affective reactions are activated as feedback is evaluated in relation to goals of the self. This leads to the creation of feedback signs which are evaluated for harm-benefit potential and the need for action. Evaluations of harm-benefit potential are reflected in the primary dimension of mood (**pleasantness**) whilst the need for action is reflected in the secondary dimension of mood (**arousal**).

These theoretical propositions suggest that the effects of feedback interventions upon task performance can be determined by four factors: **feedback intervention cues**, the **nature of the task** and **situational variables** (including **personality**).

Feedback Intervention Cues

Cues in the feedback intervention message determine which level of the hierarchy of feedback loops receives the most attention. Cues that direct attention to the self (e.g. normative feedback, discouragement) are likely to worsen performance unless the task is simple or attention is directed back down the hierarchy. Cues that direct attention to motivational processes (e.g. feedback interventions that provide information on improvements in performance compared to a previous trial) should improve performance. Cues that direct attention to learning processes (e.g. feedback on performance on task components) may disrupt performance, but may also enhance performance in cases where a solution is provided (overcoming the need for hypothesis testing).

Task Characteristics

If task completion is dependent on large amount of cognitive resources or upon intelligence level, feedback interventions may not be successful in enhancing performance even if they successfully enhance motivation.

Situational Variables

The clarity or ambiguity of the feedback-standard gap influences feedback intervention effectiveness. If the standard is ambiguous, attention may be focussed upon self-related processes rather than on motivational processes. Clear goal-setting can overcome this.

Personality

Numerous personality characteristics can have a potential influence on the effects of feedback interventions. Different personality characteristics have different salient self-goals that are sensitive to certain feedback intervention cues. For instance, low self-esteem might divert attention to the self upon receipt of a negative feedback intervention.

A Schematic Representation of Feedback Intervention Theory

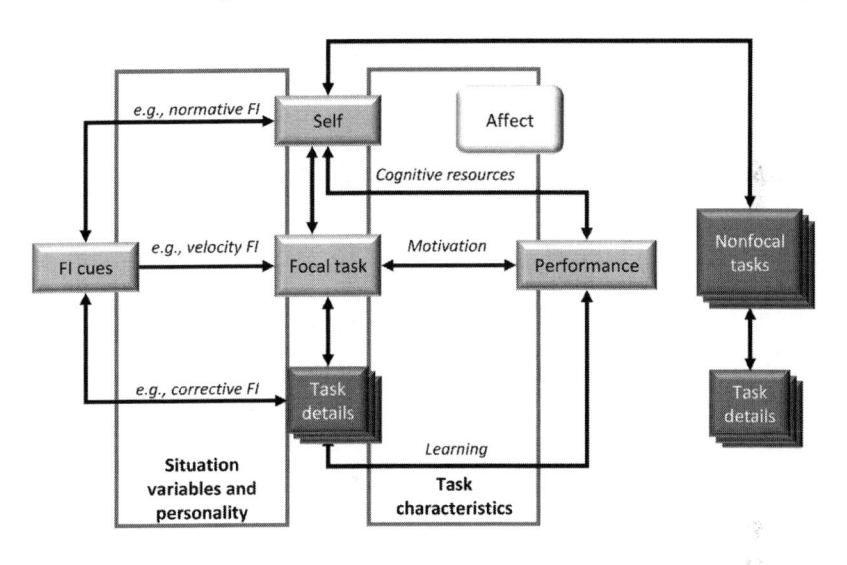

[Diagram showing feedback intervention theory with the following elements:
- FI cues connecting to Self (e.g., normative FI), Focal task (e.g., velocity FI), and Task details (e.g., corrective FI)
- Self connects to Focal task via Cognitive resources
- Focal task connects to Performance via Motivation
- Performance connects back to Task details via Learning
- Affect box near Self
- Nonfocal tasks with Task details on the right side
- Labels at bottom: Situation variables and personality, Task characteristics]

Note: FI=feedback intervention

Source: Kluger, A. N., & DeNisi, A. (1996). The effects of feedback interventions on performance: A historical review, a meta-analysis, and a preliminary feedback intervention theory. *Psychological Bulletin*, *119*(2), 254–284. Originally published by APA and reprinted here with permission.

Contributing Theories:

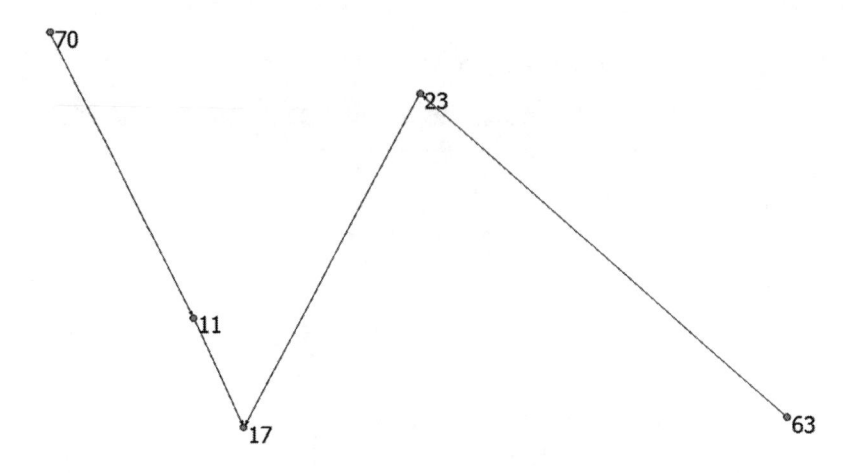

As outlined in the network diagram, the following theories included within this book were identified as contributing to the development of the Feedback Intervention Theory:

11. Control Theory

23. Goal Setting Theory

Taken from:

Kluger, A. N., & DeNisi, A. (1996). The effects of feedback interventions on performance: A historical review, a meta-analysis, and a preliminary feedback intervention theory. *Psychological Bulletin*, 119(2), 254–284.

18. Focus Theory of Normative Conduct (Cialdini et al.)

Constructs
- Descriptive norms
    o Provincial norms
- Injunctive norms
- Personal norms
- Norm focus

Brief Summary

The Focus Theory of Normative Conduct aims to explain how norms (i.e. what is most commonly done and what is most acceptable in a culture) influence behaviour. Four types of norms are described: descriptive (beliefs about what is typically done), injunctive (beliefs about what is approved or disapproved of), personal (personal beliefs and values about behaviour) and provincial (beliefs about what is typically done within a specific environment).

Description

The Focus Theory of Normative Conduct aims to provide an explanation for how norms influence behaviour. It also aims to account for why behaviour may not always conform to societal norms and how different types of (possibly conflicting) norms influence behaviour. The influence of norms on behaviour varies according to the type(s) of norms involved, and the degree to which a person's attention is drawn to the norm (**norm focus**). Four types of norms are described: **descriptive norms, injunctive norms, personal norms** and **provincial norms**.

Descriptive Norms

Descriptive norms can be defined as what is typically done, or what is 'normal' within a culture. Descriptive norms motivate behaviour by providing people with information about what actions are effective and/or adaptive in a given situation. Descriptive norms allow for quick decision-making and informational processing, as people can simply observe what the majority of others are doing in a situation and make decisions about the best course of action based on this information. Descriptive norms have the strongest influence on behaviour if they are demonstrated by someone who a person perceives as similar to themselves (e.g. same gender, ethnicity, religion, age group etc.).

Provincial Norms

Provincial norms are a sub-type of descriptive norms. Provincial norms refer to what others typically do in a specific environment (e.g. in a specific neighbourhood, in a hotel).

Injunctive Norms

Injunctive norms are what is typically approved or disapproved of within a culture and refer to the moral rules of a group. Behaviour is motivated by providing or withholding the opportunity for social acceptance. People may be influenced by these anticipated reactions of others even when their behaviour is unlikely to be witnessed by others.

Personal Norms

Personal norms are similar to injunctive norms, in that they refer to morally sanctioned ways of acting in specific situations. However, they focus on a person's beliefs or values about appropriate behaviour, and their expected self-criticism or self-approval following anti-norm or pro-norm actions.

Norm Focus

The strength of any norm's influence on behaviour is dependent upon the degree to which a person's attention is attracted to, or 'focused' on the norm at that moment. For example, raising awareness of the importance of recycling will strengthen the effect of an injunctive norm not to litter.

Contributing Theories:

None of the theories included within this book were identified as contributing to the development of Focus Theory of Normative Conduct.

Taken from:

Cialdini, R.B., Kallgren, C.A. & Reno, R.R. (1991). A Focus Theory of Normative Conduct: A Theoretical Refinement and Re-evaluation of the Role of Norms in Human Behaviour. *Advances in Experimental Social Psychology*, 24, 201-234.

Supplemented by:

Cialdini, R.B. (2012). The focus theory of normative conduct. In P. Van Lange, A. Kruglanski, & E. Higgins (Eds.), *Handbook of theories of social psychology* (pp. 295-313). London: SAGE Publications.

19. General Theory of Crime (Gottfredson & Hirschi)

Constructs

- High self-control
- Low self-control
    - o   Impulsive
    - o   Insensitive
    - o   Physical
    - o   Risk-taker
    - o   Short-sighted
    - o   Non-verbal
- Criminal behaviour
- Analogous behaviour
- Child-rearing practices
    - o   Monitoring
    - o   Recognition
    - o   Punishment

Brief Summary

The General Theory of Crime aims to explain what causes people to engage in criminal behaviour. Its central tenet is that those with low self-control are more likely to engage in criminal acts than those with high self-control and that low self-control is a function of child-rearing practices.

Description

The General Theory of Crime was developed to explain the reason why people engage in **criminal behaviour**. The central proposition of the theory is that **low self-control** is the primary determinant of criminal behaviour. Low self-control is seen as a trait that is established in early life, and that remains largely stable throughout a person's lifespan. Low self-control, defined as a tendency to respond to salient stimuli in the immediate environment, has a strong influence on criminal behaviour because criminal behaviour provides immediate gratification of a person's desires. Conversely, people with **high self-control** are characterised by a tendency to defer gratification of their desires.

Six traits characterise people with low self-control: **impulsive; insensitive; physical** (i.e. adventuresome and active rather than cautious and cognitive); **risk-takers; short-sighted** (i.e. a focus on short-term benefits of their actions overshadows the long-term consequences) and **non-verbal** (i.e. they tend to respond to conflict physically rather than verbally). It is these traits that influence a person's tendency to engage in criminal behaviour or '**analogous behaviour**' (i.e. acts that are not illegal but are similar to criminal acts as they have similar immediate and long-term benefits). People with low self-control will focus on the immediate benefits that result from these analogous behaviours, rather than the long-term consequences, in the same way as they would do with criminal actions. For instance, a person with low self-control is more likely to smoke, gamble, or engage in illicit sex, as they are more focused on the immediate gains or pleasures derived from these acts.

The primary cause of individual differences in self-control is differences in **child-rearing practices** as opposed to training, instruction, or socialisation. Adequate child-rearing practices to foster self-control involve the **monitoring** of a child's behaviour, the **recognition** of deviant behaviour and the **punishment** of deviant behaviour. If these conditions are not met, a child is more likely to develop low self-control and thus more likely to engage in criminal behaviour in later years.

Contributing Theories:

None of the theories included within this book were identified as contributing to the development of the General Theory of Crime.

Taken from:

Gottfredson, M.R. & Hirschi, T. (1990). *A general theory of crime*. Stanford, CA, US: Stanford University Press.

20. General Theory of Deviant Behaviour (Kaplan)

Constructs
- Self-attitudes
    - o Positive self-attitudes
    - o Negative self-attitudes
- Self-esteem motive
- Psychosocial and membership group experiences
    - o Attitudes of others
    - o Valued qualities or successes
    - o Ability to use controls and defences
- Perceived cause of negative self-attitudes
- Perceived availability of alternative, self-enhancing normative behaviour patterns
- Perceived availability of alternative, self-enhancing deviant behaviour patterns
- Deviant behaviour
    - o Avoidance function
    - o Attack function
    - o Substitution function

Brief Summary

The General Theory of Deviant Behaviour aims to explain why people engage in deviant behaviour. The theory proposes that negative self-attitudes (the emotions resulting from people's evaluations of their own attributes or behaviours) are the primary motivation for engaging in deviant behaviours, as engaging in such behaviours can enhance people's self-attitudes.

Description

The General Theory of Deviant Behaviour proposes that negative **self-attitudes** are the primary determinant of deviant behaviour (e.g. illicit drug use, aggression, criminal acts). Self-attitudes are defined as a person's positive or negative emotions arising from self-evaluation of their own attributes or behaviours (for instance, self-derogation is an example of a negative self-attitude and high self-esteem is an example of a positive self-attitude). The influence of self-attitudes upon behaviour is mediated by the **self-esteem motive**. This is the desire to maintain or increase **positive self-attitudes**, and to avoid developing **negative self-attitudes**.

Stable negative self-attitudes arise from **psychosocial and membership group experiences**. The main determinants of positivity or negativity of self-attitudes are: the **attitudes of others**, personal valued **qualities or successes** and personal **ability to use controls and defences**. Thus, a person is more likely to develop negative self-attitudes if important others have negative attitudes towards them, if they do not possess the attributes or achieve the successes that they personally value, and if their ability to defend themselves against or cope with self-devaluing experiences (i.e. ability to view experiences in a way that does not undermine self-attitude) is poor. Due to the self-esteem motive, people with negative self-attitudes will feel distressed and be motivated to behave in ways that foster the development of positive-self attitudes in order to reduce this distress.

People who have developed negative self-attitudes are more likely to engage in **deviant behaviour** than those who have developed positive self-attitudes. The extent to which people with negative self-attitudes will engage in deviant behaviour is determined by three main factors. First, if the **perceived cause of negative self-attitudes** is associated with the normative environment, they will be more likely to engage in deviant behaviour. Secondly, if the **perceived availability of alternative, self-enhancing normative behaviour patterns** is low, they will be more likely to engage in deviant behaviour. Thirdly, if the perceived availability of alternative, self-enhancing deviant behaviour patterns is high they will be more likely to engage in deviant behaviour.

Deviant behaviours reduce negative self-attitudes and the associated distress because they have three functions – an **avoidance function**, an **attack function** and a **substitution function**. The avoidance function can involve intrapersonal or interpersonal activities. For example, the deviant behaviour may distort perceptions of attributes or behaviours that are generally considered undesirable or unacceptable, or cause a person to interpret them as justified by circumstance (intrapersonal). Alternatively, the deviant behaviour might facilitate avoidance of specific social interactions in which negative attitudes about the person are expressed (interpersonal). Deviant behaviour can also reduce negative self-attitudes by attacking the cause of negative self-attitudes (i.e. the attack function). For instance, people might engage in hostile or physically aggressive behaviour directed towards group members that are perceived to be responsible for the development of negative self-attitudes. Similarly, if negative self-attitudes have been caused by a failure to meet normative standards, the attack function may involve the rejection of those normative standards by the adoption of a 'deviant' identity. A person may for example, decrease the value they previously placed on normative standards or on group members. They may alternatively express hostility or physical aggression to group members or to physical representations of normative standards. The attack and avoidance functions are facilitated by the substitution function. This involves forging new group memberships in which standards are easier to achieve and within which other group members are more likely to offer positive attitudinal responses to a person.

The likelihood that a person will maintain their engagement in initial deviant behaviours is determined by the effect of their initial deviant responses upon their self-attitudes. If self-attitudes are enhanced, a person is likely to continue to engage in the pattern of deviant behaviour. If self-attitudes are not enhanced or are devalued, a person will search for other deviant responses that are more effective in enhancing their self-worth. In such cases the likelihood of a person reverting to normative patterns of behaviour is low, as normative behaviours will be unable to enhance self-attitudes.

Contributing Theories:

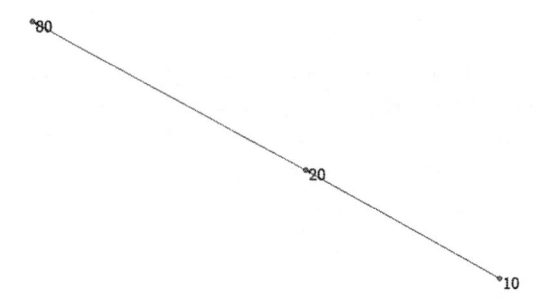

- 80
- 20
- 10

As outlined in the network diagram, the following theory included within this book was identified as contributing to the development of General Theory of Deviant Behaviour:

10. Containment Theory

Taken from:

Kaplan, H.B. (1972). Toward a general theory of psychosocial deviance: the case of aggressive behaviour. *Social Science & Medicine*, 6, 593-617.

Supplemented by:

Kaplan, H.B. (1982). Self-attitudes and deviant behaviour: New directions for theory and research. *Youth Society*, 14(2), 185-211.

Kaplan, H.B., Martin, S.S. & Robbins, C. (1982). Application of a general theory of deviant behaviour: self-derogation and adolescent drug use. *Journal of Health and Social Behaviour*, 23(4), 274-294.

21. Goal Directed Theory (Bagozzi)

Constructs

- Decisions with respect to means
    - Appraisal of means
        - Self-efficacies with respect to means
        - Instrumental beliefs
        - Affect towards means
    - Choice among means
    - Intention to perform means
- Instrumental acts
    - Planning
    - Monitoring activities
    - Guidance and control processes
- Motivational processes
    - Commitment
        - Emotional commitment
        - Ego preoccupation
    - Effort
    - Commitment to role identities
    - Cognitive representations
    - Self-schemata
    - Scripts
- Facilitating and inhibiting conditions
- Goal achievement

Brief Summary

Goal Directed Theory describes the factors that influence the performance of goal-directed behaviours. People form intentions to try and reach a goal based on appraisals of the means available to help them reach that goal. A number of factors determine whether or not these intentions are translated into goal achievement.

Description

Goal Directed Theory describes the factors that influence the performance of goal-directed behaviours. Decisions relating to the pursuit of a goal are made following a person's appraisal of their means to pursue that goal. These decisions are central determinants of goal-directed behaviours and relate to **means, instrumental acts** and **motivational processes.**

Means

When a person forms an intention to pursue a goal, decisions about how to achieve that goal are made on the basis of an appraisal of the **means** available to facilitate reaching that goal. Means are appraised using three distinct processes. First, a person makes judgements about their ability to perform each of the available means, and their confidence in doing so. This process is called **self-efficacies** with respect to **means**. Second, judgements are made about whether each of the means is likely to lead to goal achievement. This is referred to as the formation of **instrumental beliefs**. Third, a person makes appraisals of the desirability of performing each of the means, based on the level of pleasure or unpleasantness associated with each. This process is called **affect towards means**. The three appraisal processes interact and determine a person's **choice among means**. The chosen mean is the one that 'scores' most highly across the three appraisals. Once a choice among means has been made, an **intention to perform means** is formed.

Instrumental Acts

Following the formation of an intention to perform means, people make attempts to perform those means, also known as **'instrumental acts'**. This stage comprises three distinct processes. First, **planning** takes place in preparation for performing means.

A person assesses how successful these means are in terms of goal achievement, and whether additional contingencies, barriers and facilitators need to be factored into decision-making. This process is called '**monitoring activities**'. Finally; **guidance and control processes** take place. Barriers to goal achievement, failures to progress towards the goal or perceived external factors that have potential to prevent goal achievement are evaluated. In response, modifications are made to the planning and implementation of instrumental acts.

Motivational Processes

Motivational processes play an important role in determining goal achievement. They have two main components: **commitment** (the 'binding' of a person to the decision to try and achieve a goal and to use certain means to do so) and **effort** (how much a person tries to achieve the goal). Commitment is separated into two components: **emotional commitment** (the level of certainty that the decision is correct) and **ego preoccupation** (the extent to which an intention or decision is perceived as important to a person, and their personal commitment to it).

A person's level of **commitment to role identities** also plays a motivational role, giving both an impetus to forming decisions to pursue a goal and sustaining efforts to achieve that goal by reinforcing and supporting a person's self-image. **Cognitive representations** (e.g. a person imagining themselves trying to perform a behaviour) play a role in intention formation. **Self-schemata** (i.e. the ideas and beliefs people hold about themselves) reinforce a person's commitment to their goals and choice of means. Finally, **scripts** (sequences of behaviours that are expected in a specific situation) translate intentions into actions, and into sustaining action.

Goal Achievement

Facilitating and inhibiting conditions can also determine goal achievement. These may include a person's relevant resources and any objective barriers to goal achievement. Facilitating and inhibiting conditions interact with the other processes to determine **goal achievement**.

A diagram of Goal Directed Theory can be found on p.197 of Bagozzi (1992).

Contributing Theories:

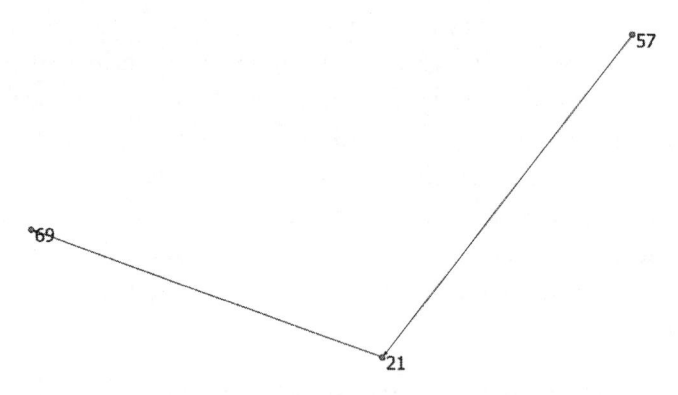

As outlined in the network diagram, the following theory included within this book was identified as contributing to the development of Goal Directed Theory:

57. Self-efficacy Theory

Taken from:

Bagozzi, R.P. (1992). The Self-Regulation of Attitudes, Intentions and Behaviour. *Social Psychology Quarterly*, 55(2), 178-204.

22. Goal-Framing Theory (Lindenberg & Steg)

Constructs

- Hedonic goals
- Gain goals
- Normative goals
- Goal frame
- Background goals
- Smart norms

Brief Summary

Goal-framing theory proposes that goals direct the information and cognitions that people attend to. The theory proposes three types of goals (hedonic, gain and normative), and states that activation of each type directs people's attention to different sub goals, cognitions and information.

Description

Goals direct people's attention, evaluations, consideration of actions/alternative actions and the cognitive accessibility of knowledge and attitudes. Three types of goals exist: **hedonic goals** (goals to instantly feel better), **gain goals** (goals to improve and protect resources) and **normative goals** (goals to act in line with what is considered acceptable).

When one of these goals is activated it becomes a **goal frame**, and begins to govern a person's sub-goals and accessibility to attitudes and knowledge. A hedonic goal frame activates sub-goals that are likely to improve how people feel in a specific situation, and to increase sensitivity to factors that have positive and negative influences on mood and pleasure levels. Hedonic goal frames have a short time horizon, and goal realisation occurs with an improvement in how a person feels. Gain goal frames activate sub-goals relating to resources (e.g. saving money), and to increase a person's sensitivity to changes in personal resources and to have a moderate to long-term time horizon. Goal realisation occurs with improvement or successful protection of personal resources.

Normative goal frames activate sub-goals relating to acting appropriately, and prompt people to consider how they should behave to be in accordance with what is considered appropriate. If norms are very abstract, they are termed '**smart norms**', as cognitive effort is required for a concrete decision regarding what action would be most appropriate. If the necessary information is not available to make this decision, people will abandon the normative goal and pursue a gain goal or hedonic goal instead.

When a goal frame is activated, sub-goals relating to the other two goal types are cognitively suppressed and become **background goals**. These may be in conflict with the goal frame, or be compatible with it. If the background goals are compatible with the goal frame, they strengthen it.

The three goal frames are not of equal strength. The hedonic goal frame is likely to be the strongest as it is directly associated with satisfying needs and is the most basic. It therefore requires minimal support from a person's social surroundings. The normative goal frame is dependent upon external support (e.g. social disapproval). The gain goal frame requires some external support (e.g. secure property rights), as it involves a person acting on behalf of their future self.

Contributing Theories:

None of the theories included within this book were identified as contributing to the development of Goal Framing Theory.

Taken from:

Lindenberg, S. & Steg, L. (2007). Normative, Gain and Hedonic Goal Frames Guiding Environmental Behaviour. *Journal of Social Issues*, 63 (1), 117-137.

23. Goal Setting Theory (Locke & Latham)

Constructs

- Goals
    - Goal difficulty
    - Goal specificity
    - Personal goals
    - Proximal goals
    - Assigned goals
- Directive function
- Energising function
- Persistence
- Task-relevant knowledge and strategies
- Commitment
    - Importance
    - Self-efficacy
- Feedback
- Task complexity
- Task performance
- External incentives
- Satisfaction
- Satisfaction paradox

Brief Summary

Goal-setting theory explains the mechanisms by which goals (defined as the object or aim of an action), affect the level of task performance and how performance can be moderated by a number of factors including the level of commitment, the importance of the goal, levels of self-efficacy, feedback and task complexity.

Description

Goal-setting theory states that conscious **goals** or intentions regulate behaviour (task performance) and describes the mechanisms through which goals influence behaviour and how characteristics of goals can influence behaviour. It specifies factors that moderate the influence of goals on behaviour, the relationship between goals and satisfaction and how goals act as mediators of incentives. Since being proposed in 1968, goal-setting theory has been revised and expanded based upon emerging evidence; the most recent version is described here.

Goal Characteristics

The goal characteristics that influence goal **performance** are **goal difficulty** and **goal specificity.** Setting difficult goals leads to better performance than setting easier goals because they lead to putting in more effort than easier goals and hence to a higher level of task performance. Setting specific leads to better performance than setting general goals such as 'to do your best'. Goals affect behaviour through four mechanisms. First, they have a **directive function**, directing attention away from irrelevant behaviour and directing effort towards goal-relevant activity. Secondly, they have an **energising function**: high goals lead to more effort being invested in task performance than low goals, and hence to a higher level of task performance. This explains the relationship between difficult or high goals and performance – higher goals lead to more effort being put into goal attainment. Thirdly, goals influence **persistence**. If no time limit is put upon goal attainment, difficult goals prolong the effort that people will put into goal attainment. Fourthly, goals stimulate the use or discovery of **task-relevant knowledge and strategies**. When task goals are set, people automatically draw on their relevant knowledge and skills, as well as applying knowledge and skills from other related contexts and new learning strategies.

Several factors moderate the relationship between goal-setting and task performance. **Commitment** to the goal strengthens the goal-performance relationship. Commitment is a function of the perceived **importance** of the goal and its expected outcomes, and of **self-efficacy** (a person's belief about whether they can attain the goal). Making a commitment in public or hearing an inspiring vision can help to increase commitment to a goal. Self-efficacy can be increased by providing training, role models and persuasive communication. **Feedback** on progress towards a goal influences performance, as knowledge of progress allows people to adjust their efforts or performance strategies if necessary. Finally, task complexity moderates the effect of goals upon performance. With greater **task complexity**, people may have to develop new strategies or learn new skills to perform the task. People's ability to do this varies greatly and hence task performance varies according to whether or not a person finds it easy or difficult to apply a new skill or strategy. Furthermore, a greater number of strategies may be needed for a very complex task. **Proximal goals** (goals that seem achievable in the short term) can facilitate performance on complex tasks because in dynamic situations it may be better to react quickly to the situation and attain the goal than strive for a more difficult, distal goal.

The effects of **external incentives** (e.g. assigned goals, monetary incentives, feedback on performance) upon task performance are mediated by **personal goals** and self-efficacy. For instance, performance on an assigned goal (i.e. a goal that is set by others) is influenced by the use of personal or self-set goals. Being assigned a difficult task may boost self-efficacy as it indicates that a leader holds confidence in a person's abilities. Similarly, effects of feedback on performance in cases where no goals are provided may be explained through the influence of self-set goals in response. Negative feedback influences self-efficacy because a person's level of self-efficacy determines whether goals are raised or lowered. For instance, when confronted by negative feedback a person with a higher level of self-efficacy (belief that s/he has the skills to achieve the goal) may result in raising the goal.

Goals can be seen as reflecting **satisfaction**, in that a person will not be satisfied unless they achieve a goal and will be dissatisfied if they fail to do so. Goals serve as a reference point for satisfaction or dissatisfaction, with satisfaction increasing the more a person exceeds a goal, and decreasing as the negative discrepancy between a set goal and achievement grows. However, a **satisfaction paradox** exists, in that people who have the best performance (i.e. those who set high goals and achieve them) are the least satisfied, because their reference point for satisfaction is much higher. This dissatisfaction motivates performance, explaining the positive effects of difficult goals upon performance.

Contributing Theories:

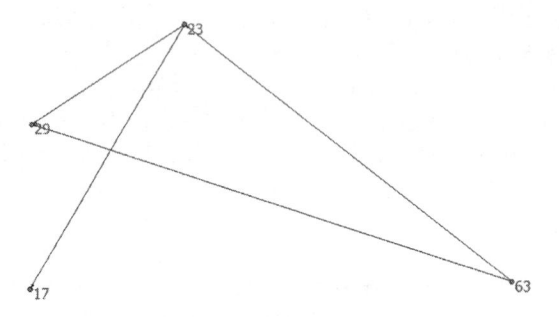

As outlined in the network diagram, the following theory included within this book was identified as contributing to the development of Goal Setting Theory:

63. Social Cognitive Theory

Taken from:

Locke, E.A. (1968). Toward a Theory of Task Motivation and Incentives. *Organisational Behaviour and Human Performance*, 3, 157-189.

Locke, E.A. & Latham, G.P. (2002). Building a Practically Useful Theory of Goal Setting and Task Motivation: A 35-Year Odyssey. *American Psychologist*, 57(9), 705-717.

24. Health Action Process Approach (Schwarzer)

Constructs

Original Theory

- Motivation phase
    - Self-efficacy
    - Outcome expectancies
        - Generalized
        - Social
            - Social pressure
            - Social support
            - Norms
    - Threat perception
        - Perceived severity
        - Perceived vulnerability
    - Intention formation
- Action phase
    - Action plans
    - Action control
    - Situational barriers
        - Actual environment
        - Perceived environment

Social support

Reformulation of Theory

- Motivational phase
    - Action self-efficacy
    - Outcome expectancies
        - Risk perception
        - Perceived severity
            - Perceived vulnerability
            - Intention
            - Volitional phase
    - Action planning
        - Coping planning

- ☐ Maintenance self-efficacy
- o Recovery self-efficacy

- Action

Brief Summary

The Health Action Process Approach is proposed as a causal model of the initiation and maintenance of health-related behaviours. The model incorporates a temporal perspective, making an explicit distinction between a motivation (or decision-making) phase and an action (or maintenance) phase.

Description

The Health Action Process Approach is proposed as a causal model that explains the determinants of the initiation and maintenance of health-related behaviours. The model incorporates a temporal perspective, making an explicit distinction between a **motivation (or decision-making) phase** and an **action (or maintenance) phase**. Successful progression through both of these phases results in long-term behaviour change.

Motivational Phase

The motivational phase is a decision-making stage, and describes the process by which people form **intentions** to either adopt a health-protective or health-promoting behaviour or to change a risky health behaviour. There are three major determinants of intention formation. The first is **self-efficacy** (i.e. a person's beliefs about their ability to successfully carry out the behaviour). The second is **outcome expectancies** (i.e. a person's beliefs about the consequences of the behaviour). Outcome expectancies are an antecedent to self-efficacy and intention, in that people tend to consider the consequences of a behaviour before considering their ability to carry it out. The constructs of self-efficacy and outcome expectancies are interrelated, with perceptions of low self-efficacy having the potential to nullify the influence of even very positive outcome expectancies. There are two types of outcome expectancies: **social** or **generalised**. 'Social outcome expectancies' include perceptions of **social pressure** (i.e. perceived expectations of others), **social support** for engaging in the behaviour, and **norms** (i.e. whether the behaviour is in line with that of referent others). 'Generalised outcome expectancies' refers to more general expectations of outcomes, and can also be described as 'optimism'.

The third determinant of intentions is **threat perception** resulting from the interplay between the **perceived severity** of an illness and **perceived vulnerability** to that illness. Threat perceptions alone are insufficient to enable intention formation. Rather, a minimum level of perceived threat is considered to be necessary to stimulate the consideration of outcome expectancies and self-efficacy, which then in turn determine intention formation.

Action Phase

The 'action phase' describes the process by which behavioural intentions are translated into actual behaviour. Once an intention has been formed, it must be translated into **actions plans** (i.e. detailed specifications of how to perform the intended behaviour). Perceptions of self-efficacy influence the formation of these action plans, as perceptions of capability to carry out the behaviour could influence the quality and quantity of the plans formed.

Following the initiation of an action plan, maintenance is dependent upon the action being controlled by **self-regulatory processes**. Without this process of **action control**, people may abandon the action due to interruptions, competing intentions or tendencies towards other actions. During action performance, self-efficacy is also influential in determining the level of effort and persistence invested in the performance. People with perceptions of poor self-efficacy are predisposed to anticipate failure, worry about their inability to perform, and abandon action. Conversely, people with greater self-efficacy are more likely to anticipate success and effectively overcome any barriers to action.

Situational barriers also have a role in the process of translating intentions into action. According to the model, situational factors are able to overwhelm self-regulatory processes and lead to failure in action performance. 'Situational barriers' can refer to barriers in the **actual environment** or **perceived environment**. The presence of **social support** can strengthen lower levels of volitional control when situational barriers are encountered.

The Reformulation of the Health Action Process Approach

The Health Action Process Approach has been reformulated, with situational barriers and social support reconceptualised. In addition, the action phase was reconceptualised as the **volitional phase** and self-efficacy was divided into three, phase-specific types of self-efficacy. **Action self-efficacy** refers to a person's beliefs in their ability to adopt a behaviour and is influential during the motivation phase, whereas **maintenance self-efficacy** and **recovery self-efficacy** are influential at the volitional phase. Maintenance self-efficacy refers to a person's beliefs in their ability to maintain a newly adopted behaviour and deal with barriers that arise during the maintenance period. Recovery self-efficacy refers to a person's beliefs in their ability to address the experience of failure and resume the behaviour after a setback. Outcome expectancies may be negative, social, physical and/or emotional. Finally, **coping planning** was incorporated as a mediator of intentions and action. Coping planning involves the anticipation of potential barriers to

ABC OF BEHAVIOUR CHANGE THEORIES

action and the generation of behavioural options to overcome these barriers.

Diagrams representing the original formulation of the Health Action Process Approach and the reformulation of the theory can be found on p. 233 of Schwarzer (1992) and on p. 6 of Schwarzer (2008), respectively.

Contributing Theories:

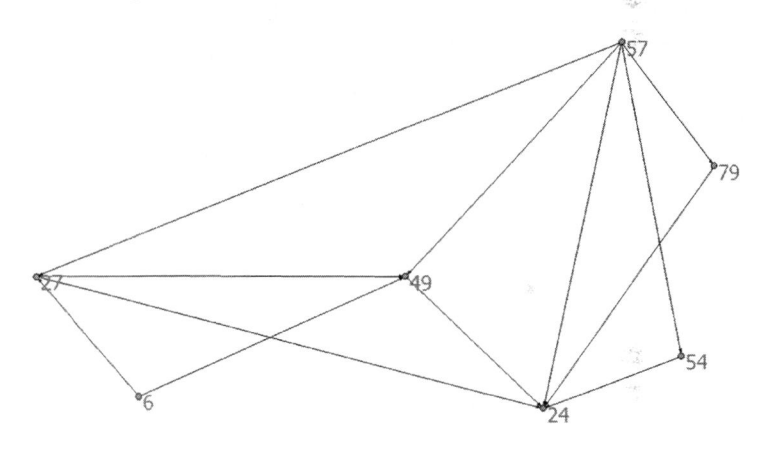

As outlined in the network diagram, the following theories included within this book were identified as contributing to the development of the Health Action Process Approach:

27. Health Belief Model

49. Protection Motivation Theory

54. Relapse Prevention Model

57. Self-efficacy Theory

79. Theory of Planned Behaviour

Taken from:

Schwarzer, R. (1992). Self-efficacy in the adoption and maintenance of health behaviours: theoretical approaches and a new model. In R. Schwarzer (Ed.), *Self-efficacy: Thought control of action* (pp. 217-243). Washington, DC: Hemisphere.

Supplemented by:

Schwarzer, R. (2008). Modeling health behaviour change: How to predict and modify the adoption and maintenance of health behaviours. *Applied Psychology: An International Review, 57*(1), 1-29.

25. Health Behaviour Goal Model (Maes & Gebhardt)

Constructs

- Personal goal structure
    - Higher order goals
    - Lower order goals
- Social influence
- Perceived health costs and benefits
- Perceived emotional costs and benefits
- Perceived competence
- Personal characteristics
- Environmental characteristics
- Stages of the process of change
    - Pre-contemplation
    - Contemplation
    - Initial behaviour change
    - Maintenance
- Initial health behaviour
- Target health behaviour
- Regulatory Processes
    - Feedback mechanisms
    - Feed forward mechanisms
    - Action control processes

Brief Summary

The Health Behaviour Goal Model is a stage model proposing that behaviour change is most likely to occur if the target change is compatible with what is important to a person and the things that they want to achieve in life.

Description

The Health Behaviour Goal Model proposes that health behaviour change is most likely to occur if the target change is compatible with a person's **personal goal structure**, which is formed by more specific goals arranged hierarchically. Goals are desired states or outcomes, whilst the personal goal structure is the things that a person feels are important to do with or in their life. The personal goal structure is organised into abstract **higher-order goals**, and more concrete **lower-order goals**. Higher-order goals are goals that are most associated with a person's self-concept, such as a person's desire to be considerate and thoughtful to others because they believe they are (or want to be) a nice person. Higher-order goals include goals relating to health (e.g. to stay healthy), well-being (e.g. to enjoy life to the fullest), personal growth (e.g. to develop talents) and social goals (e.g. to be a good father). Lower-order goals result from these higher-order goals, and are sub-goals that contribute to attaining higher order goals. Lower-order goals can exist at varied levels of specificity and relate more to daily activities (e.g. studying, washing the dishes, watching television).

If behaviour change targets conflict with higher-order goals, progress towards change is unlikely. Conflicts between valued lower-order goals and behaviour targets (e.g. having a goal to watch television but a target to exercise) may also impede progress towards behaviour change. If the target is accepted as a goal, cases of goal conflict such as this can result in emotional distress, particularly if goal conflict is sustained. The likelihood of achieving a goal is higher when the change target involves the adoption a new behaviour (as opposed to the cessation of an existing behaviour), when it is perceived to be important and when it is perceived to be relatively easy to achieve in a reasonably short amount of time.

The process of behaviour change is also influenced by the expected consequences of the target behaviour. There are four categories of expected consequences: the **perceived health costs and benefits**, the **perceived emotional costs and benefits, social influence** and **perceived competence**'. The perceived health costs and benefits include all expected health outcomes of the behaviour (e.g. starting running might improve cardiovascular health, but could also result in injury). The perceived emotional costs and benefits include all expected emotional outcomes of the behaviour, and expected influences upon well-being. 'Social influence' refers to a person's expectations of how their social environment might respond to their adoption of the target behaviour (e.g. expectations of support from family when adopting a healthier diet). Finally, 'perceived competence' is defined as a person's assessment of their ability to adopt the target behaviour. The latter includes assessments of self-regulatory mechanisms, which may be involved in overcoming internal or external barriers to change.

These four types of expectancies are related to a person's personal goal structure. For instance, higher-order health goals are likely to relate to perceived health costs and benefits; higher-order social goals are likely to relate to 'social influence'. The more that the expected consequences are consistent with higher-order goals, the greater influence they will have upon behaviour change. The four categories of expected consequences are also interrelated. For instance, social influences may alter perceptions of the costs and benefits of a behaviour when a significant other makes it clear that s/he would prefer a person to stop smoking.

A person's personal goal structure can be altered by **environmental characteristics and personal characteristics**. Environmental characteristics are aspects of the environment that either facilitate or impede adoption of the target behaviour. Personal characteristics include sociodemographic characteristics, personal attribute and goal orientations, and may be changeable over time through learning processes. Changes in either environmental or personal characteristics can lead to changes in the personal goal structure and may also influence the expected consequences of a behaviour. Environmental and personality characteristics act as cues to action, and can be either internal (e.g. physical symptoms) or external (e.g. health messages). These cues can either lead to the perception of a new challenge (e.g. wanting to learn a new behaviour to achieve a goal) or perception of a threat that must be avoided (e.g. wanting to change behaviour to avoid negative consequences). If a new goal is valued (or if perceptions of threat are high), the priority of goals in the personal goal structure may be realigned. Expected consequences may also change, with both of these changes having the potential to trigger the process of behaviour change.

The process of change occurs in four distinct stages, drawing on the Transtheoretical Model to define the stages. The starting point of change is termed the **initial health behaviour** (i.e. actual behaviour prior to change, such as smoking), and the end point is termed the **target health behaviour** (e.g. sustained smoking cessation). The stages are (1) the **precontemplative stage**, (2) the **contemplative stage**, (3) **initial behaviour change stage** and (4) the **maintenance stage**. In the precontemplative stage, a person has no desire to change their behaviour. In the contemplative stage, a person is motivated to change their behaviour but has not yet made any changes. In the initial behaviour change stage, a person begins to make changes in their behaviour and thus starts to progress towards the target behaviour. In the maintenance stage, behaviour change in line with the target behaviour is sustained long-term. Relapse is possible at any stage.

At each stage, people assess whether it is still beneficial to progress towards behaviour change, and adjust their behaviour accordingly. These adjustments will either involve further progress to the target behaviour, or goal abandonment. Assessments at each stage are based on both the consistency between the target behaviour and the personal goal structure, and the expected immediate consequences of the target behaviour. According to the model, assessments involve three distinct regulatory processes: **feedback mechanisms** (where current behaviour is compared against an emotional or achievement standard), **feedforward mechanisms** (guided by the context- and capability-related expected consequences of the behaviour) and **action control processes** (which control cognitive, emotional and behavioural barriers to behaviour change, facilitating progression).

The strength of influence that each of the factors has is different at each stage in the behaviour change process. For instance, changes in personal and environmental characteristics are particularly important in the initial behaviour change stage.

A diagram of the Health Behaviour Goal Model can be found on p. 358 of Maes & Gebhardt (2000).

Contributing Theories:

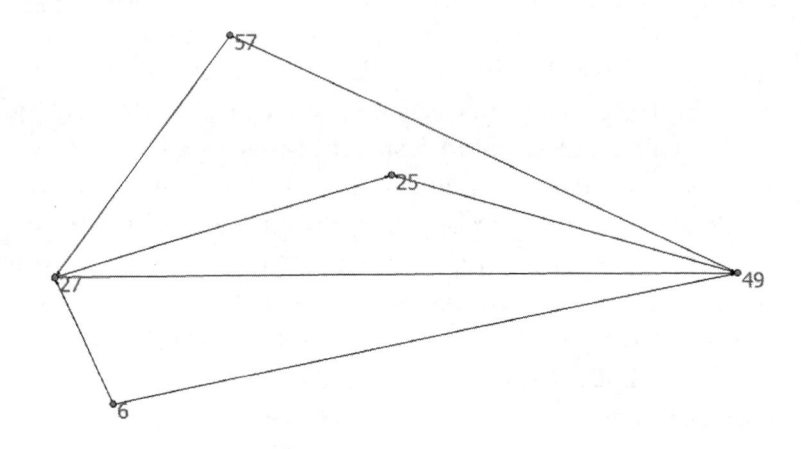

As outlined in the network diagram, the following theories included within this book were identified as contributing to the development of the Health Behaviour Goal Model:

27. Health Belief Model

49. Protection Motivation Theory

Taken from:

Maes, S. & Gebhardt, W. (2000). Self-Regulation and Health Behaviour: The Health Behaviour Goal Model. In M. Boekaerts, P. Pintrich & M. Zeidner (Eds.), *Handbook of Self-Regulation* (pp. 348-368). San Diego, CA, US: Academic Press.

26. Health Behaviour Internalisation Model (Bellg)

Constructs

- Internalisation and self-regulation of new health behaviour
    - External regulation
    - Introjected self-regulation
    - Integrated self-regulation
- Self needs
    - Identity
    - Self-determination
    - Security
    - Support
- Behaviour-related needs
    - Preference
    - Context
    - Competence
        - Self-efficacy
        - Able to carry out the behaviour well and relatively easily
        - Ability
    - Coping
- Health behaviour maintenance

Brief Summary

The Health Behaviour Internalisation Model is a model of behavioural regulation. It proposes that the regulation of behaviour lies along a continuum from external regulation (i.e. behaviour is regulated by an external source) to integrated self-regulation (i.e. behaviour is regulated by the self and is consistent with a person's values and identity). A person's position on this continuum determines the likelihood of behaviour maintenance.

Description

The Health Behaviour Internalisation Model aims to explain the factors that influence the maintenance of newly adopted health behaviours. The maintenance of new behaviours is proposed to occur through a gradual process of **internalisation** where external attitudes, beliefs or behavioural regulations in the social environment are transformed into personal values or goals that are regulated by the self. The regulation of behaviour exists along a continuum, from **external regulation** to **introjected self-regulation** and then **integrated self-regulation**.

External Regulation and Self-Regulation

Externally-regulated behaviours are those in which a person perceives an external contingency that requires them to adopt a new behaviour, arising either from another person or environmental circumstances. The perceived consequences of externally-regulated behaviours are outside a person's sense of self. For instance, a person might change their behaviour to avoid a heart attack or to please another person. Thus, the behaviour is a response to an anticipated external social reward or health contingency, and is self-regulated with respect to those anticipated consequences. Externally-regulated behaviours are unstable and vulnerable to change if the anticipated consequences change. They are often characterised by conflict. For instance, people may be resentful of intrusion and argue with others that provide or communicate the reward or contingency, or passively agree to change without ultimately doing so.

Introjected self-regulated behaviours are those in which the regulation of the behaviour has been internalised, but in which experiences of conflict and control are retained. Conflict may arise if people feel that adopting a new behaviour will result in some form of deprivation (e.g. giving up favourite foods or eating out with friends when on a diet). Experiences of control are retained despite motivation for the behaviour originating internally (i.e. from within a person). For instance, experiences of control may arise from feelings of guilt, shame or subjective pressure. In cases of introjected self-regulation, failure to meet behaviour change goals (e.g. weight loss) is likely to be perceived as personal failure rather than a failure of strategy, and success is likely to be experienced as relief from subjective pressure rather that a sense of accomplishment.

At the opposite end of the continuum is integrated self-regulation, in which a new behaviour has become integrated with a person's values and sense of self. When self-regulation is integrated, people do not feel controlled to engage in the behaviour or feel conflict about the behaviour. The motivation for the behaviour originates internally and the behaviour is valued because of its consistency with other values. Integrated self-regulation holds the greatest likelihood of resulting in long-term **health behaviour maintenance**.

Factors Influencing Internalisation and Self-Regulation

There are two sets of motivational variables that influence the internalisation process: **self-needs** and **behaviour-related needs**. Meeting these needs facilitates a higher quality of internalisation (i.e. integrated self-regulation).

Self-needs include the needs for **ownership**, **self-determination**, **security** and **support**. The need for ownership refers to the need to engage in a new health behaviour for personal reasons, rather than for reasons given by another person. The need for self-determination refers to the need to possess a sense of personal agency and initiative in relation to adopting the new behaviour, as opposed to engaging in the behaviour in response to real or imagined pressure, or feelings of shame or guilt. The need for security is triggered by perceptions of a health threat, and refers to the need to establish a sense of security when faced with a health threat. Without doing this, feelings of fear and anxiety may create a sense of pressure and control, leading to introjected self-regulation. Finally, the need for support is defined as the need for support from family, friends or caregivers to meet self-needs and behaviour-related needs in a manner that promotes integrated self-regulation.

Behaviour-related needs include the needs for **preference, context, competence** and **coping**. The need for preference refers to the need for a new behaviour to be consistent with, rather than contrary to, a person's tastes. The need for context refers to a need for a person to be satisfied with the context in which the new health behaviour occurs (e.g. a person might find exercising in a gym boring, but enjoy running outdoors). The need for competence refers to three factors: the need to have the **ability** to engage in the health behaviour, the need to be **able to carry out the behaviour well and relatively easily** and the need for a sense of **self-efficacy** (i.e. confidence in ability to maintain healthy behaviours, even in the face of difficulty). Finally, the need for coping is influential as many people engage in unhealthy behaviours as a method of **coping** with other conditions (e.g. smoking to cope with stress). If the new behaviour involves cessation of an unhealthy coping method then a new, healthier coping method will be needed.

A diagram of the Health Behaviour Internalisation Model can be found on p. 113 of Bellg (2003).

Contributing Theories:

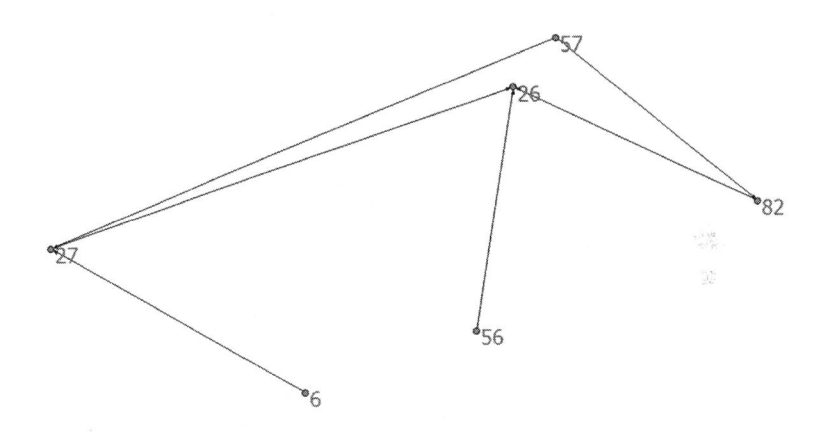

As outlined in the network diagram, the following theories included within this book were identified as contributing to the development of the Health Behaviour Internalisation Model:

27. Health Belief Model

56. Self-Determination Theory

82. Transtheoretical Model of Behaviour Change

Taken from:

Bellg, A.J. (2003) Maintenance of health behaviour in preventative cardiology: Internalisation and self-regulation of new behaviours. *Behaviour Modification*, 27: 103.

27. Health Belief Model (Rosenstock)

Constructs

- Demographic variables
- Socio-psychological variables
- Structural variables
- Perceived threat
    - Perceived susceptibility
    - Perceived severity
- Perceived benefits
- Perceived barriers
- Self-efficacy
- Cues to action
    - Internal
    - External
- Likelihood of preventative action

Brief Summary

The Health Belief Model explains health-risk reducing behaviours. Its core proposal is that people are most likely to take preventative action if they perceive the threat of the health risk to be serious, that they are personally susceptible and if they feel there are fewer costs than benefits to engaging in protective action.

Description

The Health Belief Model was developed to predict the likelihood of people undertaking the recommended action to avoid a health threat (i.e. disease). According to the model, the **likelihood of preventive action** is primarily determined by specific beliefs: **perceived susceptibility** (to the disease), **perceived severity** (of the disease), **perceived benefits** (of taking action) and **perceived barriers** (to taking action).

Perceived Susceptibility and Severity

Perceived susceptibility is the extent to which a person believes they are at risk of contracting the relevant disease. Perceived severity is a person's perception of the seriousness of the disease, both in terms of the emotional arousal elicited by thoughts of the disease and the anticipated difficulties that could be created by the disease (e.g. reduced physical and mental functioning, job implications, implications for family life). Perceptions of susceptibility and severity are partially dependent upon knowledge about the disease, and together reflect perceptions of the overall **threat** posed by the disease.

Perceived Benefits and Barriers

Belief in a personal susceptibility to a disease that is also believed to be severe provides a force leading to action. However, the course of action is directed by perceived benefits and barriers. Perceived benefits are beliefs about the relative effectiveness of known options to reducing the health threat, and are distinct from objective facts. An option is likely to be favoured if it relates to a reduction in perceptions of susceptibility or severity. Perceived benefits are influenced by social norms and social pressures in a person's social group(s).

Perceived barriers are beliefs about the negative aspects of taking protective health action (e.g. inconvenience, expense, discomfort). Even in cases where preventative action is perceived as beneficial, these beliefs can present barriers to action and may arouse feelings of conflict, which may be resolved in one of several ways. If the readiness to act is high and perceived barriers are minimal, the preventative action is likely to be undertaken. However, if the readiness to act is low while perceived barriers are strong, the barriers may prevent action. In cases where readiness to act is great and perceived barriers are both great, conflict may be harder to resolve. In some circumstances where perceived barriers are strong, alternative preventive actions may be available which present fewer perceived barriers, presenting a means of resolving conflict. However, if such alternative actions are not available, people might engage in efforts to avoid the negative emotions associated with perceptions of threat such as denial.

Cues to Action

In cases where perceptions of severity, susceptibility and benefit are high, and perceived barriers are weak, a further force is necessary to deliver the impetus, or 'trigger', to take action. This variable is termed '**cues to action**'. Cues are either **internal** (e.g. perceptions of pain, discomfort or other bodily states) or **external** (e.g. interactions with others, mass-media campaigns, screening reminders). The strength of such a cue necessary to trigger action varies according to levels of perceived susceptibility and severity. Where perceptions of susceptibility or severity are weak, intense cues may be necessary. With higher levels of perceived susceptibility and severity, minor stimuli may suffice.

Other Variables

The core variables (i.e. perceived severity, susceptibility, benefits and barriers) are influenced by **demographic variables** (e.g. age, gender, ethnicity), **socio-psychological variables** (e.g. personality, socio-economic status, peer pressure) and '**structural variables**' (e.g. knowledge about the relevant disease, prior experience of the disease).

A later version of the model added the construct of **self-efficacy** (defined as a person's beliefs about whether or not they are capable of taking the preventative action), proposing a positive relationship with a person's likelihood of taking action.

A diagram of the Health Belief Model can be found on p. 7 of Rosenstock (1974).

Contributing Theories:

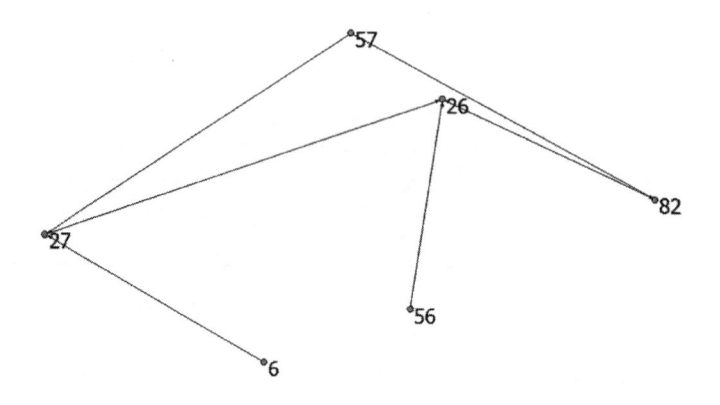

As outlined in the network diagram, the following theories included within this book were identified as contributing to the development of the Health Belief Model:

6. Change Theory

57. Self-Efficacy Theory

Taken from:

Rosenstock, I. (1974). Historical Origins of the Health Belief Model. *Health Education Monographs*, 2(4), 328-335.

Supplemented by:

Rosenstock, I.M., Strecher, V.J. & Becker, M.H. (1988). Social learning theory and the health belief model. *Health Education Quarterly,* *15*(2), 175-183.

28. Health Promotion Model (Pender et al.)

Constructs
- Individual characteristics and experiences
    o Prior related behaviour
    o Personal factors
        ▫ Biological
        ▫ Psychological
        ▫ Sociocultural
- Behaviour-specific cognitions and affect
    o Perceived benefits of action
    o Perceived barriers to action
    o Perceived self-efficacy
    o Activity-related affect
        ▫ Act-related
        ▫ Self-related
        ▫ Context-related
    o Interpersonal influences
        ▫ Norms
        ▫ Modelling
        ▫ Social support
    o Situational influences
    o Commitment to plan of action
    o Immediate competing demands and preferences
        ▫ Competing demands
        ▫ Competing preferences
        ▫ Self-regulatory ability
- Behavioural outcome
    o Health promoting behaviour

Brief Summary

The Health Promotion Model aims to explain the factors underlying motivation to engage in health-promoting behaviours. The model emphasises the role of person-environment interactions in motivating health-promoting behaviour. It describes eight behaviour-specific beliefs which are proposed to determine the health-promoting behaviour, and to be modifiable targets for behaviour change interventions.

Description

The Health Promotion Model aims to explain the factors that motivate people to engage in health-promoting behaviours, and was designed to provide a framework for nurses to use when attempting to increase patients' health-promoting behaviours. It is an approach-oriented model of behaviour, and does not consider the role of fear or threat in motivating behaviour. Thus, the model is applicable to any health-promoting behaviour except for those in which fear or threat are a primary source of motivation for behaviour. It aims to describe people's interactions with their physical and interpersonal environments during attempts to improve health. Factors influencing health-promoting behaviour are arranged in three categories: **'individual characteristics and experiences'**, **'behaviour-specific cognitions and affect'** and **'behavioural outcome'**.

The model is based upon a number of assumptions, which aim to integrate the perspectives of behavioural science and nursing into the model. These assumptions emphasise the active role that a person has in initiating and maintaining health-promoting behaviour, and in shaping their own environment to support health-promoting behaviours. These assumptions are that people; (1) seek to create a lifestyle and living environment through which their health potential can be maximised, (2) are capable of evaluating their own capabilities and reflective self-awareness, (3) value positive growth and strive for a subjectively acceptable balance between change and stability, (4) actively strive to regulate their own behaviour, and (5) interact with their environment, such that they modify and are modified by their environment over time. Health professionals are assumed to be part of an interpersonal environment, which can influence people throughout their lifetime, and an essential prerequisite of behaviour change is assumed to be the self-initiated modification of interactions between a person and their environment.

Individual Characteristics and Experiences

Individual characteristics and experiences include a person's **prior related behaviour** (i.e. the frequency with which they have engaged in the same or similar behaviours in the past) and '**personal factors**'. Personal factors include **biological, psychological** and **sociocultural factors** (e.g. gender, socioeconomic status, ethnicity, personality characteristics). Prior behaviour has both direct and indirect effects on future behaviour. Direct effects occur through mechanisms such as habit formation, whilst indirect effects occur by influencing **perceived self-efficacy, perceived benefits of action, perceived barriers to action,** and **activity-related affect.** Personal factors may have an indirect effect on behaviour by shaping people's cognitions, affect and health behaviours.

Behaviour-Specific Cognitions and Affect

There are eight types of cognitions and affect that have both direct and indirect effects upon health-promoting behaviour. Their terms and definitions are outlined below.

- **Perceived benefits of action:** Beliefs about the positive or reinforcing outcomes of engaging in a health-promoting behaviour. In addition to directly influencing health promoting-behaviours, perceived benefits have an indirect effect by influencing the strength of a person's commitment to a plan of action (to engage in a health-promoting behaviour). Positive perceptions of the benefits of action are necessary for behaviour to occur, but are insufficient to motivate behaviour alone.

- **Perceived barriers to action:** Beliefs about barriers to engaging in the health-promoting behaviour, and about personal costs associated with engaging in the behaviour. Examples of perceived barriers include perceptions relating to the unavailability, inconvenience, or expense of a health promoting behaviour. They may also include loss of satisfaction relating to the cessation of a health-damaging behaviour (e.g. stopping smoking). Perceived barriers influence behaviour directly by serving as barriers to engaging in the behaviour, and indirectly by decreasing a person's commitment to a plan of action.

- **Perceived self-efficacy:** Beliefs about their ability to successfully carry out a health-promoting behaviour. Perceptions of self-efficacy are positively influenced by activity-related affect, and vice versa. Self-efficacy influences behaviour directly by motivating action, and indirectly through positive influences on person's perceptions of barriers to action and their commitment to plans of action.

- **Activity-related affect:** The feelings or emotions that a person experiences before, during, or after a health-promoting behaviour. Activity-related affect consists of **act-related** affect (i.e. emotional responses to the behaviour itself), **self-related** affect (i.e. emotional responses to the self engaging in the behaviour) and **context-related** affect (i.e. emotional responses to the environment in which the behaviour takes place). Affective responses to behaviours become stored in memory and associated with thoughts about the behaviour. The feelings that subsequently arise from thoughts of the behaviour determine the likelihood of a person repeating or maintaining that behaviour. Positive feelings increase the likelihood that a person will repeat a behaviour, whilst negative feelings decrease the likelihood. Activity-related affect influences behaviour both directly and indirectly, the latter through effects on perceived self-efficacy and commitment to a plan of action.

- **Interpersonal influences:** Perceptions of the beliefs, attitudes and behaviours of others in relation to the health-promoting behaviour. Interpersonal influences include **norms** (i.e. the expectations of important others), **modelling** (i.e. vicarious learning through observation of others' behaviour) and **social support** (i.e. emotional encouragement and practical support).

The most important sources of interpersonal influences are family, peers and healthcare providers. Interpersonal influences affect behaviour directly and indirectly, the latter through the effects of encouragement to commit to a plan of action or felt social pressures to engage in a behaviour.

- **Situational influences:** Perceptions of the environment in which a behaviour takes place, specifically how compatible or incompatible a person feels they are with that environment. Such perceptions might include perceptions of the availability of environmental options for the behaviour, or perceptions of the aesthetic features of the environment associated with a behaviour. Situational influences affect behaviour directly (e.g. by containing cues to a behaviour or through organisational rules about the behaviour), and indirectly by enforcing commitment to a plan of action.

- **Commitment to plan of action:** the commitment to carry out a particular behaviour in a particular context despite any competing desires, in conjunction with the formulation of strategies for successfully performing the behaviour.

- **Immediate competing demands and preferences:** alternative behaviours that intrude into a person's thoughts immediately prior to engaging in behaviour. **Competing demands** are those things that a person has no control over, such as childcare responsibilities. **Competing preferences** are alternative behaviours over which a person has control, but that have highly reinforcing properties. A person's ability to overcome competing preferences is dependent upon their **self-regulatory ability**. Competing demands and preferences influence behaviour via a detrimental influence upon commitment to a plan of action.

Behavioural Outcome

The 'behavioural outcome' component is the endpoint of the model. It refers to engagement in **health-promoting behaviour**, which ultimately results in improved health outcomes.

A diagram of the Health Promotion Model can be found on p. 60 of Pender, Murdaugh & Parsons (2002).

Contributing Theories:

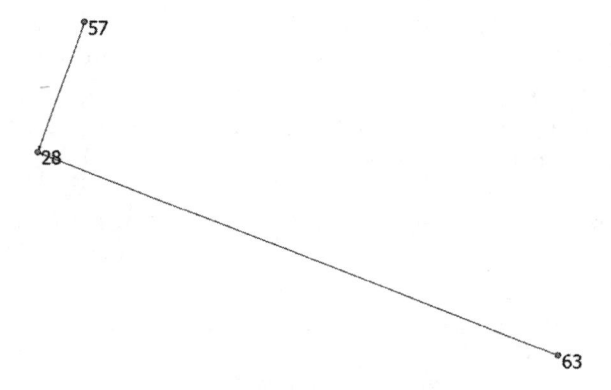

As outlined in the network diagram, the following theories included within this book were identified as contributing to the development of the Health Promotion Model:

57. Self-Efficacy Theory

63. Social Cognitive Theory

Taken from:

Pender, N.J., Murdaugh, C., & Parsons, M.A. (2002). *Health Promotion in Nursing Practice* (4th ed.). Upper Saddle River, NJ, US: Pearson Education Inc.

29. I-Change Model (De Vries et al.)

Constructs
- Predisposing factors
    - Behavioural factors
    - Psychological factors
    - Biological factors
    - Social and cultural factors
- Information factors
    - Message
    - Channel
    - Source
- Awareness factors
    - Knowledge
    - Cues to action
    - Risk perception
- Motivation
    - Attitudes
        - Rational/cognitive pros & cons
        - Emotional pros & cons
        - Response efficacy
    - Social Influences
        - Norms
        - Modelling
        - Pressure/support
    - Self-efficacy
        - Routine
        - Social
        - Situational
        - Stress
- Ability factors
    - Action plans
    - Skills
- Barriers
- Intention
    - Precontemplation
    - Contemplation
    - Preparation

- Behavioural state
    - Trial
    - Maintenance

Brief Summary

The I-Change Model integrates several models of behaviour change and aims to identify psychological and social determinants of behaviour. It was developed from the Attitude-Social Influence-Efficacy model which proposes that attitudes, social influences and self-efficacy are the primary determinants of behaviour and that behaviour change or initiation occurs in a number of stages.

Description

The I-Change Model (or Integrated Change Model) was derived from the Attitude-Social Influence-Efficacy Model, which in turn was an extension of the Theory of Reasoned Action. The I-Change model states that the primary determinant of **behaviour** is a person's **intention** to carry out that behaviour. Behaviour itself is conceptualised as having two categories: '**trial**' and '**maintenance**'. Intention has different states: '**precontemplation**' (no intention to take action in the foreseeable future [i.e. next 6 months]), '**contemplation**' (intention to take action in the next 6 months) and '**preparation**' (intention to take action in the immediate future [i.e. next month]). Intentions may not always transfer into behaviour – **ability factors** and **barriers** to action determine the likelihood of them doing so. Ability factors include a person's ability to prepare and carry out plans for carrying out the behaviour (**action plans** or implementation intentions) and their **behavioural skills**. When **ability factors** are high and barriers are low, the likelihood of intentions being translated into behaviour is at its highest.

The primary determinant of intentions is **motivation**. Motivation is in turn determined by three factors: **attitudes, social influences** and **self-efficacy**. Attitudes arise from the perceived **emotional**

and cognitive/rational pros and cons of carrying out a given behaviour, and from perceptions of **response efficacy** (whether carrying out the behaviour will result in the desired outcome). Social influences encompass others' perceptions of the behaviour (**social norms**), observation of others carrying out the behaviour (**social modelling**) and the pressures or support from others to execute the behaviour (**pressure/support**). **Self-efficacy** is a person's perception of their ability to carry out the behaviour. There are four types of self-efficacy: **routine, social, situational** and **stress.**

Motivation factors are determined by the more distal **awareness factors, information factors** and **predisposing factors.** Awareness factors include **knowledge, risk perceptions** and '**cues to action**'. Information factors include the **message** (e.g. level of discrepancy between message and opinions of target group), the **channel** (e.g. mass media strategies) and the **source** (e.g. reliability of source). Predisposing factors are **behavioural** (e.g. lifestyle, pervious experiences), **psychological** (e.g. attributions, personality), **biological** (e.g. gender, age, genetic predisposition) and **social and cultural** (e.g. socio-economic status, policies).

A diagram of the I-Change Model can be found on p.155 of De Vries, Mesters, van de Steeg, & Honing (2005).

Contributing Theories:

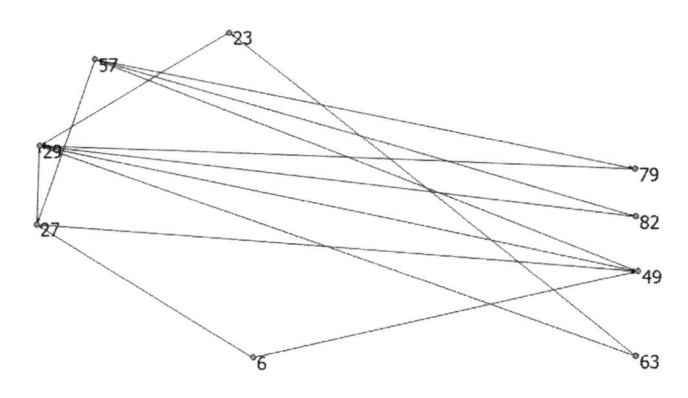

As outlined in the network diagram, the following theories included within this book were identified as contributing to the development of the I-Change Model:

23. Goal Setting Theory

27. Health Belief Model

49. Protection Motivation Theory

63. Social Cognitive Theory

79. Theory of Planned Behaviour

82. Transtheoretical Model of Behaviour Change

Taken from:

De Vries, H., Mesters, I., van de Steeg, H. & Honing, C. (2005). The general public's information needs and perceptions regarding hereditary cancer: an application of the Integrated Change Model. *Patient Education and Counseling*, 56, 154-165.

Supplemented by:

De Vries, H., Dijkstra, M. & Kuhlman, P. (1988). Self-efficacy: the third factor besides attitude and subjective norm as a predictor of behavioural intentions. *Health Education Research: Theory & Practice*, 3(3), 273-282.

De Vries, H., Mudde, A.N. and Dijkstra, A. (2000). The attitude–social influence–efficacy model applied to the prediction of motivational transitions in the process of smoking cessation. In Norman, P., Abraham, C. and Conner, M. (eds), *Understanding and Changing Health Behaviour: From Health Beliefs to Self-regulation*. Harwood Academic, Amsterdam, pp. 165–187

30. Information-Motivation-Behavioural Skills Model (Fisher & Fisher)

Constructs

- Information
    - Information about means of transmission
    - Information about means of prevention
- Motivation
    - Attitudes
    - Social norms
- Behavioural Skills
    - Self-acceptance of sexuality
    - Acquisition of behaviourally relevant information
    - Bringing up/negotiating AIDS prevention with partner
    - Public prevention acts
    - Consistent AIDS prevention
    - Self- and Partner-reinforcement
    - Group-specific skills
    - Self-efficacy

Brief Summary

The Information-Motivation-Behavioural Skills Model of AIDS-risk reduction behaviour is based on the Theory of Reasoned Action. The three main factors that affect behaviour are proposed to be information, motivation and behavioural skills. To exert an influence on behaviour, these three factors must be specific to the situation and the population in which the behaviour occurs.

Description

The Information-Motivation-Behavioural Skills Model proposes that there are three fundamental, independent determinants of AIDS preventive behaviour. First, **information** (or knowledge) about the means of AIDS transmission and prevention is an essential prerequisite for reducing AIDS-risk behaviour. However, information is a necessary but not sufficient requirement for risk-reduction behaviour. **Motivation** to change AIDS-risk behaviour is necessary for people to act upon this knowledge. Thirdly, possessing the necessary **behavioural skills** to perform AIDS-preventative acts is required for a knowledgeable and motivated person to take preventative action.

Information and motivation exert an influence on behaviour through behavioural skills, by activating the necessary skills for reducing risk behaviours and maintaining behaviour change. Risk-reduction information and risk-reduction motivation can directly influence risk-reduction behaviour, particularly behaviour change that does not require complex or difficult skills.

The three core constructs are generalised determinants of behaviour that can be applied to any population to identify how best to promote preventative behaviour within that population. However, the constructs are more strongly predictive of behaviour when the specific needs and characteristics of a target group are identified (e.g. level of knowledge, specific motivational issues and specific behavioural skills). Each of the three determinants (and the causal paths amongst them) will be more influential in some populations, and for some behaviours, than others.

Information

Except when AIDS-risk reduction requires a relatively simple behaviour, AIDS information is a necessary condition for AIDS-risk reduction behaviours to occur (but is not sufficient on its own). The types of information needed are (1) specific **knowledge about to the processes by which AIDS is transmitted** and (2) specific **knowledge about the processes by which AIDS is prevented**.

Motivation

Motivation is a function of a person's **attitudes** towards prevention (e.g. feelings of favourableness or unfavourableness to preventative behaviours), their **social norms** (i.e. perceptions of others' beliefs about AIDS prevention) and the perceived costs and benefits of prevention. Even well-informed people with the necessary behavioural skills to engage in AIDS-risk reduction behaviours must be motivated in order to initiate and maintain AIDS-preventative behaviours.

Behavioural Skills

Behavioural skills are a critical determinant of AIDS prevention practices. These are:

- **Self-acceptance of sexuality:** The acknowledgement that one is sexually active and thus should consider AIDS prevention.

- **Acquisition of behaviourally relevant information:** Having the skills to access accurate information about methods of AIDS prevention

- **Bringing up/negotiating AIDS prevention with partner:** The ability to discuss and agree upon AIDS-preventative actions with a sexual partner, and to remove oneself from situations in which safe sex cannot be agreed upon.

- **Public prevention acts:** The ability to carry out public AIDS-preventative behaviours such as purchasing condoms and undergoing HIV testing.

- **Consistent AIDS prevention:** The ability to carry out AIDS-preventative behaviours consistently.

- **Self- and partner-reinforcement:** The ability to reinforce oneself and one's partner.

- **Group-specific skills:** Additional AIDS-prevention-relevant skills that are specific to certain groups of people (e.g. substance abuse status, gender, ethnicity).

- **Self-efficacy:** A person must also possess self-belief in their ability to use these skills effectively in order to carry the behaviours out.

The Information-Motivation-Behavioural Skills Model

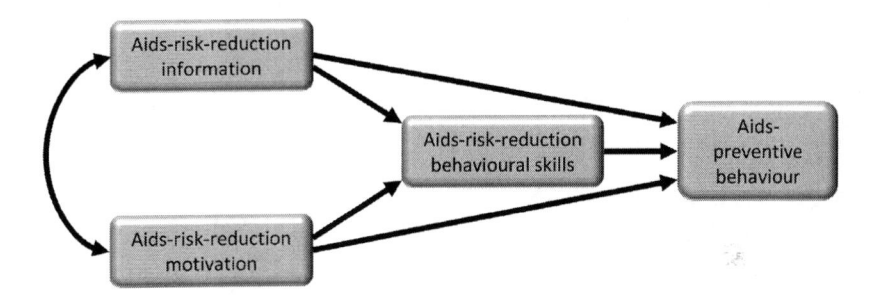

Source: Fisher, J.D. & Fisher, W.A. (1992). Changing AIDS-risk behaviour. *Psychological Bulletin*, 111(3), 455-474. Originally published by APA and reprinted here with permission.

Contributing Theories:

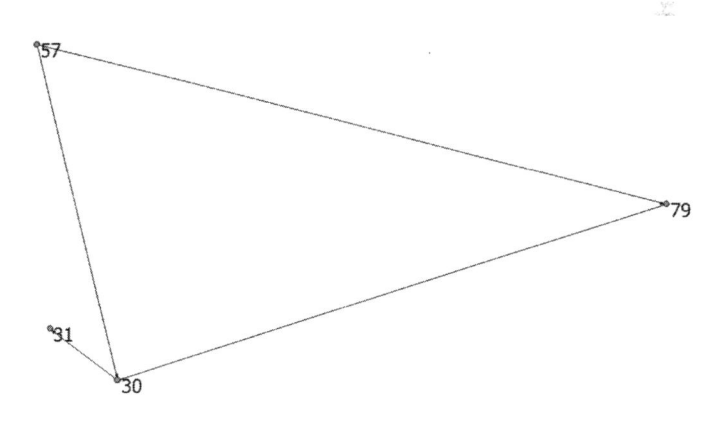

As outlined in the network diagram, the following theories included within this book were identified as contributing to the development of the Information-Motivation-Behavioural Skills Model:

57. Self-Efficacy Theory

79. Theory of Planned Behaviour

Taken from:

Fisher, J.D. & Fisher, W.A. (1992). Changing AIDS-risk behaviour. *Psychological Bulletin,* 111(3), 455-474.

31. Information-Motivation-Behavioural Skills Model of Adherence (Fisher et al.)

Constructs

- Information
    - Accuracy of information
    - Adherence-related heuristics
    - Implicit theories
- Motivation
    - Personal motivation
        - Beliefs
        - Evaluations
    - Social motivation
        - Perceived social support
        - Motivation to comply
- Behavioural skills
    - Objective abilities
    - Perceived self-efficacy
- Adherence behaviour
- Health outcomes
    - Viral load
    - CD-4 count
    - Drug resistance
    - Physical health
    - Subjective health
    - Quality of life
- Moderating factors
    - Psychological health
    - Stability of living situation
    - Access to medical care
    - Substance use/addiction

Brief Summary

The Information-Motivation-Behavioural skills model of adherence aims to explain and predict adherence to highly-active anti-retroviral therapy (HAART), with a view to informing how it can best be promoted. The three main factors that affect adherence are information, motivation and behavioural skills.

Description

According to the Information-Motivation-Behavioural skills model of highly active antiretroviral therapy (HAART) adherence, information, motivation and behavioural skills are fundamental determinants of HAART adherence among HIV-infected people. HIV-positive individuals who are well-informed about HAART, motivated to adhere to HAART and possess the behavioural skills to do so are more likely to adhere to HAART over time. Conversely, people lacking in these domains are unlikely to adhere to their medication regimen.

Information relating to HAART is necessary for optimum adherence. The **accuracy of information** can either facilitate adherence or present barriers to adherence. Accurate information about the adequate adherence levels, how to take medications and about potential side effects facilitates adherence. Inaccurate information or a lack of information about these factors may present a barrier. People may also possess HAART **adherence-related heuristics** which allow for somewhat automatic decision-making regarding adherence. If such heuristics are incorrect (e.g. "I am feeling well so my medication levels must be correct"), they may negatively influence HAART adherence. Adherence-related **implicit theories** may be detrimental to HAART adherence; these are more complex sets of belief about adherence that can be applied to decision-making with some cognitive effort (e.g. "Occasionally skipping my medication will strengthen my immune system").

Motivation comprises both **personal motivation** and **social motivation** to adhere to HAART. Personal motivation arises from a person's attitudes towards adherence – that is their **beliefs** about the possible outcomes of adherence/nonadherence and their **evaluations** of these outcomes. Social motivation is defined as a person's level of **perceived social support** from important others and their **motivation to comply** with these others.

Behavioural skills are necessary for adherence to HAART. This includes a person's **objective abilities** to acquire, access and self-administer medication in line with their prescribed regimen, and their **perceived self-efficacy** (i.e. beliefs about their ability to carry out specific behaviours) to do so. The objective and perceived abilities required to perform the behaviour may be numerous and include factors such as keeping medication accessible, self-cueing and self-administering the medications, incorporating the regimen into daily life, coping with the side-effects of medications, updating knowledge of HAART, mobilising support, being able to communicate with health care providers and reinforcing self-beliefs.

Information and motivation influence **adherence behaviour** indirectly through their influence on behavioural skills - they facilitate the application of behavioural skills such as the acquisition and storage of medication. Behavioural skills are the primary determinants of adherence behaviour although information and motivation may also directly influence adherence to a lesser extent when behavioural skills are not necessary (i.e. for less complex/novel behaviours). Adherence to HAART has a direct influence on objective and subjective health outcomes; including **viral load, CD-4 count, drug resistance, physical health, subjective health** and **quality of life.** These outcomes further influence information, motivation and behavioural skills via a feedback loop. For example, positive subjective or objective health outcomes as a result of optimum adherence may improve confidence in information, strengthen motivational factors and reinforce behavioural skills factors. Positive health outcomes will lead to increased adherence and maintenance of adherence, whilst negative health outcomes may have a detrimental effect.

Personal and environmental **moderating factors** can also play a role in influencing adherence, including **psychological health, stability of living circumstances, access to medical care** and **substance use/addiction.** In situations of psychological ill-health, unstable living circumstances, poor access to medical or substance use/addiction, these factors can influence adherence behaviour indirectly through their effects on information, motivation factors and behaviour skills. These factors may make adherence hard to achieve regardless of the status of information, motivation and behavioural skills factors.

The IMB model of adherence to antiretroviral medication

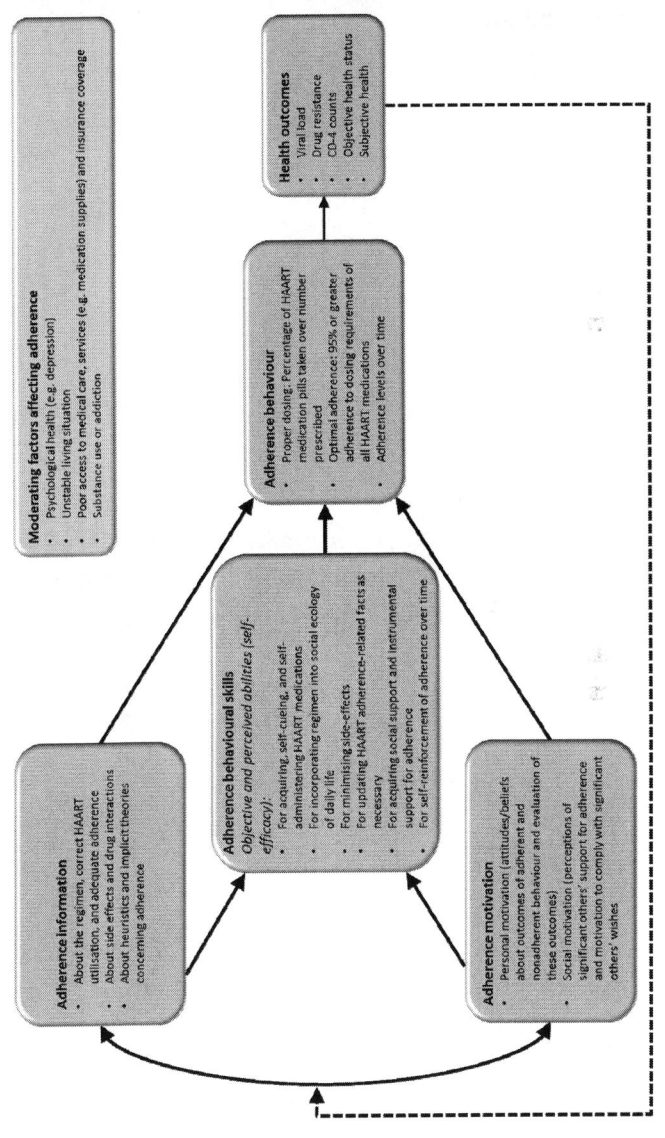

Source: Fisher, J.D. & Fisher, W.A. (1992). Fisher, J.D., Fisher, W.A., Amico, K.R., & Harman, J.J. (2006). An Information-Motivation-Behavioural Skills Model of Adherence to Antiretroviral Therapy. *Health Psychology*, 25(4), 462-473. Originally published by APA and reprinted here with permission.

Contributing Theories:

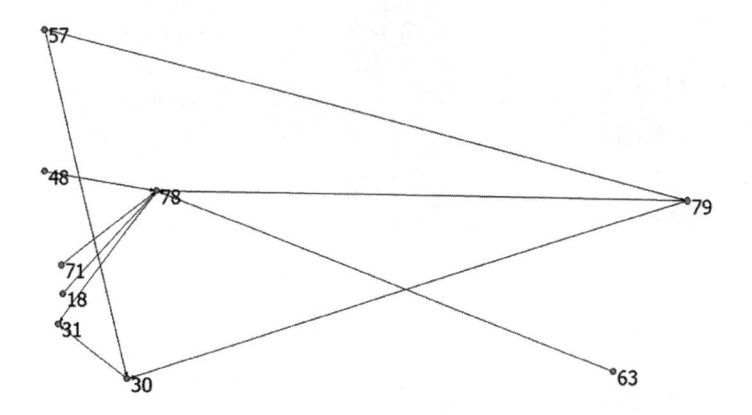

As outlined in the network diagram, the following theories included within this book were identified as contributing to the development of the Information-Motivation-Behavioural Skills Model of Adherence:

29. Information-Motivation-Behavioural Skills Model

79. Theory of Planned Behaviour

Taken from:

Fisher, J.D., Fisher, W.A., Amico, K.R., & Harman, J.J. (2006). An Information-Motivation-Behavioural Skills Model of Adherence to Antiretroviral Therapy. *Health Psychology*, 25(4), 462-473.

32. Integrated Theoretical Model for Alcohol and Other Drug Abuse Prevention (Gonzalez)

Constructs

- Intrapersonal factors
    - Severity of problem
    - Personal susceptibility
    - Behavioural options
    - Efficacy expectations
        - Self-efficacy
        - Outcome expectations
    - Behavioural skills
- Supportive environment
- Environmental factors
    - Environmental pressures
    - Interpersonal situations
    - Health-enhancing activities
- Behaviour change

Brief Summary

The Integrated Theoretical Model for Alcohol and Other Drug Abuse Prevention is a combination of the Health Belief Model, Social Learning Theory and Problem Behaviour Theory and aims to provide a framework for the prevention of alcohol and drug abuse in university campuses. The model emphasises the importance of both intrapersonal and environmental factors in facilitating behaviour change.

Description

The Integrated Theoretical Model for Alcohol and Other Drug Abuse Prevention is a combination of the Health Belief Model, Social Learning Theory and Problem Behaviour Theory. The model emphasises the importance of both **intrapersonal factors** and **environmental factors** in influencing **behaviour change**, preventing alcohol and drug abuse prevention in university campuses, and aims to provide a framework for the design of interventions to facilitate reductions in alcohol and drug abuse.

Intrapersonal Factors

People will not be motivated to change problem alcohol- and drug-related behaviour unless they perceive the problem to be serious (**severity of problem**), feel personally susceptible to the problem (**personal susceptibility**) and perceive alternative **behavioural options** that are beneficial. Perceptions of personal susceptibility are the most influential determinant of motivation to change.

The translation of motivation to change into actual behaviour change is dependent upon a person's **efficacy expectations** and **behavioural skills**. Efficacy expectations include self-efficacy (i.e. a person's beliefs about their ability to change their behaviour) and **outcome expectations** (i.e. a person's beliefs about whether behaviour change will lead to the desired outcome). Outcome expectations influence both motivation to change and behaviour change. However, positive outcome expectations and high levels of motivation only lead to behaviour change when the behaviour change is easy to achieve. When behaviours are difficult to modify, self-efficacy becomes much more influential than outcome expectations and adequate behavioural skills such as assertiveness and interpersonal communication are also necessary for behaviour change.

Environmental Factors

People will be unable to change behaviour unless they do so within a **supportive environment** (i.e. one that supports moderation in alcohol consumption and does not tolerate the use of illicit drugs). Behaviour and behaviour change is also influenced by environmental pressures (e.g. pro-drug role models and peer pressure), interpersonal situations (e.g. peer interaction, communication with parents or teachers, drug-avoiding socialising) and health-enhancing activities (e.g. attendance at drug-free social event, participation in wellness programs). Resistance of negative environmental pressures, enhancement of interpersonal situations and participation in health-enhancing activities will facilitate behaviour change towards a reduction in problematic alcohol consumption and illicit drug use.

A diagram of the Integrated Theoretical Model for Alcohol and Other Drug Abuse Prevention can be found on p.495 of Gonzalez (1989).

Contributing Theories:

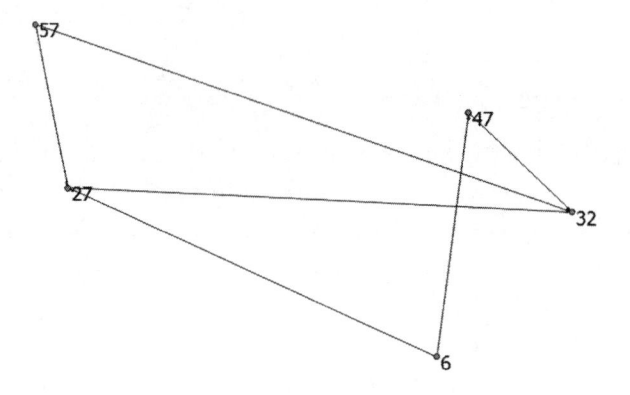

As outlined in the network diagram, the following theories included within this book were identified as contributing to the development of the Integrated Theoretical Model for Alcohol and Other Drug Abuse Prevention:

27. Health Belief Model

45. Problem Behaviour Theory

57. Self-Efficacy Theory

Taken from:

Gonzalez GM. (1989). An integrated theoretical model for alcohol and other drug abuse prevention on the college campus. *Journal of College Student Development*, 30, 492-503.

33. Integrated Theory of Drinking Behaviour (Wagenaar & Perry)

Constructs

- Perceptions and cognitions
- Social interactions
- Models of drinking
- Formal social controls
- Legal availability
- Economic availability
- Physical availability
- Social structures
- Social integration
- Public policy
- Market mechanisms
- Biological and pharmacological factors
- Social roles
- Conditioned responses
- General beliefs, perceptions and personality characteristics
- Drinking behaviour

Brief Summary

The Integrated Theory of Drinking Behaviour is a 'meta-theory' that integrates ideas from a range of other theories of drinking and aims to identify the factors that determine alcohol consumption in young people. The model emphasises the role of social interactions in determining drinking behaviour, and the importance of changing socio-environmental conditions in attempts to facilitate long-term reductions in alcohol consumption.

Description

The Integrated Theory of Drinking Behaviour aims to provide a framework for further research and theory creation, and as a guide for designing interventions to reduce alcohol consumption. **Drinking behaviour** is directly influenced by people's alcohol-related **perceptions and cognitions**. Specifically, a person is likely to drink alcohol when they anticipate there will be positive and reinforcing effects, when they understand alcohol consumption in terms of its socially shared positive meanings, and when the perceived rewards of doing so outweigh the perceived costs. Alcohol-related perceptions are directly determined by a number of social influences: **social interaction** with important others, observation of **models of drinking** (e.g. parents, peers, media programming, contemporary literature) and **formal social controls** such as laws and policies (including the probability of detection by formal social controls and the level of threat posed by them).

Educational interventions alone will not be sufficient to change beliefs and attitudes related to alcohol consumption, as social structures, public policy, role-models and other factors in the environment will remain unchanged. In addition, some factors may impact upon drinking behaviour directly rather than indirectly through their influence on cognitions and perceptions. The **legal availability** (e.g. minimum drinking age, hours of sale), **economic availability** (e.g. retail price of alcohol) and **physical availability** (e.g. proximity to outlets) of alcohol are all proposed to directly influence drinking behaviour, as well as having an indirect influence by creating perceptions.

The model operates at both the societal (macro) level and at the individual (micro) level. At the macro level, **public policy, social structures,** and **market mechanisms** are important environmental antecedents of drinking behaviour. Public policy influences drinking behaviour through direct effects on formal social controls and the legal, economic and physical availability of alcohol. Social structures (class, school, neighbourhood) directly influence **social integration** (connectedness, bonding) which in turn affects the level of **social interactions** with peers, parents and significant others). Individual beliefs and perceptions about alcohol are influenced by these social interactions and by the **social roles** of a person (e.g., level of conventionality, whether a person is working or a student). Role models of drinking are also important determinants of drinking behaviour as they influence alcohol-related cognitions and perceptions. Models of drinking may be provided by reference groups such as parents, siblings and peers, but may also be portrayed in the media and through marketing.

At the micro level of influence are **biological and pharmacological factors, conditioned responses** and **general beliefs, perceptions and personality characteristics.** Biological factors play a role because consuming alcohol may be intrinsically rewarding due to the psychopharmacological action of alcohol on the body. However, this biological influence is relatively small compared with the greater importance of socially learned meanings and expectations. Personality, self-esteem and locus of control are also associated with drinking behaviour, but are not causal factors as both personality characteristics and drinking behaviour are influenced by common antecedent factors in the environment.

A diagram of the Integrated Theory of Drinking Behaviour can be found on p.322 of Wagenaar & Perry (1994).

Contributing Theories:

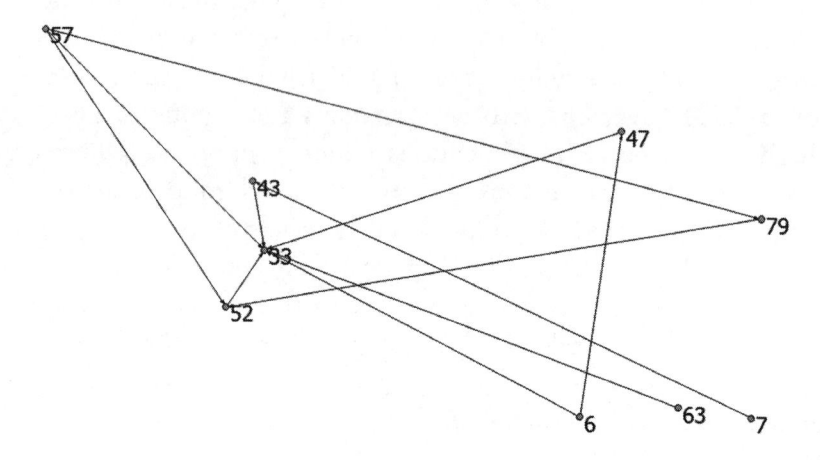

As outlined in the network diagram, the following theories included within this book were identified as contributing to the development of the Information-Motivation-Behavioural Skills Model of Adherence:

6. Change Theory

43. Operant Learning Theory

47. Problem Behaviour Theory

52. Rational Addiction Model

Taken from:

Wagenaar, A.C. & Perry, C. L. (1994). Community Strategies for the Reduction of Youth Drinking: Theory and Application. *Journal of Research on Adolescence*, 4(2), 319–345.

34. Integrated Theory of Health Behaviour Change (Ryan)

Constructs

- Knowledge and beliefs
    o Condition specific knowledge
    o Personal perceptions
        ☐ Self-efficacy
        ☐ Outcome expectancy
        ☐ Goal congruence
- Self-regulation skill and ability
    o Goal setting
    o Self-monitoring
    o Reflective thinking
    o Decision making
    o Planning
    o Plan enactment
    o Self-evaluation
    o Management of emotions
- Social facilitation
    o Social influence
    o Social support
        ☐ Emotional
        ☐ Instrumental
        ☐ Informational
- Engagement in self-management of behaviour
- Health status

Brief Summary

The Integrated Theory of Health Behaviour Change aims to explain the adoption of self-management behaviours. Three main factors are proposed to facilitate behaviour change: knowledge and beliefs, self-regulatory skills and abilities, and social facilitation.

Description

The Integrated Theory of Health Behaviour Change integrates concepts from numerous theories of behaviour and behaviour change, with a focus on the promotion of self-management strategies for people with chronic disease. Behaviour change is seen as a dynamic and iterative process in which motivation to change is a necessary precursor of behaviour change. Self-reflection and positive social influences are influential in facilitating motivation and willingness to change, and in sustaining behaviour change attempts.

Three main factors have a positive influence on health behaviour change: **knowledge and beliefs, self-regulation skill and ability** and **social facilitation.** The proximal outcome of these factors is **engagement in self-management behaviour** specific to a particular condition or health behaviour, which over time is seen to influence the more distal outcome of **health status**. 'Knowledge and beliefs', 'self-regulation skill and ability' and 'social facilitation' are related not only to outcomes, but also to each other and a number of more specific constructs.

Knowledge and Beliefs

Knowledge is factual and condition-specific information, whilst **beliefs** are a person's perceptions regarding their specific condition or health behaviour. If knowledge and beliefs are enhanced, increases will occur in a person's **understanding** of the behaviour or condition, their behaviour-specific **self-efficacy**, their **outcome expectancy** and their **goal congruence**. 'Self-efficacy' is a person's confidence in their ability to successfully carry out the behaviour, even under conditions of stress. 'Outcome expectancy' is a person's belief that carrying out the behaviour will lead to the desired results. Finally, 'goal congruence' is the resolution of confusion and anxiety arising from any competing demands associated with a person's health goals. For example, a person may have a goal to reduce or maintain their weight and a goal to increase their calcium intake. Increasing calcium intake by increasing calcium consumption with dairy foods could be problematic, and so the person must find a way to manage their weight and their calcium intake to make these goals congruent.

Self-Regulation Skill and Ability

Self-regulation is the process by which people incorporate behaviour change into their everyday lives, involving: **self-monitoring, goal setting, reflective thinking, decision making, planning, plan enactment, self-evaluation** and the **management of emotions** arising as a result of the behaviour change.

Social Facilitation

'Social facilitation' incorporates **social influence** and **social support**. Social influence can result in engagement in health behaviour when a credible source (i.e. a person who is perceived as in a position of authority who holds the relevant health knowledge) influences a person's thoughts and motivation. Social influences can arise from numerous sources, including (but not limited to) healthcare professionals, family members, peers and the media. Social support also facilitates performance of the desired health behaviour, and exists in three distinct: **emotional, instrumental** and **informational**.

Relationships between Constructs

Knowledge alone is insufficient to lead to health behaviour change. However, knowledge and beliefs influence engagement in self-regulatory activities, with engagement in self-regulation skills and abilities in turn improving self-management behaviour. Positive influences from social facilitation have a beneficial effect upon both self-regulation and actual self-management behaviour. Carrying out self-management behaviours directly and positively influences health status.

A diagram of the Integrated Theory of Health Behaviour Change can be found on p.164 of Ryan (2009).

Contributing Theories:

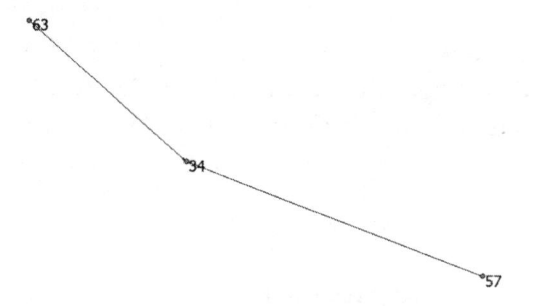

As outlined in the network diagram, the following theories included within this book were identified as contributing to the development of the Integrated Theory of Health Behaviour Change:

57. Self-Efficacy Theory

63. Social Cognitive Theory

Taken from:

Ryan, P. (2009). Integrated Theory of Health Behaviour Change: Background and Intervention Development. *Clinical Nurse Specialist*, 23(3), 161-172.

35. Integrative Model of Behavioural Prediction (Fishbein)

Constructs

- Background variables
    - Demographic variables
    - Attitudes towards targets
    - Personality traits
    - Individual differences
- Behavioural beliefs and their evaluative aspects
- Normative beliefs and motivation to comply
- Efficacy beliefs
- Attitude
- Perceived norms
- Self-efficacy
- Intention
- Skills
- Environmental constraints
- Behaviour

Brief Summary

The Integrative Model of Behavioural Prediction is a development of the Theory of Planned Behaviour. The model emphasises the importance of two additional factors, environmental constraints and skills/ability, which influence behaviour over and above the effect of behavioural intentions.

Description

The Integrative Model of Behavioural Prediction is as an integration of theories of behaviour/behaviour change, aiming to provide a theoretical basis for the design of behaviour change interventions.

Intentions (to perform a behaviour), **environmental constraints** preventing that behaviour being carried out and **skills** facilitating performance of the behaviour are the primary determinants of that behaviour. When intentions are strong, environmental constraints are minimised and skills are present, the probability of the behaviour occurring is high. If a person's intentions are strong but they are unable to act on them, it is likely due to a lack of skills and the presence of environmental constraints.

Intentions are a function of **attitudes**, **perceived norms** and **self-efficacy**. Attitude is defined as a person's feelings about how favourable or unfavourable performing the behaviour would be. The perceived norm is the felt social pressure regarding performance of the behaviour and has two aspects; a person's perceptions of what others think they should do and their perception of what others are doing (in relation to the behaviour in question). Self-efficacy refers to a person's beliefs about whether they can perform the behaviour, even under difficult circumstances. More positive attitudes, perceived norms to carry out the behaviour and greater self-efficacy will result in stronger intentions. These three variables will have varying relative influence upon intentions, depending upon the behaviour and the population in question.

These determinants of intention arise from a number of underlying factors. Attitudes are a function of evaluations of the possible outcomes of the behaviour, termed '**behavioural beliefs and their evaluative aspects**' (i.e. beliefs that the behaviour will lead to positive outcomes and prevent negative ones result in more positive attitudes). Perceived norms arise from a person's beliefs about what specific others think they should do, and a person's motivation to comply with those others (**normative beliefs and motivation to comply**). Self-efficacy is determined by a person's perceptions of their skills and ability to carry out the behaviour even if specific barriers are present (**efficacy beliefs**).

The model outlines a number of **background variables** that indirectly influence behaviour, which are proposed to play a role in shaping beliefs about specific behaviours. These include **demographic variables** (e.g. gender, culture, socio-economic status), **attitudes towards targets** (e.g. people with favourable attitudes towards family planning may hold different attitudes towards one specific behaviour but similar attitudes towards another), **personality traits**, and other **individual differences** (e.g. differing perceptions of risk).

A diagram of the Integrative Model of Behavioural Prediction can be found on p.274 of Fishbein (2000).

Contributing Theories:

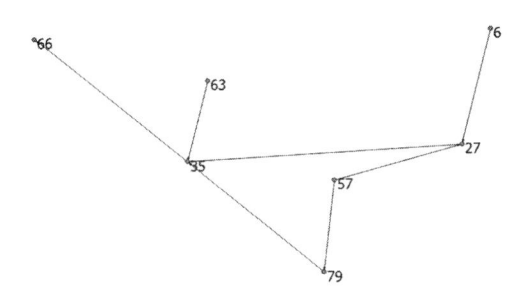

As outlined in the network diagram, the following theories included within this book were identified as contributing to the development of the Integrative Model of Behavioural Prediction:

27. Health Belief Model

63. Social Cognitive Theory

79. Theory of Planned Behaviour

Taken from:

Fishbein, M. (2000). The role of theory in HIV prevention. *Aids Care*, 12(3), 273-278.

36. Integrative Model of Factors Influencing Smoking Behaviours (Flay et al.)

Constructs

- Stages in the development of adolescent smoking behaviour
    - Preparation and anticipation
        - Knowledge
        - Values
        - Beliefs
        - Attitudes
        - Intentions
    - Initiation
    - Experimentation
    - Regular smoking (becoming)
- Influences on smoking behaviour
    - Family influences
    - Peer influences
    - Selection of peers
    - Self-image
    - Social competence
    - Attitudes
    - Environment
    - Socioeconomic status
    - Social motives
    - Perceived physiological effects
    - Personality factors
    - Social reinforcement
- Adult smoking

Brief Summary

The Integrative Model of Factors Influencing Smoking Behaviour aims to identify the determinants of smoking behaviour during adolescence, and to describe the developmental stages in which smoking behaviour occurs. It proposes four stages in the acquisition of smoking behaviour: preparation and anticipation, initiation, experimentation, and regular smoking. It proposes different types of influence in transition between the different stages.

Description

The Integrative Model of Factors Influencing Smoking Behaviours describes four sequential **stages** in which smoking behaviour in adolescents develops, and outlines the social, psychological and environmental factors that are influential at the different stages of smoking behaviour. These stages are:

- **Preparation and anticipation.** This stage involves learning experiences during childhood, provided by a person's environment (e.g. smoking-related family influences and vicarious experiences of smoking). **Knowledge**, **values**, **beliefs**, **attitudes** and **intentions** relating to smoking behaviour are developed during this stage.

- **Initiation.** This is the stage in which smoking behaviour is first tried.

- **Experimentation.** The experimentation stage may or may not occur after initiation. For some people, their first experience of smoking may put them off trying the behaviour again and experimentation will not occur. Others may progress to the experimentation stage and continue to try smoking.

- **Regular smoking (becoming).** If experimentation with smoking continues for long enough, then people will eventually progress to the 'becoming' stage, where they become regular smokers.

Family influences are most influential in the preparation stage, but their influence decreases as smoking behaviour develops. At the initiation stage, **peer pressure** and problems with social **competence** or **self-image** become most influential in determining smoking behaviour. Children may start smoking to improve their self-image, particularly if they have low performance in school or in the eyes of adults, or if they have low approval from peers. **Attitudes** formed during the preparation and anticipation stage may also have an indirect influence at the initiation stage, as they can play a role in a child's choice of peers. **Socioeconomic status** also has an indirect influence during the initiation stage - it determines the **environment** in which a child exists, which in turn limits the **selection of peers**. Further, socioeconomic status determines the likelihood of whether or not a child's parents smoke.

At the experimentation stage, peer pressure remains an important factor in determining smoking behaviour. However the extent to which peer pressure is influential in this stage depends upon other **social motives** for smoking and upon the **perceived physiological effects** of the first few cigarettes. **Personality factors** and peer influences have an indirect effect upon smoking behaviour during the experimentation stage as they both play a role in determining social motives, and personality factors may influence perceptions of the physiological effects of smoking.

In the maintenance stage, **social reinforcements** become the most influential factor in determining whether experimentation develops into regular smoking. In addition to social reinforcement for smoking, perceptions of physiological effect and peer pressure may also play a role in determining whether an adolescent becomes a regular smoker. As an adolescent becomes an adult, the physiological effects of smoking upon emotional states become the most important factor in determining **adult smoking** behaviour, whilst social factors become less influential.

A diagram of the Integrative Model of Factors Influencing Smoking Behaviours can be found on p.144 of Flay, D'Avernas, Best, Kersell, & Ryan (1983).

Contributing Theories:

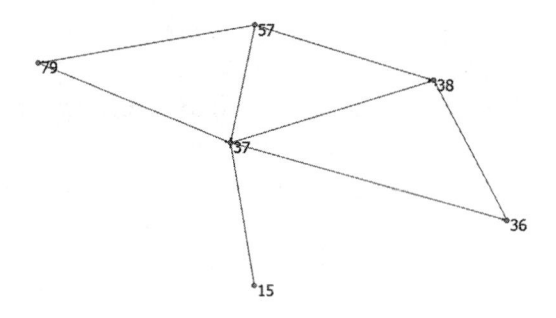

As outlined in the network diagram, the following theory included within this book was identified as contributing to the development of the Integrative Model of Factors Influencing Smoking:

37. Integrative Model of Health Attitude and Behaviour Change

Taken from:

Flay, B. R., D'Avernas, J. R., Best, J. A., Kersell, M. W. & Ryan, K. B. (1983). Cigarette smoking: why young people do it and ways of preventing it. In P. Mcgrath & P. Firestone (Eds.) *Pediatric and Adolescent Behavioural Medicine* (pp. 132-183). New York: Springer-Verlag.

37. Integrative Model of Health Attitude and Behaviour Change (Flay)

Constructs
- Source variables
- Message variables
- Channel variables
- Audience variables
- Information
- Attention
- Comprehension
- Acceptance
- Exposure
- Awareness
- Knowledge
- Beliefs
- Attitudes
    o Values
    o Evaluations
    o Expectancies
- Intentions
- Behaviour
- Social normative beliefs
- Weight
- Personality factors
- Self-efficacy
- Available behavioural alternatives
- Available materials
- Trial behaviour
- Repeated behaviour
- Reinforcements
- Consistency

Brief Summary

The Integrative Model of Health Attitude and Behaviour Change integrates several theories from social and behavioural psychology and describes how mass media health promotion campaigns can lead to changes in health-related attitudes and behaviours. Change occurs in sequential stages: messages influence knowledge, beliefs and attitudes, leading to changes in behavioural intentions and finally behaviour change.

Description

The Integrative Model of Health Attitude and Behaviour Change aims to describe the factors that influence whether health promotion campaigns are successful in changing people's health-related attitudes and behaviours. The model integrates ideas from the Extended Information Processing Model, the Theory of Reasoned Action and other socio-cognitive theories of behaviour.

Behaviour change occurs in a series of stages, with completion of one stage increasing the likelihood of progressing to the next. Message variables influence **awareness, knowledge**, and **beliefs**. In turn, values, value expectancies and beliefs influence attitudes. **Social normative beliefs**, **attitudes** and **personality** predict **intentions**. **Trial behaviour** is predicted by intentions, **available materials** and **available behavioural alternatives**. Finally, trial behaviour is maintained if it is appropriately reinforced. Further specifics of each part of the model are described below.

The first part of the model focuses on characteristics of the message - **source variables, message variables, channel variables** and **audience variables** – and how through exposure these create awareness, increase knowledge and inform beliefs. The process follows a causal chain with four steps. First, **exposure** to

information in a message will lead to awareness of that message, under the condition that a person **attends** to that message. Second, awareness will result in knowledge change, so long as the message is **comprehended**. Third, knowledge change will lead to change in beliefs, under the condition that the content of the message is **accepted**. Changes in beliefs may (or may not) lead to changes in attitudes, then intentions, then behaviour. Beliefs are weighted by the **value** that a person places upon the attributes of an object or the expected consequences of an action (i.e. their **evaluation** of an object/action), and attitudes are the multiplicative function of evaluations and **expectancies** (i.e. beliefs about the probable consequences of behaviour).

Behavioural intentions mediate the influence of attitude change upon behaviour. Behavioural intentions are an additive function of attitudes **and social normative beliefs** (i.e. social norms, influences or pressures). The relative influence of each upon intentions varies according to their **weight**, which is dependent upon factors such as the behaviour in question, the situation and personality factors. Personality factors moderate the weight (importance) of an attitude, as well as directly influence **self-efficacy** (defined as the possession or acquisition of control over the behaviour).

At least one of two conditions must be met for changes in behavioural intentions to lead to changes in actual behaviour. A person must have the necessary level of self-efficacy, and/or have **available behavioural alternatives** for coping with barriers to the behaviour (e.g. possession of the necessary coping skills to resist social pressures). The presence of **available materials** may also have an influence at this stage. Trying a behaviour (termed **trial behaviour**) does not necessarily lead to maintenance of that behaviour; behavioural maintenance is dependent on both the behaviour being **repeated** and **reinforced**.

Because of a need for **consistency**, changes in any one variable in the model will create changes in the others. Thus, changes in variables may occur in any order.

A diagram of the Integrative Model of Health Attitude and Behaviour Change can be found on p. 70 of Flay (1981).

Contributing Theories:

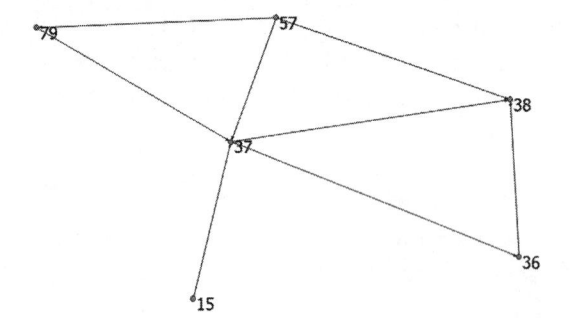

As outlined in the network diagram, the following theories included within this book were identified as contributing to the development of the Integrative Model of Health Attitude and Behaviour Change and Behaviour Change:

15. Extended Information Processing Model

57. Self-efficacy Theory

79. Theory of Planned Behaviour

Taken from:

Flay, B. R. (1981). On improving the chances of mass media health promotion programs causing meaningful changes in behaviour. In M. Meyer (Ed.), *Health Education by Television and Radio* (pp. 56-91). Munich: K.G. Saur Verlag.

38. Integrative Model of Factors Influencing Smoking And Attitude And Health Behaviour Change (Flay et al.)

Constructs
- Major influences on smoking
    - Socioeconomic status
    - Selection of peers
    - Selection of significant others
    - Family influences
    - Peer influences
    - Self-image
    - Personality
    - Physiological reaction
    - Physiological reinforcement
- Mediating variables
    - Social normative beliefs
    - Available behavioural alternatives
    - Available materials
    - Self-efficacy
    - Social reinforcements
    - 'Weights'
- Stage of behaviour
    - Knowledge
    - Values
    - Beliefs
    - Attitudes
    - Intentions
    - Trial behaviour
    - Repeated behaviour

- Stage of smoking
  - Preparation
  - Anticipation
  - Initiation
  - Experimentation
  - Learning
  - Becoming
  - Habituation
  - Maintenance

Brief Summary

The Integrative Model of Factors Influencing Smoking and Attitude and Health Behaviour Change aims to explain (1) the factors influencing smoking behaviour during adolescence, proposing stages in which smoking behaviour develops, and (2) the processes by which smoking-related attitudes and behaviour may change. It identifies a range of major influences (e.g. peer influence) and mediating variables (e.g. self-efficacy).

Description

The Integrative Model of Factors Influencing Smoking and Attitude and Health Behaviour Change is a combination of the 'Integrative Model of Factors Influencing Smoking' and the 'Integrative Model of Health Attitude and Behaviour Change'. It provides a basis for the development and evaluation of smoking prevention interventions for adolescents, by providing an account of the factors influencing both the development of smoking behaviour and attitudinal and behavioural change.

The development of smoking behaviour during adolescence occurs in five sequential stages, with different factors influential in determining smoking behaviour at each of these stages. Each 'stage of smoking' in the model is accompanied by a 'stage of behaviour'.

The theory does not provide an account of the interrelations between major influences on smoking behaviour, nor detailed descriptions of the constructs within it. Therefore, it is necessary to refer to descriptions of the original two theories it is based upon.

Major Influences on Smoking Behaviour

The major influences on smoking behaviour (i.e. whether or not a person will progress through the stages above to become a smoker) are:

- **Socioeconomic status**
- **Selection of peers**
- **Selection of significant others**
- **Family influences**
- **Peer influences**
- **Self-image**
- **Personality**
- **Physiological reactions to smoking**
- **Physiological reinforcement for smoking**

Mediating Variables

The main mediating variables are:

- **Weights** – Beliefs are 'weighted' by the value that a person attributes to relevant object or to the anticipated consequences of a relevant action (i.e. their evaluation of an object/action).

- Social normative beliefs
- Available behavioural alternatives
- Available materials
- Self-efficacy
- Social reinforcements

Stages of Behaviour and Smoking

The adoption of behaviour occurs in four sequential stages. The first stage is the development of **knowledge, values, beliefs** and **attitudes**. This is then followed by the formation of **intentions**, then '**trial behaviour**' (i.e. the first time that a person engages in the behaviour), and finally **repeated behaviour**.

Each behaviour stage is reflected by specific stages in the development of smoking behaviour. The development of knowledge, values, beliefs and attitudes can be seen as the '**preparation**' stage of smoking. Intention formation is reflective of the '**anticipation**' stage of smoking. The 'trial behaviour' stage can be seen as the '**initiation**' stage of smoking. Finally, the 'repeated behaviour' stage encompasses the sequential stages of '**experimentation**', '**learning**', '**becoming**', '**habituation**' and '**maintenance**'.

A diagram of the Integrative Model of Factors Influencing Smoking Behaviours and Health Attitude and Behaviour Change can be found on p.170 of Flay, D'Avernas, Best, Kersell, & Ryan (1983).

Contributing Theories:

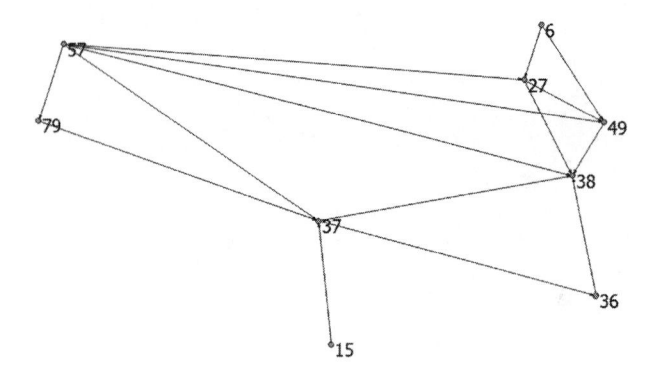

As outlined in the network diagram, the following theories included within this book were identified as contributing to the development of the Integrative Model of Factors Influencing Smoking and Health Attitude and Behaviour Change:

27. Health Belief Model

49. Protection Motivation Theory

57. Self-efficacy Theory

Taken from:

Flay, B. R., D'Avernas, J. R., Best, J. A., Kersell, M. W. & Ryan, K. B. (1983). Cigarette smoking: why young people do it and ways of preventing it. In P. McGrath and P. Firestone (Eds.) *Paediatric and Adolescent Behavioural Medicine* (pp. 132-183). New York: Springer-Verlag.

39. Model of Pro-Environmental Behaviour (Kollmuss & Agyeman)

Constructs

- Internal factors
    - Personality traits
    - Value system
        - Pro-environmental Consciousness
            - Knowledge
            - Values
            - Attitudes
            - Emotional involvement
- Indirect pro-environmental actions
- External factors
    - Infrastructure
    - Political factors
    - Social and cultural factors
    - Economic situation
- Barriers
    - Lack of knowledge
    - Emotional blocking of new knowledge
    - Existing values prevent learning
    - Existing knowledge contradicts environmental values
    - Emotional blocking of environmental values and attitudes
    - Existing values prevent emotional involvement
    - Lack of internal incentives
    - Negative or insufficient feedback about behaviour
    - Lack of environmental consciousness
    - Lack of external possibilities and incentives
    - Old behaviour patterns
- Pro-environmental behaviour

Brief Summary

The Model of Pro-Environmental Behaviour proposes a number of intrapersonal (e.g. personality) and external factors (e.g. the economic situation) that can contribute to environmentally friendly behaviour, alongside a number of intrapersonal and external barriers to pro-environmental behaviour.

Description

The Model of Pro-Environmental Behaviour provides a theoretical account of **internal factors** and **external factors** that determine **pro-environmental behaviour**. Internal factors include **personality traits** and broad personal values (termed the **value system**). Within these personal values is '**pro-environmental consciousness**': a complex made up of environmentally-related **knowledge, values** and **attitudes**, and environmental **emotional involvement**. External factors comprise factors such as **political factors, infrastructure, social and cultural factors**, and **economic situation**.

Both internal and external factors have direct, independent influences on pro-environmental behaviour. However, their effects upon behaviour are most positive when internal factors and external factors work synergistically. Pro-environmental behaviour may also occur for non-environmentally motivated reasons (e.g. using less power due to financial constraints). Internal factors and external factors can also influence each other. For instance, internal factors can affect external factors when **indirect pro-environmental actions** are carried out (e.g. taking political action). Pro-environmental behaviour can also further influence internal factors via a feedback system.

There are a number of **barriers** to pro-environmental behaviour, with barriers that influence the relationship between internal/external factors and pro-environmental behaviour distinguished from barriers that operate within the complex of 'pro-environmental consciousness'. Barriers within the 'pro-environmental consciousness' complex are:

- **Emotional blocking of new knowledge:** prevents emotional involvement from influencing knowledge.

- **Lack of knowledge:** prevents knowledge from influencing emotional involvement.

- **Existing values prevent learning** and **existing knowledge contradicts environmental values:** influences the interaction between personal values and knowledge.

- **Emotional blocking of environmental values and attitudes** and **existing values prevent emotional involvement:** influences the interaction between emotional involvement and value and attitudes.

Barriers between internal factors and pro-environmental behaviour include '**negative or insufficient feedback about behaviour**' (which prevents the feedback system from operating), '**lack of internal incentives**' and '**lack of environmental consciousness**'. '**Lack of external possibilities and incentives**' is a barrier to external factors influencing pro-environmental behaviour. The strongest barrier in the model is '**old behaviour patterns**' (also termed 'old habits'), which operates between pro-environmental behaviour and both internal and external factors.

A diagram of the Model of Pro-environmental Behaviour can be found on p.257 of Kollmuss & Agyeman (2002).

Contributing Theories:

None of the theories included within this book were identified as contributing to the development of the Model of Pro-Environmental Behaviour.

Taken from:

Kollmuss, A. & Agyeman, J. (2002). Mind the Gap: why do people act environmentally and what are the barriers to pro-environmental behaviour? *Environmental Education Research*, 8(3), 239-260.

40. Motivation-Opportunities-Abilities Model (Ölander & Thøgersen)

Constructs

- Motivation
    - Attitude towards the behaviour
        - Beliefs
        - Evaluations of outcomes
    - Social Norm
    - Intention
- Opportunity
- Ability
    - Habit
    - Task knowledge
- Behaviour

Brief Summary

The Motivation-Opportunity-Abilities model provides a theoretical account of consumer engagement in pro-environmental behaviours, and proposes that behaviour is dependent upon the presence of motivation, ability and opportunity. Motivation arises from a range of factors including intentions, social norms, attitudes. Ability involves habits and task knowledge. Opportunity refers to the external factors necessary for the behaviour to occur.

Description

The Motivation-Opportunity-Abilities model was developed to provide an integrative theory of human behaviours which have an impact on the environment (e.g. waste handling and recycling). The model builds on motivational theories of behaviour by incorporating an 'ability' construct and an 'opportunity' construct, based on the rationale that this could improve the model's power to predict **behaviour**. There are three classes of variables used to understand the determinants of environmental behaviour: **motivation, ability** and **opportunity.**

Motivation

The 'motivation' class of variables incorporates **intentions** (to engage in a certain behaviour), **social norms** (a person's perceptions of what others want them to do), **attitudes** towards the behaviour, **beliefs** about the behaviour and **evaluations of the possible outcomes** of the behaviour. Attitudes are a function of beliefs and evaluations of outcomes. In turn, intentions are determined by social norms and attitudes. It should be noted that whilst the motivation component of the model is based on the Theory of Reasoned Action, the model acknowledges that alternative models of motivation could be just as relevant.

Ability

A person must possess the ability to carry out the behaviour for intention to lead to behaviour. 'Ability' encompasses two constructs: **habits** and **task knowledge**. Habits are routines that allow behaviours to be performed automatically with minimal conscious effort. Task knowledge is a person's knowledge about how to accurately perform the behaviour. Ability independently influences behaviour and moderates the intention-behaviour relationship.

Opportunity

Opportunity is defined as the presence of objective conditions that are necessary for the behaviour to occur. For example, for people to recycle their waste, recycling bins and collection systems must be in place.

Relationships between Determinants

The translation of motivational factors (represented in intentions) into behaviour is moderated by opportunity and ability. Additionally, experiences of carrying out the behaviour provide feedback which influences beliefs, evaluation outcomes, and ability. For example, a change in beliefs may occur if the behaviour is not viewed to be as rewarding as was initially believed. Likewise, beliefs and evaluations may also change after the behaviour is carried out multiple times and becomes easier to implement. In this case, behaviour feeds back to beliefs and evaluations via ability.

A diagram of the Motivation-Opportunities-Abilities Model can be found on p.361 of Ölander & Thøgersen (1995).

Contributing Theories:

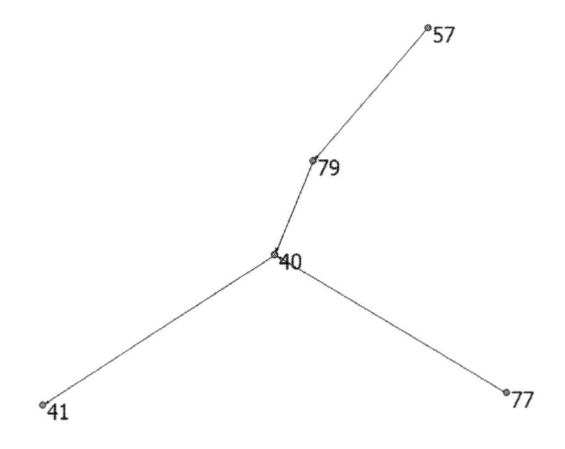

As outlined in the network diagram, the following theories included within this book were identified as contributing to the development of the Motivation-Opportunities-Abilities Model:

77. Theory of Interpersonal Behaviour

79. Theory of Planned Behaviour

Taken from:

Ölander, F. & Thøgersen, J. (1995). Understanding of consumer behaviour as a prerequisite for environmental protection. Journal of Consumer Policy, 18, 345-385.

41. Needs-Opportunities-Abilities Model (Gatersleben & Vlek)

Constructs
- Macro-level factors
    - o Technology
    - o Economy
    - o Demography
    - o Institutions
    - o Culture
- Needs
    - o Social relations
    - o Development/education
    - o Comfort
    - o Pleasure/arousal
    - o Beauty
    - o Work/labour
    - o Health
    - o Privacy
    - o Money
    - o Status
    - o Safety
    - o Nature/environment
    - o Freedom/control
    - o Leisure time
    - o Social justice
- Opportunities
    - o Financial
    - o Temporal
    - o Spatial

- - o Cognitive
  - o Physical
- Abilities
- Motivation
- Behavioural control
- Intention
- Consumer behaviour
- Consequences

Brief Summary

Based on the Motivation-Opportunities-Abilities Model, the Needs-Opportunities-Abilities model aims to identify the factors that determine consumer behaviour. It proposes that consumption is determined by the needs, opportunities and abilities of a person or a household. The model recognises the importance of a wide range of internal and external factors and the interactions between them.

Description

The Needs-Opportunities-Abilities model provides an explanation of the factors underlying consumer behaviours (i.e. household consumption behaviour), and is based on the Motivation-Opportunities-Abilities model. A person's **motivation** to engage in consumer behaviour arises from **needs** and **opportunities**. That is, a person becomes motivated to purchase goods when those goods fulfil certain needs, and they have the opportunity to purchase them. However, motivation alone is insufficient to lead to consumer behaviour – a person must also have a certain level of **behavioural control**. The level of behavioural control that a person possesses is determined by their **opportunities** and **abilities** to engage in the consumer behaviour.

If a person has the necessary levels of both motivation and behavioural control, they will form a behavioural **intention**, which in turn determines **consumer behaviour**. Consumer behaviour then leads to **consequences**, both in relation to a person's quality of life and to environmental quality.

The societal context also influences behaviour through effects on needs, opportunity and ability. The societal context is made up of **five macro-level factors: technology, economy, demography, institutions** and **culture**.

Needs

Needs are defined as objectives that people strive to achieve in order to improve or maintain their wellbeing or quality of life. There are 15 such objectives, which represent the factors considered to be important in Western culture:

- **Social relations**: Having good relationships with family, friends and peers and the opportunity to improve these relationships and to establish new ones.

- **Development/education**: The opportunity to receive a good education and to develop general knowledge.

- **Comfort**: Everyday life being easy and comfortable.

- **Pleasure/arousal:** Everyday life providing experiences that are enjoyable and exciting.

- **Beauty:** Being able to experience and enjoy beautiful things inside and around the home.

- **Work/labour**: Having a good job that is enjoyable, and being able to perform that job well.

- **Health:** Having good health and adequate, accessible healthcare.

- **Privacy:** When people have the ability to be themselves, do things for themselves and have their own place.

- **Money:** Having sufficient money to buy and do things that are necessary and things that are enjoyable.

- **Status:** Receiving the appreciation of others due to personal skills, achievements or possessions.

- **Safety:** Having personal safety and protection from crime and accidents both at home and outside.

- **Nature/environment:** Being in an environment which provides clean air, water and soil, and healthy animals and plants.

- **Freedom/control:** When a person has the freedom to control the course of their life, to make their own decisions and to do the things they would like to do.

- **Leisure time:** Sufficient leisure time.

- **Social justice:** Living in an environment which provides equal opportunities and the right to own and do things.

Opportunities

Opportunities are defined as external conditions which facilitate consumer behaviour – for instance the objective availability and accessibility of goods or services, or accessibility to the financial means needed for purchasing goods.

Abilities

Abilities refer to either people or to households, and are defined as the internal capacities needed to purchase goods or services. Six categories of abilities are outlined: **financial** (i.e. income, credit, loans), **temporal** (availability of time in which to engage in consumer behaviour), **spatial** (referring both to the availability of space in which to store good and the distance between the home and shops and services), **cognitive** (having the cognitive ability to engage in consumer behaviour) and **physical** (having the necessary health, fitness to engage in consumer behaviour, and necessary licenses or permits to do so).

Macro-level Factors

Developments in technology, economy, demography, institutions and culture can influence changes in people's needs, opportunities and abilities, which in turn influence consumer behaviour. For example, mass production can lead to reductions in the cost of goods, which increases consumer ability and opportunity. Similarly, technological and economic developments can lead to increased availability of services and materials, which increases consumer opportunity.

A diagram of the Needs-Opportunities-Abilities Model can be found on p.146 of Gatersleben & Vlek (1998).

Contributing Theories:

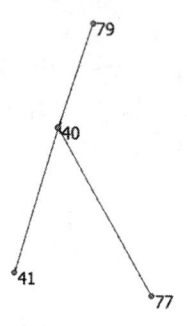

```
      79
       •
        \
         \
       •40
       /  \
      /    \
     /      \
    •        \
    41        •77
```

As outlined in the network diagram, the following theory included within this book was identified as contributing to the development of the Needs-Opportunities-Abilities Model:

40. Motivation-Opportunities-Abilities Model

Taken from:

Gatersleben, B & Vlek, C. (1998). Household Consumption, Quality of Life, and Environmental Impacts: A Psychological Perspective and Empirical Study. In K.J. Noorman & T.S. Uiterkamp. (Eds.). *Green Households?: Domestic Consumers, Environment and Sustainability* (pp. 141-183). London, UK: Earthscan Publications.

42. Norm Activation Theory (Schwartz)

Constructs

- Perception of need and responsibility
    - Awareness of need
    - Perception that need can be relieved by action
    - Recognition of own ability to provide relief
    - Arousal of some sense of responsibility to respond
        - Causal responsibility
        - Distinctive suitability
        - Accountability
        - Directed appeal
- Activation of norms
    - Personal norms
    - Social norms
    - Specific norms
- Assessment, evaluation and reassessment
    - Assessment and evaluation of responses
        - Costs and benefits
            - Social
            - Physical
            - Psychological
                - Moral
    - Reassessment and redefinition of the situation
        - Denial of the state of need
        - Denial of responsibility to respond
        - Denial of the suitability of norms
- Action or inaction response

Brief Summary

Norm Activation Theory aims to explain the decision-making process underlying altruistic behaviours. The central proposal of the theory is that when people perceive others to be in need, their responses are guided by the activation of personal norms which elicit a sense of responsibility to act in a certain way.

Description

Norm Activation Theory proposes that altruistic behaviours are influenced by the activation of personal norms in response to perceptions of others' need. Personal norms are those which relate to a person's self-concept. For instance, a person who thinks of themselves as a kind and responsible person would feel an obligation to comply with internalised norms that live up to that self-image, such as comforting others. These norms influence behaviour as a cognitive decision-making process. This process occurs in four major sequential stages. The first involves a person's **perception of need and responsibility**. The second involves the **activation of norms**. The third involves the **assessment, evaluation and reassessment**. The fourth and final stage is the **action or inaction response**. The cognitive processes in these stages may occur either consciously or unconsciously.

Perception of Need and Responsibility

The first stage includes four sub-stages. The first is **awareness of need**, where a person must become aware of the need of another individual, group or entity before norm activation can occur. 'Need' is defined as the possible or actual deprivation of a necessary or wanted resource. A greater intensity of need increases the likelihood that a person will respond to that need.

The second sub-stage of the decision-making process is the **perception that need can be relieved by action**. This involves a person recognising that action can be taken in response to the need. The type of possible actions that are considered in this stage determine the type of norms that are activated, with the norms that influence behaviour being action-specific.

The third sub-stage, '**recognition of own ability to provide relief**' involves a person recognising that they are capable of performing the actions (identified in the previous stage) necessary to provide relief. These perceptions of action-specific ability may be influenced by a person's overall sense of personal competence (i.e. perceived competence in other, irrelevant domains).

The fourth sub-stage involves the **arousal of some sense of responsibility to respond**. This arousal of responsibility may occur in response to various conditions. Arousal of responsibility occurs readily in some people who have passed through the first three stages, requiring only some evidence of need. Arousal of responsibility may occur due to **causal responsibility** (i.e. when a person is responsible for causing the other's need), **distinctive suitability** (i.e. a person feeling distinctively suitable for responding to the need due to unique skills, knowledge or availability), **accountability** (i.e. when a person is made accountable for the outcomes of the entity in need) or **directed appeal** (i.e. receiving a direct appeal from the individual or entity in need).

Activation of Norms

Passing through all of the first four sub-stages is prerequisite to progression to the second stage: the activation of norms. In relation to altruistic behaviour, it is **personal norms** that direct behaviour. Personal norms are defined as those which are related to a person's self-concept (i.e. the type of person they see themself as), and are influenced to some degree by **social norms** (i.e. what is deemed to be acceptable behaviour in a group or society). The activation of norms leads to a sense of obligation to respond to need. Norms may be either previously established or newly generated on the base of existing values and norms. In addition, **specific norms** are activated that relate to different possible courses of action. Thus, a person has a differing sense of obligation to act for different action possibilities which are generated by different specific personal norms.

Assessment, Evaluation and Reassessment of Potential Responses

The third stage of assessment, evaluation and reassessment includes two sub-stages. The first is the **assessment and evaluation of responses**, in which the outcomes of all possible response actions are assessed, including not acting and evaluates them in terms of their potential **costs and benefits**. Costs and benefits can be **social, physical, psychological** and **moral.** Perceptions of social costs and benefits are guided by social norms, and include anticipations of praise, blame, promotion and prosecution. Physical costs and benefits include effort expenditure, time loss, excitement and exhilaration. Psychological costs and benefits relate to the consequences of a course of action to a person's self-concept, such as loss of self-esteem or a sense of achievement. Moral costs and benefits are a specific type of psychological costs and benefits, and relate to a person's self-perception of how they respond to the welfare of others (e.g. perceptions of personal kindness and responsibility). Moral costs and benefits are the only type that are unique to personal norms, and are anticipated to arise from compliance or non-compliance with personal norms.

In the second sub-stage of this stage, people engage in a **reassessment and redefinition of the situation**. This occurs when the moral costs of not responding to need and the balance of the costs of response actions are both high. Here, a person experiences a sense of conflict wherein satisfaction of their sense of moral obligation (i.e. compliance with personal norms) is only achievable by experiencing substantial social, physical and psychological costs. People in this type of situation will often attempt to relieve this conflict by deactivating their personal norms through a process of redefinition, thus reducing the anticipated moral costs. There are three methods by which this can be achieved, each of which relates to the prerequisites of norm activation: **denial of the state of need** (this is made more difficult by the presence of factors which increase the saliency of needs), **denial of responsibility to respond** (again, factors that enhance the saliency of responsibility such as causal responsibility, distinctive suitability, accountability and direct appeals make the denial of responsibility more difficult) and **denial of the suitability of norms**. The latter may occur through the consideration of additional alternative actions, which could modify the outcome of a person's cost-benefit analysis. Anticipated outcomes of actions may also activate personal norms that conflict with a person's initial sense of obligation to respond to a need.

Following the 'reassessment and redefinition' sub-stage, the 'assessment and evaluation' sub-stage is re-entered, as an altered definition of the situation will have generated new possibilities for response options. At this point, an ideal response may now become apparent, or the balance of costs and benefits may still be inconclusive. If the latter is the case, people will go on to make further reassessments. The more delayed a response decision is, the greater the likelihood of inaction.

Action or Inaction Response

A person may decide to act directly after the activation of personal norms, following the 'assessment and evaluation' stage or following the 'reassessment and redefinition' stage. Inaction can occur either as a result of a decision not to act, or because a person is continuing to assess, evaluate and reassess options for action.

Contributing Theories:

None of the theories included within this book were identified as contributing to the development of Norm Activation Theory.

Taken from:

Schwartz, S. (1975). The Justice of Need and the Activation of Humanitarian Norms. *Journal of Social Issues*, 31(3), 111-136.

43. Operant Learning Theory (Skinner)

Constructs

- Responses
- Consequences
    - o   Positive reinforcers
    - o   Negative reinforcers
    - o   Positive punishment
    - o   Negative punishment
- Reinforcement
- Operant behaviour
- Operant conditioning
- Operant extinction
- Conditioned reinforcers
- Generalised reinforcers
- Differential reinforcement
- Intermittent reinforcement
    - o   Fixed-interval reinforcement
    - o   Variable-interval reinforcement
    - o   Fixed-ratio reinforcement
    - o   Variable-ratio reinforcement
    - o   Combined schedule reinforcement
- Operant discrimination

Brief Summary

Operant Conditioning Theory is a learning theory that describes the process by which the frequency of behaviours can be modified through schedules of reinforcement, involving reward or punishment. The theory also details how behaviour can be 'shaped' using these processes.

Description

Operant Conditioning Theory describes how the probability of a behaviour being carried out can be changed by the **consequences** of that behaviour. In the theory, single behaviours are termed '**responses**'. If **reinforcement** (i.e. a reinforcing consequence such as the provision of food) occurs every time a person carries out a certain response (e.g. pressing a button) the probability of a similar response occurring in the future will increase. This behaviour that has undergone reinforcement is termed **operant behaviour**, as it operates upon the environment to generate certain consequences. The process that results in a change in behavioural frequency is termed **operant conditioning**.

Reinforcers and Punishment

Consequences that are capable of reinforcing behaviour (i.e. increasing the frequency of behaviour) are termed 'reinforcers', for example by their ability to reduce a state of deprivation. **Positive reinforcers** refer to consequences in which something is added to the environment (e.g. food, water). **Negative reinforcers** refer to consequences in which something aversive is taken away from the environment (e.g. the removal of a bright light, a loud sound, or a painful stimulus). Consequences that function to suppress behaviour, or decrease its frequency, are termed 'punishment'. Punishment can be achieved in two ways: by the addition of a negative reinforcer (**positive punishment**) or by the removal of a positive reinforcer (**negative punishment**).

Operant Extinction

If reinforcement for an operant behaviour is stopped then the frequency of that behaviour will reduce. This process is referred to as '**operant extinction**'. The amount of time it takes for extinction to occur is positively related to the amount of time the behaviour had previously been reinforced for.

Conditioned and Generalised Reinforcers

Previously neutral stimuli can become reinforcing by being paired with a reinforcer. For example, if a sound is played every time a primary reinforcer is presented, the sound itself will ultimately become reinforcing (i.e. a **conditioned reinforcer**). Conditioned reinforcers may not always be introduced under controlled circumstances – they may be stimuli present in a person's normal context or generated by their normal behaviour. A conditioned reinforcer can also become a **generalised reinforcer** when it is paired with multiple primary reinforcers.

Differential Reinforcement

Differential reinforcement is when behaviour is reinforced only in certain situations. This process can be used to modify the intensity or form of behaviours. For instance, if throwing a ball is only reinforced when the ball lands with a certain accuracy, differential reinforcement can be used to increase the skill with which the ball is thrown. Similarly, if pulling a lever is only reinforced when the lever is extended fully, this differential reinforcement increases the intensity of the behaviour.

Intermittent Reinforcement

Day-to-day behaviour may not always be reinforced with every occurrence, but rather intermittently. There are various forms of **intermittent reinforcement**, each of which has unique effects on behaviour.

- **Fixed-interval reinforcement:** Behaviour is reinforced at regular intervals (e.g. every two minutes). The closer together the intervals are, the more frequently a person will respond. With continued fixed-interval reinforcement, people will stop responding immediately after a reinforcement, and begin again once an interval of time has elapsed.

- **Variable-interval reinforcement:** Behaviour is reinforced at a specific interval on average (e.g. the average interval overall is five minutes, but intervals vary between one and ten minutes). This will lead to a situation where behaviour is sometime reinforced immediately, and sometimes not until after some time has passed. This schedule of reinforcement results in very persistent repetitions of responses.

- **Fixed-ratio reinforcement:** Behaviour is reinforced after a certain number of responses (e.g. every fifteenth response is reinforced). This leads to a very high rate of responding as the rate of reinforcement increases with the rate of responding. However, very high ratios of reinforcement may result in rapid extinction once reinforcement ceases. In addition, the high rate of responding generated by fixed-ratio reinforcement may ultimately result in exhaustion and thus a declining rate of responding.

- **Variable-ratio reinforcement:** The ratio of reinforcement varies around a mean, similar to variable-interval reinforcement. As the probability of reinforcement at any time remains constant, this results in a more consistent rate of responding than fixed-ratio reinforcement.

- **Combined schedule reinforcement:** A combination of interval and ratio reinforcement (i.e. reinforcement is determined by a combination of the passage of time and by the number of responses that have occurred since the last reinforcement). This results in an unstable rate of responding.

Operant Discrimination

Operant discrimination refers to situations in which the reinforcement of a behaviour is contingent upon the presence of another environmental stimulus (e.g. a light being on). If behaviour is only reinforced in the presence of certain stimuli, that behaviour will ultimately only be carried out when the stimulus is present.

Contributing Theories:

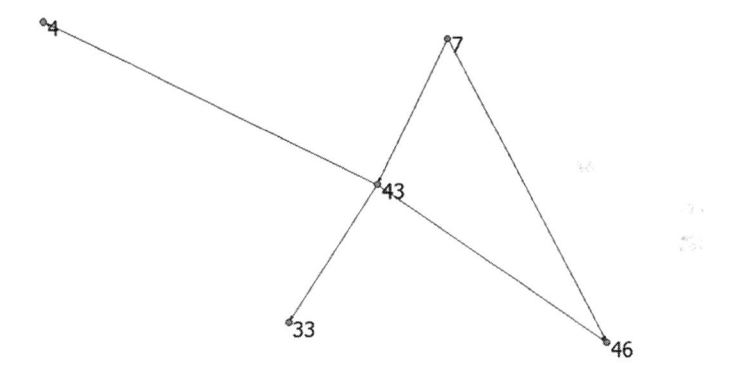

As outlined in the network diagram, the following theory included within this book was identified as contributing to the development of Operant Learning Theory:

7. Classical Conditioning

Taken from:

Skinner, B.F. (1938). The Behaviour of Organisms: An Experimental Analysis. New York: Appleton-Century-Crofts.

Skinner, B.F. (1953). *Science and Human Behaviour.* New York: The Free Press.

44. Precaution Adoption Process Model (Weinstein & Sandman)

Constructs

- Stage 1: Unaware
- Stage 2: Unengaged
- Stage 3: Undecided
- Stage 4: Decided not to act
- Stage 5: Decided to act
- Stage 6: Acting
- Stage 7: Maintenance

Brief Summary

The Precaution Adoption Process Model proposes that the decision-making and behaviour change process in relation to the adoption of health-protective behaviours occurs in seven distinct stages. The stages range from being unaware of the threat through to maintenance of the newly adopted behaviour. People at each stage vary in terms of their beliefs and knowledge.

Description

The Precaution Adoption Process Model is a stage theory of behaviour change. It is a theoretical model comprising the decision-making and behaviour-change stages involved in determining whether protective action is taken in response to a health threat. There are seven stages: **unaware, unengaged, undecided, decided not to act, decided to act, acting** and **maintenance**. People have different patterns of beliefs, knowledge and behaviours at each stage. The seven stages are:

- **Stage 1 (Unaware):** People in this stage are unaware of the health threat and have formed no opinion about it.

- **Stage 2 (Unengaged):** People in this stage are aware of the health threat and have begun to form an opinion about it. They are not however, personally engaged with the issue and have not begun considering whether to take action.

- **Stage 3 (Undecided):** People in this stage have become engaged by the issue but have not yet formed an opinion on how to act to avert the threat. It is important to distinguish between those who have never considered an action and those who have thought about an action but not yet made a decision to act. The two groups are likely to differ in levels of knowledge, and different methods of intervention would be require to promote consideration of an issue that would be needed to promote decision-making.

- **Stage 4 (Decided not to act):** The 'Precaution Adoption Process' stops when people make a decision not to act at this stage.

- **Stage 5 (Decided to act):** People in this stage have formed an intention to act but have not yet taken any action to avert the threat.

- **Stage 6 (Acting):** People in this stage have initiated protective action to avert the health threat.

- **Stage 7 (Maintenance):** People in this stage are successfully repeating the protective action over time.

Examples of the factors influencing movement across the stages include media messages about the threat and protective behaviours, which may stimulate progression from Stage 1 to Stage 2. Similarly, beliefs about personal susceptibility to a threat are likely to be important in transitioning from Stage 3 to Stage 4 or 5; and social influences might play a role in transitions across all stages.

The model serves as an assessment framework to determine which stage people are at, but makes no formal or definitive propositions about factors involved in stage-to-stage progression. Factors that influence transition through the stages differ across populations and behaviours. The population- and behaviour-specific factors should be identified and used to inform the design and/or tailoring of interventions.

A diagram of the Precaution Adoption Process Approach can be found on p.146 of Glanz, Rimer & Viswanath (2008).

Contributing Theories:

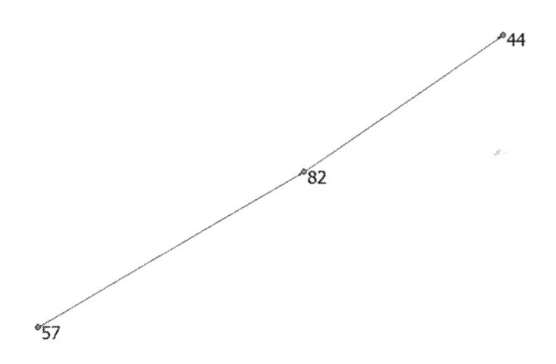

44
82
57

As outlined in the network diagram, the following theory included within this book was identified as contributing to the development of the Precaution Adoption Process Model:

82. Transtheoretical Model of Behaviour Change

Taken from:

Weinstein, N. D., & Sandman, P. M. (1992). A model of the precaution adoption process: Evidence from home radon testing. *Health Psychology, 11(3),* 170-80.

Supplemented by:

Weinstein, N.D., Sandman, P.M. & Blalock, S.J. (2008). The Precaution Adoption Process Model. In K. Glanz, B.K. Rimer & K. Viswanath (Eds.). *Health Behaviour and Health Education: Theory, Research and Practice* (4th Ed., pp. 123-148). San Francisco, USA: John Wiley & Sons, Inc.

45. Pressure System Model (Katz)

Constructs

- Motivation
    - o Beliefs about importance
    - o Beliefs about personal risk
    - o Beliefs about the efficacy of change
- Resistance
    - o Capability to change
    - o Locus of control
    - o Fixed impediments to change
- Stages of change
    - o Precontemplative
    - o Contemplative
    - o Preparative
    - o Behaviour change
    - o Maintenance
    - o Relapse
    - o Termination
- Clinical scenarios
    - o Precontemplative with no prior behaviour change attempts
    - o Contemplative or preparative with no prior behaviour change attempts
    - o Behaviour modification or maintenance of behaviour change
    - o Lapse
    - o Precontemplative or contemplative with prior behaviour change attempts
- Self-esteem
- Self-efficacy

Brief Summary

The Pressure System Model is a theory of behaviour change which proposes that behaviour change is determined by opposing forces of motivation and resistance. It aims to provide a guide for behaviour change counselling in primary care, and classifies five categories of people in the behaviour change process, with suggested counselling strategies for each.

Description

The Pressure System Model is based upon the Transtheoretical Model, incorporating some elements of other models of health behaviour. It aims to provide a guide for the provision of behavioural counselling in primary care, taking into account the restrictions unique to primary care.

Behaviour change can be understood as a function of the relative amounts of two diametrically opposed sources of pressure: **motivation** and **resistance** to change. Health-promoting or -protective behaviour change will occur if motivation exceeds resistance, but will not occur if resistance exceeds motivation. Motivation cannot be raised infinitely, so at high enough levels of resistance behaviour change will not occur regardless of motivation strength.

Motivation has three components: **beliefs about importance** (perceptions of how important the health condition to be avoided is), **beliefs about personal risk** (perceptions of one's personal risk of experiencing the health condition) and **beliefs about the efficacy of change** (perceptions of whether change will lead to the desired health outcome). If a person's beliefs in these three areas are pro behaviour change, behaviour change will be seen as desirable. Sources of resistance include both internal and external obstacles to change: **capability to change**, **locus of control** and fixed **impediments to change**. People with an external locus of control believe that they have little control over their behaviour, and so have little capability to change. Fixed impediments (e.g. the convenience of fast food, lack of time for exercise) can also present a barrier to change. In cases where resistance is so high that it cannot be overcome by increased motivation, identifying the most surmountable impediments and ways to overcome them is necessary to facilitate behaviour change.

Behaviour change occurs in seven stages. Each stage represents different categories of the balance between resistance and motivation. People are in the **precontemplative** stage when the difficulty of change is perceived to outweigh the benefits of change (resulting in an unwillingness to change), or when alternative behaviours are unfamiliar (resulting in a lack of awareness about the possibility of change). Progress to the **contemplative** stage (aware of the need for change, thinking about changing) and then the **preparative** stage (taking preparative action for change) occurs when new information and experiences raises motivation whilst resistance remains stable. **Behaviour change** occurs when motivation exceeds resistance, and **maintenance** of behaviour change occurs for as long as motivation outweighs resistance. If no temptation to return to the previous behaviour is felt, then people will reach the **termination** stage, which refers to successful behaviour change. However, in cases where resistance 'overtakes' motivation, **relapse** can occur. Repeated relapses may lead to regression to earlier stages in the model.

People can be classified as belonging to one of five discrete categories, or '**clinical scenarios**' using these stages (except termination, where no behaviour change strategy is needed). Different behavioural counselling strategies (i.e. focusing on either increasing motivation, decreasing resistance or both) are suggested for each of the categories.

A diagram illustrating the forces of motivation and resistance in the Pressure System Model can be found on p.69 of Katz (2001).

Contributing Theories:

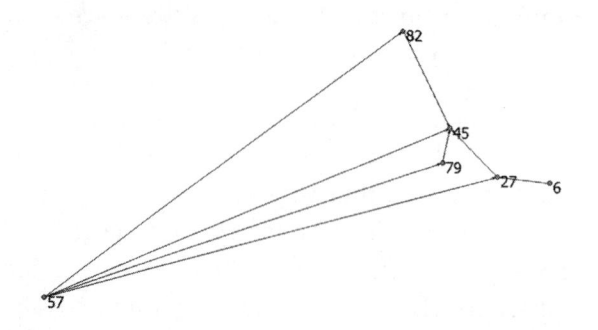

As outlined in the network diagram, the following theories included within this book were identified as contributing to the development of the Pressure System Model:

27. Health Belief Model

57. Self-Efficacy Theory

79. Theory of Planned Behaviour

82. Transtheoretical Model of Behaviour Change

Taken from:

Katz, D.L. (2001). Behaviour modification in primary care: The pressure system model. *Preventative Medicine, 32,* 66-72.

46. PRIME Theory (West)

Constructs

- Dispositions
  - States
  - Traits
- Internal environment
  - Mental representations
    - Images
    - Beliefs
  - Feelings
    - Sensations
      - Pleasure
      - Satisfaction
      - Pain
      - Discomfort
    - Emotions
      - Generalised
        - Happiness
        - Sadness
        - Anxiety
        - Depression
      - Targeted
        - Liking
        - Disliking
    - Drive states
  - Identity
    - Self-thoughts
      - Self-labels
      - Self-attributes
        - Self-efficacy
        - Self-esteem
      - Personal rules

- ☐ Self-images
- ☐ Self-feelings
  - o Arousal
  - o Mental energy/ego depletion
- External environment
  - o Stimuli
    - ☐ Information
    - ☐ Triggers
      - • Reminders
    - ☐ Rewards
    - ☐ Punishments
    - ☐ Models
  - o Context
    - ☐ Culture
    - ☐ Norms
    - ☐ Situations
- Motivational system
  - o Plans/intentions
    - ☐ Choice
  - o Evaluations
    - ☐ Values
  - o Motives/desires
    - ☐ Wants
    - ☐ Needs
  - o Impulses/inhibition
    - ☐ Urge
    - ☐ Habit
    - ☐ Instinct
  - o Responses
    - ☐ Reflexes
  - o Self-control
  - o Addiction

- Behaviour
    - o Behaviour pattern
- Change processes
    - o Chreods
    - o Critical periods
    - o Balancing input
    - o Reflective change processes
        - ☐ Analysis
        - ☐ Inference
    - o Automatic change processes
        - ☐ Perception
        - ☐ Memory
        - ☐ Habituation
        - ☐ Sensitisation
        - ☐ Associative learning
            - • Operant conditioning
            - • Classical conditioning
        - ☐ Imitation
        - ☐ Maturation
        - ☐ Dissonance reduction
        - ☐ Physical intervention
        - ☐ Chemical intervention

Brief Summary

The PRIME Theory of Motivation is a general theory of motivation, which provides a framework in which more specific theories of choice, self-control, habits, emotions and drives can be integrated. It proposes that there are five sub-systems making up the human motivational system. Going from most proximal to most distal in terms of moment-to-moment influence on behaviour these involve: response co-ordination, impulses/inhibition, motives (wants and needs), evaluations (beliefs about what is good or bad), and plans (self-conscious intentions). These interact with each other and are influenced by the immediate internal and external environment. The motivational system is changed by a range of processes including associative learning, imitation, habituation, and inference. Identity (mental representations of ourselves and feelings associated with these) is a particularly important source of motives and the source of self-control. The operation of the system is inherently unstable and requires constant 'balancing input' to avoid going down maladaptive 'chreods'.

Description

PRIME Theory is a general theory of motivation, this being defined as the brain processes that energise and direct behaviour. It fits within the broader COM-B model of behaviour in which capability, motivation and opportunity interact as a system to generate behaviour.

Levels of the Motivational System

According to PRIME Theory, the human **motivational system** consists of a chain of five interacting subsystems whose initials make the PRIME acronym.

At the highest level of adaptability, there is a subsystem that generates **plans** which are self-conscious intentions to do or not do something. At the other end of the chain is the subsystem that organises and executes **responses**. This involves starting, modifying or stopping actions. Responses arise from simple reflexes and from the output from a subsystem which generates a number of potentially competing or additive **impulses and inhibitions**. It is the strongest of these which control our responses.

Impulses and inhibitions are influenced by internal and external stimuli and also by the output of the subsystem that generates

motives (also known colloquially as 'desires'). These are feelings of want or need. Wants involve mental representations of something and associated feelings of anticipated pleasure or satisfaction with that thing; needs are feelings of anticipated relief from mental or physical discomfort arising from some actual or imagined event or situation. Wants and needs are influenced by internal and external stimuli, including reminders, physical sensations and drive states. Particularly important are generalised positive and negative emotional states such as happiness and sadness, which lead by association to targeted emotional states of liking and disliking.

They are also influenced by the output from the subsystem that generates **evaluations**. Evaluations are a type of belief. Beliefs are propositional mental representations (i.e. ones that can be expressed through language, as distinct from 'images' (not necessarily visual) that are experienced iconically). Evaluations involve in their meaning a degree of 'good' and 'bad'. Evaluations are generated by analysis and inference, as well as by wants and needs, and internal and external stimuli. They are also influenced by plans, which lie at the top of the chain of subsystems. Plans are formed when there is a desire to engage in an act but the time is not right at the moment. This may be because of competing desires or because the conditions when the act would be desirable do not yet exist.

Thus if someone remembers a plan to do something at a particular time, this generates a positive evaluation of this act which in turn creates a level of desire to do it which in turn may generate an impulse to do it. Whether or not the act is undertaken will depend on competing plans, evaluations, motives and impulses and inhibitions at the time.

Identity and Self-control

PRIME Theory acknowledges that identity (defined as beliefs and images about oneself and feelings about these) are an important source of potentially very strong wants and needs. It is the source of self-control, which is defined as acting in accordance with self-conscious plans in the face of competing desires, impulses and inhibitions arising from other sources.

Self-control is therefore dependent on remembering plans and them generating sufficiently strong wants and needs to win through to behaviour at the relevant moments. The strength of attachment to aspects of identity that underlie plans influences the strength of wants and needs arising from them. Moreover, plans that have clear boundaries which means that they are remembered and applicable to all relevant situations will have greater control over behaviour.

The Moment to Moment Control of Behaviour

PRIME Theory is firmly rooted in time and recognises that outputs of components of the motivational system exist only when they are generated. Thus, for example, evaluations only exist when we are prompted to form them, and the same is true for plans, motives and impulses and inhibitions. This places a greater emphasis on the immediate internal and external environment in controlling behaviour than theories which assume that their components (e.g. attitudes and self-efficacy) have trait-like qualities.

Consistency in behaviour lies in more or less stable dispositions for components of the motivational system to respond in particular ways to particular stimuli. When these dispositions are enduring, they are considered to be traits and when they themselves are generated current stimuli they are thought of as states.

A key proposition arising out of the moment-to-moment control of behaviour and the structure of the motivational system is what PRIME Theory refers to as the first law of motivation: 'At every moment we act in pursuit of what we most want or need at that moment'. Under this proposition control over behaviour largely involves shaping these momentary wants and needs.

Changing Dispositions and Chreods

PRIME Theory recognises that there are multiple ways in which dispositions for components of the system to respond to stimuli change over time and in response to events. The system as a whole is fundamentally unstable, and like a 'fly-by-wire' aircraft requires constant 'balancing input' to prevent it going down paths or 'chreods' that are maladaptive.

The processes of change are drawn from the broad psychology literature and all have been shown to be important. They include 'automatic' processes (not requiring self-conscious thought) such as perception (acquiring information from the senses), memory (storing information), habituation (becoming less responsive with repeated occurrences of a stimulus), sensitisation (becoming more responsive with repeated occurrences of a stimulus), associative learning (underpinning operant and classical conditioning), imitation (mirroring a stimulus), dissonance reduction (forming or changing beliefs to reduce emotional or motivational conflict), maturation (growing up and growing old), and physical and chemical interventions (e.g. brain injury and ingestion of drugs or toxins). Reflective processes are inference (induction and deduction) and analysis (calculation, comparison, judgement and estimation).

Addiction

PRIME Theory was developed in part to help understand and combat addition. It defines addiction as a chronic condition in which people experience repeated powerful motivation, learned through experience, to engage in a purposeful behaviour to a degree that carries significant risk of harm which undermines and overwhelms attempts at restraint. It is a disorder of the motivational system that involves an interaction between stimuli in the current environment and disorders in one or more of the processes underlying plans, evaluations, motives, impulses and inhibitions.

The structure of the human motivational system in PRIME theory.

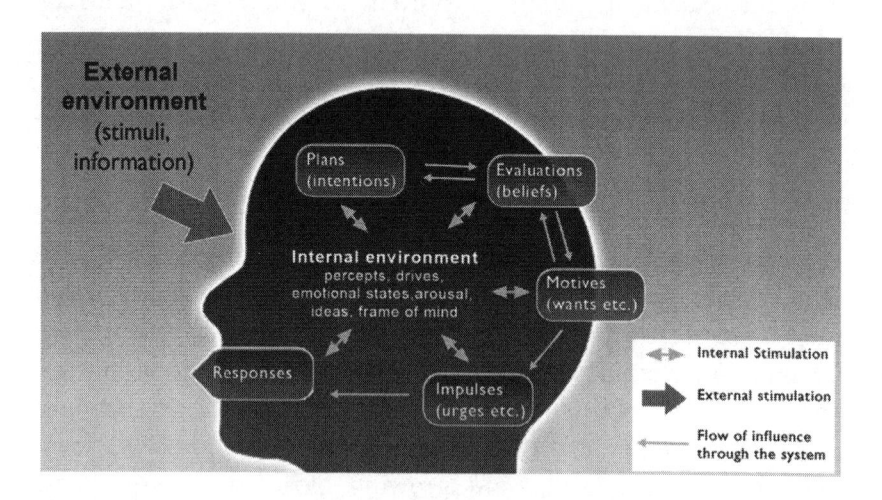

Source: www.primetheory.com. Reprinted with permission from Professor Robert West.

Contributing Theories:

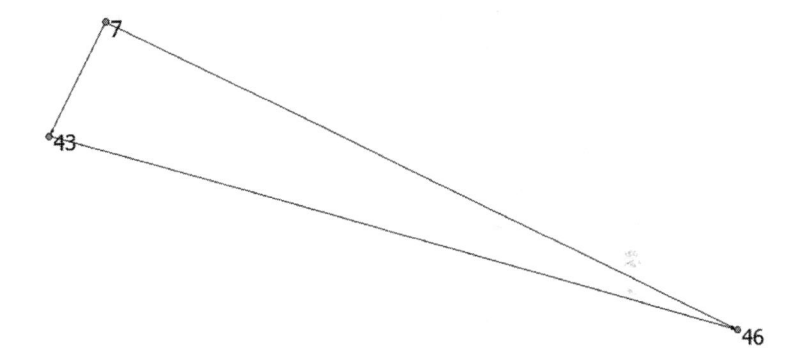

As outlined in the network diagram, the following theories included within this book were identified as contributing to the development of PRIME Theory:

7. Classical Conditioning

43. Operant Learning Theory

Taken from:

West, R. & Brown, J. (2013). *Theory of Addiction* (2nd ed.). Oxford, UK: Wiley-Blackwell.

47. Problem Behaviour Theory (Jessor)

Constructs

Original Theory

- Instigations
- Controls
- Psychosocial proneness
    - Behavioural proneness
    - Environmental proneness
    - Personality proneness
- Demography-Social Structure
    - Father's education
    - Father's occupation
    - Father's religious group
    - Mother's education
    - Mother's religious group
    - Hollingshead index
    - Family structure
- Socialisation
    - Parental ideology
        - Maternal traditional beliefs
        - Maternal religiosity
        - Maternal tolerance of deviance
        - Paternal traditional beliefs
        - Paternal religiosity
    - Home climate
        - Maternal controls-regulations
        - Maternal affectional interaction
    - Peer influence
        - Friends' interests
    - Media influence
        - Involvement with television
- Personality system
    - Motivational-instigation structure
        - Value on academic achievement
        - Value on independence
        - Value on affection
        - Independence-achievement value discrepancy

- Expectation for academic achievement
- Expectation for independence
- Expectation for affection
  - Personal belief structure
    - Social criticism
    - Alienation
    - Self-esteem
    - Locus of control
  - Personal control structure
    - Attitudinal tolerance of deviance
    - Religiosity
    - Positive-negative functions discrepancy
- Perceived environment system
  - Distal structure
    - Parental support
    - Parental controls
    - Friends support
    - Friends controls
    - Parent-friends compatibility
    - Parent-friends influence
  - Proximal structure
    - Parent approval of problem behaviour
    - Friends approval of problem behaviour
    - Friends modelling problem behaviour
- Behaviour system
  - Problem behaviour structure
  - Conventional behaviour structure

Reformulation of Theory

- Risk factors
- Protective factors
- Biology and genetics
- Social environment
- Perceived environment
- Personality
- Behaviour
- Adolescent risk behaviours/lifestyles
- Health/life-compromising outcomes

Brief Summary

Problem Behaviour Theory aims to identify the underlying factors explaining problem (i.e. deviant) behaviour during adolescence. The theory proposes that three 'systems' interact to determine a person's 'proneness' to problem behaviour: personality factors, behavioural factors and social-environmental factors. Each of these systems comprises variables that act as either instigations to or controls against problem behaviour.

Description

Problem Behaviour Theory explains the factors underlying problem behaviour during adolescence. According to the theory, 'problem behaviour' (e.g. illicit drug use, delinquency, behaviour that deviates from societal norms) is the product of three systems: the **behaviour system**, the **personality system** and **perceived environment system**. Each of these systems encompasses variables that are proposed to represent either **instigations** to problem behaviour or **controls** against problem behaviour. According to the theory, the relative balance of these instigation and control variables result in a dynamic state termed 'proneness' (i.e. the likelihood or risk of the occurrence of problem behaviour). More specifically, **behavioural proneness, environmental proneness** and **personality proneness** together contribute to a person's **psychosocial proneness** to problem behaviour.

Demographic variables and socialisation are distal influences on behaviour, termed the 'demography-social structure' and 'socialisation'. Their influences are largely mediated by the three main systems in the model, but the roles of individual variables within them are not outlined (therefore not listed here but in the construct list above).

Variables within the 'personality system' represent socio-cognitive risk factors that are related to social meanings and developmental experience. This system contains three components: (1) the **motivational-instigation structure**, (2) the **personal belief structure** and (3) the **personal control structure**.

The motivational-instigation structure relates to a person's motivational orientation, and is a function of the goals that a person is working towards and the outcomes they anticipate from achieving these goals. Variables within this structure include value on academic achievement, **value on independence, value on affection, independence-achievement value discrepancy, expectation for academic achievement, expectation for independence** and **expectation for affection**. Goals for academic achievement and independence are particularly influential, with low expectations for achieving valued goals being an instigation for problem behaviour.

The personal belief and personal control structures act as controls again problem behaviour, with the latter having a more proximal influence on behaviour and the former a more distal one. Variables in the personal belief structure include **social criticism** (i.e. rejection of societal norms and values), **alienation** (i.e. a sense of isolation and meaninglessness in everyday roles), **self-esteem** and **locus of control** (i.e. internal or external locus of control). Variables in the personal control structure include **attitudinal tolerance of deviance, religiosity** and **positive-negative functions discrepancy** (this relates to having lower levels of control when the positive aspects of problem behaviour are perceived as outweighing the negative).

Personality proneness is highest when a person places a low value on academic achievement, a high value on independence, has lower expectations of achieving academic and independence goals, has high levels of social criticism, has greater feelings of alienation, has low self-esteem, has an externalised locus of control, tolerates deviance, has lower levels of religiosity and has a greater positive-negative functions discrepancy.

Variables within the 'perceived environment system' relate to perceptions of external factors such as support, controls and the expectations of others. This system comprises two components: the **distal structure** and the **proximal structure**.

Variables in the distal structure relate to whether a person's social context is more oriented towards their family or towards their peers, and include **parental support, parental controls, friends support, friends controls, parent-friends compatibility** and **parent-friends influence**. A peer-oriented social context is a risk factor for problem behaviour as this reduces associations with conventional norms, reduces control over problem behaviours and increases exposure to models of problem behaviour. Variables in the proximal structure relate to the availability of models, supports and approval for problem behaviour, and include **parent approval of problem behaviour, friends approval of problem behaviour** and **friends modelling problem behaviour.**

Thus, greater environmental proneness is a function of lower levels of parental support and controls, lower levels of controls from friends, lower compatibility between parents and friends, a greater influence of friend than of parents, lower levels of parental disapproval of problem behaviour and greater levels of approval for and modelling of problem behaviour by friends.

The behaviour system comprises two components: the **problem behaviour structure** and the **conventional behaviour structure**. The former relates to behaviours such as illicit drug use, problematic alcohol consumption and general deviant behaviour, whilst the latter relates to behaviours such as academic performance. Higher behavioural proneness arises for higher levels of engagement in other problem behaviour and lower levels of engagement in conventional behaviours.

The Reformulation of Problem Behaviour Theory

Modifications to Problem Behaviour Theory include 'instigations' and 'controls' being reconceptualised as **risk factors** and **protective factors**, the restructuring of 'systems' into five categories of risk and protective factors, and the addition of two, expanded, outcome variable categories: **adolescent risk behaviours/lifestyles** (e.g. problem behaviour such as illicit drug use, health-related behaviour such as unhealthy eating and school-related behaviour such as truancy) and **health/life-compromising outcomes** (e.g. illness or disease, school failure, poor personal development and poor preparation for adulthood and employability). The latter is seen to be directly determined by the former.

The five categories of risk/protective factors are: **biology and genetics, social environment, perceived environment, personality** and **behaviour.** Each domain encompasses both risk and protective factors. Specific variables within each domain are included for illustrative purposes (e.g. family history of alcoholism as a risk factor in the biology/genetics domain; models for conventional behaviour as a protective factor in the perceived environment domain). However, the domains represent a framework for integrating risk and protective factors identified in the literature rather than identifying specific variables that increase or decrease risk. Each domain has both a direct effect upon adolescent risk behaviour as well as an indirect effect through interactive influences upon the other domains. Protective factors have an additional indirect effect upon behaviour by 'buffering' the influence of risk factors.

Diagrams representing the original formulation of Problem Behaviour Theory and the reformulation of the theory can be found on p.333 of Jessor (1987) and on p.602 of Jessor (1991), respectively.

Contributing Theories:

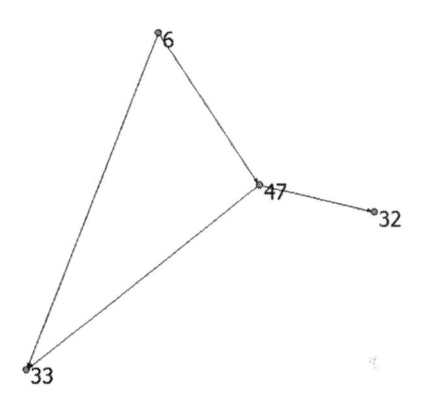

As outlined in the network diagram, the following theory included within this book was identified as contributing to the development of Problem Behaviour Theory:

6. Change Theory

Taken from:

Jessor, R. (1987). Problem-Behaviour Theory, Psychosocial Development and Adolescent Problem Drinking. *British Journal of Addiction*, 331-342.

Supplemented by:

Jessor, R. (1991). Risk Behaviour in Adolescence: A Psychosocial Framework for Understanding and Action. *Journal of Adolescent Health*, 12, 597-605.

48. Prospect Theory (Kahneman & Tversky)

Constructs

- Certainty effect
- Isolation effect
- Editing phase
    - Coding
        - Gains
        - Losses
        - Reference point
    - Combination
    - Segregation
    - Cancellation
    - Simplification
    - Detection of dominance
- Evaluation phase
    - Decision weight
    - Subjective value
- Probability
- Outcomes
- Prospects
- Edited prospects
- Choice

Brief Summary

Prospect theory is a theory of how people make decisions under uncertainty. It is a development from Subjective Expected Utility Theory and proposes that people weigh up the expected positive and negative outcomes of the options and compare them. It postulates: 1) a function relating subjective utility to objective value in which a given objective outcome has a differential impact depending on whether it is seen as avoiding a loss or making a gain, 2) a general tendency for priority to be given to loss aversion and for gains to be overweighted relative to their expected utility when they are certain rather than probabilistic; and 3) the utility of a gain to be a decelerating function of its value and the utility of a loss to be an accelerating function of its value.

Description

Prospect theory aims to describe how people make decisions under uncreatainty. People choose between probabilistic alternatives by evaluating potential losses and gains. Whilst the theory was developed to account for simple **prospects** (defined as a contract that yields **outcome** with **probability** (i.e. the probability of the outcome occurring)) with financial outcomes and objectively stated probabilities, the authors state that it can be applied to more complex decision-making processes.

The way information is framed influences how people evaluate the probability of the outcome occurring. There are two types of framing effects. The **certainty effect** occurs when positive gains are described, and refers to people's tendency to overweight outcomes considered to be certain compared to outcomes that are presented as probabilistic. The **isolation effect** occurs when people are presented with alternatives, and refers to people's tendency to ignore the shared characteristics of the alternatives and focus on the differences between them in order to simplify choices. This leads to inconsistent preferences.

The decision-making process occurs in two stages: the **editing phase**, which simplifies the subsequent **evaluation phase**.

Stage One: Editing

In the editing phase, a preliminary analysis of available prospects is conducted, often resulting in a simpler representation of these prospects. According to prospect theory, the purpose of this phase is to organise and reformulate options, so that subsequent evaluation and **choice** is simplified. The process of editing involves a number of operations:

- **Coding.** People tend to perceive outcomes as either **gains** or **losses**, as opposed to final states. Gains or losses are defined in comparison to a neutral **reference point**, which will usually be the same as a person's current assets. In these cases, gains or losses will be equal to actual outcomes. However, the reference point location may be influenced by a person's expectations and the formulation of available prospects, which would in turn influence perceived gains and losses.

- **Combination.** If available outcomes are identical, prospects can be simplified by combining the probabilities of these outcomes, and evaluating them in this combined form. For example, if two identical prospects of a .25 probability of winning £100 are presented, this will be evaluated as a prospect of a .50 probability of winning £100.

- **Segregation.** Prospect choices can contain a riskless component and a risky component, and during the editing process the riskless component is separated from the risky component. For instance, the prospect of either a .80 probability of winning £300 or a .20 probability of winning £200 is perceived as a guaranteed gain of £200 and a risky prospect of a .20 probability of gaining £100.

- **Cancellation.** When there is a choice between alternative prospects, people will disregard any shared components of the alternatives. An example of this would be when two games, each with two stages, are played sequentially. If the first stage of each game is identical, people tend to ignore it because it is common to both games and instead they focus on the second stage of the game which is different. Editing information in this way simplifies decisions but this may lead to non-rational behaviour. For example, players may ignore a bonus that would accrue from the first stage.

- **Simplification.** People are likely to simplify prospects by the rounding of probabilities and/or outcomes (e.g. a .49 probability of gaining £101 becomes a .50 probability of gaining £100). People may also simplify by disregarding extremely unlikely outcomes.

- **Detection of dominance.** People may scan their available prospects to assess whether any alternatives are dominated, and disregard those that are.

These editing processes are performed whenever possible, as they facilitate the evaluation of prospects. Some editing processes can prevent or allow the use of others, as components are discarded or prospects reduced. Thus, final edited prospects will vary depending upon the sequence in which editing operations are applied.

Stage Two: Evaluation

In the evaluation phase, edited prospects are evaluated and the prospect with the greatest value is chosen. The overall value of a prospect is a function of the **decision weight** (the impact of the probability on the total value of a prospect) assigned to it and the **subjective value** of the outcome.

Prospects may be strictly positive (all outcomes are positive), strictly negative (all outcomes are negative) or regular (neither strictly positive nor strictly negative. The basic equation of prospect theory describes exactly how the overall value of a regular prospect is determined (where **V** is the overall value, x and y are outcomes, p and q are the respective probabilities, π is the decision weight and v is the subjective value):

$$V(x, p; y, q) = \pi(p) v(x) + \pi(q) v(y)$$

In cases where prospects are strictly negative or strictly positive, prospect theory states that the overall value is determined differently:

$$V(x, p; y, q) = v(y) + \pi(p) [v(x) - v(y)]$$

The second equation states that the values of strictly positive or negative prospects are equal to the value of the riskless components plus the value-difference between outcomes, multiplied by the decision weight assigned to the most extreme outcome.

The Value Function

Values are determined by changes in wealth or welfare, as opposed to final outcomes. Value is seen as a function of the reference position (current assets) and the magnitude of change from that position offered by outcomes. Thus, the value function in the equations of prospects theory differs according to assets. However, mild and moderate variations in assets do not alter prospect preferences greatly.

The perceived magnitude of change influences the value function, leading to the proposition that the value function for changes above the reference point is usually concave, and usually convex for change below the reference point. For instance, the difference between a gain of £100 or £200 seems much larger than the difference between a gain of £1,100 or £1,200. As losses are more salient than gains, the value function below the reference point is steeper than that above.

The Weighting Function

Decision weights are a function of probability. However, they are not an exactly linear function as the simplification of prospects during the editing process leads to prospects with extreme probabilities being over-weighted or ignored. Prospects with very low probabilities may be either ignored or over-weighted, whilst the difference between high probabilities and absolute certainty may be ignored or exaggerated.

Diagrams representing the value function and the weighting function can be found on p. 279 and p.283 of Kahneman & Tversky (1979).

Contributing Theories:

None of the theories included within this book were identified as contributing to the development of Prospect Theory.

Taken from:

Kahneman, D & Tversky, A. (1979). Prospect theory. An analysis of decision under risk. *Econometrica*, 47(2), 263-292.

49. Protection Motivation Theory (Rogers)

Constructs

- Initiating sources
    - Environmental sources
        - Verbal persuasion
        - Observational learning
    - Intrapersonal sources
        - Personality factors
        - Prior experience
- Maladaptive response
    - Threat appraisal
        - Intrinsic rewards
        - Extrinsic rewards
        - Severity
        - Vulnerability
        - Fear arousal
- Adaptive response
    - Coping appraisal
        - Response efficacy
        - Self-efficacy
        - Response costs
- Protection motivation
- Action or inhibition of action

Brief Summary

Protection Motivation Theory provides a model of the cognitive processes that occur in reaction to messages designed to instil fear ("fear appeals") or health threats. Specifically, it proposes a theoretical account of the cognitive appraisal of maladaptive and adaptive responses to threat, and their influence on behaviour.

Description

Protection Motivation Theory provides a model of the cognitive processes that occur in reaction to health threats. It assumes that behaviour is a result of decision-making processes based on assessments of the expected consequences of a behaviour and the value of those consequences. The earliest version of the model describes the cognitive processes that lead to attitude change following messages designed to instil fear ("fear appeals"). Three variables are cognitively appraised: the severity of an event, the probability that the event will occur if no protective behaviour is carried out and the availability and effectiveness of coping or protective responses. These, and the resultant appraisals, combine multiplicatively to determine 'protection motivation'. Protection motivation stimulates, sustains and motivates action. The amount of protection motivation elicited determines the strength of intentions to act.

A later revision of the theory expands on this. Cognitive appraisal is initiated by sources of information, which can be **environmental sources** (**observational learning**, **verbal persuasion**) or **intrapersonal sources** (similar **prior experiences**, **personality factors**). These sources initiate two appraisal processes: **threat appraisal** and **coping appraisal**. During threat appraisal, factors that increase or decrease the likelihood of the **maladaptive response** (e.g. continuing to smoke) are appraised. Factors that facilitate the maladaptive response are **intrinsic rewards** (e.g. the bodily pleasure gained from smoking) and **extrinsic rewards** (e.g. social approval for smoking). The factors that decrease the probability of the maladaptive response occurring are the **severity** of the threat and perceptions of **vulnerability** (i.e. likelihood of being exposed) to the threat.

Factors that influence a person's ability to cope with a threat, and thus increase or decrease the likelihood of the **adaptive response** (e.g. stopping smoking), are appraised. Factors that facilitate coping responses are **response efficacy** (beliefs about how effective a coping response will be in averting the threat) and **self-efficacy** (a person's beliefs about whether they capable or incapable of performing the coping response). Factors that decrease the likelihood of the coping response occurring are the appraised costs of the coping response (e.g. inconvenience, expense, discomfort).

Protection motivation arises as a function of these two appraisal processes (i.e. high protection motivation will be elicited by high perceptions of severity, vulnerability, response efficacy and self-efficacy and low perceptions of intrinsic/extrinsic rewards and costs). If levels of perceived efficacy are low, protection motivation will not be elicited regardless of severity/vulnerability perceptions due to feelings of inability and helplessness, and the maladaptive response may be elicited. **Fear arousal** also plays a role in appraisals of threat, influencing appraisals of severity but not having a direct influence on protection motivation or action.

Action is determined by protection motivation, and may involve single, multiple and/or repeated acts. Decision-making about taking action may not be rational, as appraisals can be biased by heuristic judgments.

A diagram of Protection Motivation Theory can be found on p.168 of Rogers (1983).

Contributing Theories:

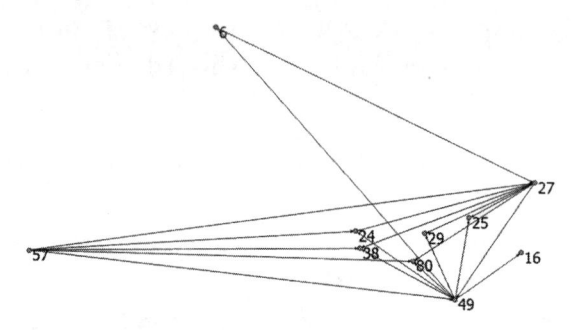

As outlined in the network diagram, the following theories included within this book were identified as contributing to the development of the Information-Motivation-Behavioural Skills Model of Adherence:

6. Change Theory

27. Health Belief Model

57. Self-Efficacy Theory

Taken from:

Rogers, R. W. (1975). A protection motivation theory of fear appeals and attitude change. *Journal of Psychology*, 91, 93-114.

Supplemented by:

Rogers, R.W. (1983) Cognitive and Physiological Processes in Fear Appeals and Attitude Change: A Revised Theory of Protection Motivation. In J. Cacioppo & R. Petty (Eds.), *Social Psychophysiology*. New York, USA: Guilford Press.

50. Prototype Willingness Model (Gerrard et al.)

Constructs

- Previous behaviour
- Reasoned path
    - Attitude
    - Subjective norm
    - Behavioural Intention
- Social reaction path
    - Risk prototypes
    - Perceptions of vulnerability
    - Behavioural Willingness
- Risk behaviour

Brief Summary

The Prototype Willingness Model provides a theoretical account of the decision-making processes involved in adolescent risk behaviour. It is a dual-process model, proposing a 'reasoned path' and a heuristically-based 'social reaction' path to risk behaviour. In the social reaction path, a risk behaviour does not result from intention but from behavioural willingness which in turn is influenced by social identity.

Description

The Prototype Willingness Model is a dual-process model of adolescent risk behaviour, which suggests there are two decision-making paths to behaviour: a **reasoned path** and a **social reaction path**.

In the reasoned path, **intentions** to carry out a behaviour are the primary determinant of **risk behaviour**. Intentions are determined by attitudes towards the behaviour and subjective norms (perceptions of what others are doing in relation to the behaviour), with more positive **attitudes** and **subjective norms** supportive of the behaviour leading to greater intentions.

In the social reaction path, risk behaviour is not a function of adolescents' intentions but rather of **behavioural willingness** (openness to engaging in the behaviour). Behavioural willingness is also proposed to play a role in the reasoned pathway by influencing intentions, and is a function of not only adolescents' attitudes and subjective norms but also additional antecedents: **risk prototypes** and **perceptions of vulnerability** to the relevant risk. Risk prototypes are 'images' or cognitive representations of the 'type' of person that engages in risk behaviours (e.g. the kind of person who is a smoker); the more favourable this image, the stronger behavioural willingness or intention is, and thus the likelihood of risk behaviour.

An adolescent's past behaviour has an influence on all the antecedents to intentions and willingness included in the model, with both the reasoned and the social reaction paths operating simultaneously. However, much greater use is made of the social reaction path until the end of adolescence whilst adults rely more on the reasoned path, a rational process of decision-making. Thus, health-risk behaviours of adolescents are more a consequence of a social environment that facilitates risk behaviour than being planned or intentional.

A diagram of the Prototype Willingness Model can be found on p.36 of Gerrard, Gibbons, Houlihan, Stock & Pomery (2008).

Contributing Theories:

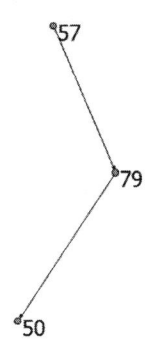

- 57
- 79
- 50

As outlined in the network diagram, the following theory included within this book was identified as contributing to the development of the Prototype Willingness Model:

79. Theory of Planned Behaviour

Taken from:

Gerrard, M., Gibbons, F.X., & Houlihan, A.E., Stock, M.L., & Pomery, E.A. (2008). A dual-process approach to health risk decision making: The prototype willingness model. *Developmental Review*, 28, 29-61.

51. Rational Addiction Model (Becker & Murphy)

Constructs

- Adjacent complementarity
- Unstable steady states
- Multiple steady states
- Rationality
- Utility
- Marginal utility
- Consumption (past and current)
- Bimodal distribution of consumption
- Time preference
    - o Present-oriented
    - o Future-oriented
- Price
- Stress
- Myopia
- Addiction (harmful and beneficial)
- Quitting
- Binging

Brief Summary

The Rational Addiction Model is an economic model of addiction based on the idea of stable rational preferences. It makes assumptions common to classical economics including the ideas that people behave rationally and possess all the relevant information to make a decision. Rationality is defined as 'a consistent plan to maximise utility over time' where utility is a measure of the benefits (or losses) as the person concerned sees them. Although addiction may seem to be irrational, the main premise of the model is that addictions are rational in that the person maximises utility consistently over time and a good is potentially addictive if increases in past consumption raise current consumption.

Description

In the Rational Addiction Model, **addiction** occurs when there is an increase **in current consumption** of a 'good' such as drugs or gambling as a result of **past consumption**. Addiction can be applied to a range of goods including drugs, watching TV, sex and food and the model can be applied to bingeing, and temporary or permanent abstention. Some addictions are harmful (heroin, alcohol) and some addictions can be beneficial (jogging, religion). The difference between harmful and beneficial addictions is the effect they have on a person's stock of capital or resources (beneficial addictions increase resources, harmful addictions decrease resources). Addicts are rational insofar as they look ahead and behave in a way that maximises their preferences and that remain stable over time. The theory is expressed as a range of equations and terms drawn from economic theory (i.e., stock, consumption, utility) to represent psychological variables (i.e., addictive goods, addiction, tolerance).

In economics, the **marginal utility** of a good or service is the gain from an increase or loss from a decrease in the consumption of that good or service. A person becomes addicted if, and only if, past consumption of the good raises the marginal utility of current consumption. This is referred to as '**adjacent complementarity**'. The addiction is stronger when adjacent complementarity (i.e. a rise in utility) in consumption increases.

Rationality

The Rational Addiction Model relies on a weak assumption of **rationality** which does not rule out strongly discounting future events; people do not take account of the future consequences of their actions and become more myopic as their preference for the present increases. It is then seen as 'rational' to ignore the future effects of a change in current consumption. Discounting future events is often regarded as irrational but it can be rational to be myopic in some circumstances; for example old people are 'rationally myopic' because they have fewer years of life remaining to them. Thus, the model predicts that if all things were equal, older people would be more likely to become addicted.

Unstable and Multiple Steady States

Unstable steady states explain rational 'pathological' addictions where a person's consumption of a good continues to increase over time, even when they fully anticipate the future. These unstable steady states lead to **multiple steady states**. There are two paths that highly addicted people can follow; abstention or a much greater level of consumption. People rarely continue to take small quantities of addictive goods. Thus, highly addictive goods are proposed to have a **bimodal distribution of consumption**, with one mode located near abstention and the other mode located near a high level of consumption.

Time Preference

Addictions involve an interaction between people and goods, in that a good may be addictive to some people but not others. 'Present-oriented' people are more likely to become addicted to harmful goods compared to 'future-oriented' people.

Harmful addiction is distinguished from **beneficial addiction** by whether consumption capital (the value of assets after depreciation) has negative or positive effects on utility and earnings. A future cost is added to the current market price of a harmful good whereas a future benefit is subtracted from the current market price of a beneficial good. Thus, an increase in the rate of preference for the present raises the demand for harmful goods and decreases the demand for beneficial goods. As a result, people such as drug addicts and smokers tend to be more **present-oriented**, whilst people such as joggers tend to be **future-oriented**.

The Effect of Price

A decline in current consumption is predicted when the price of a good increases. There is good evidence that an anticipated increase in the future price of an addictive good reduces the consumption of that good and the longer that future price change is anticipated, the bigger is the effect on current consumption. These negative effects of anticipated future price changes distinguish between rational addiction and rational habit formation

Stress and Start of Addiction

The consumption of harmful addictive goods may be triggered by **stress**-inducing events such as divorce, bereavement, and unemployment. If these events lower utility while raising the marginal utility of addictive goods then changes in life cycle events have the same effect on consumption as changes in price. Therefore, even people with the same utility function and the same wealth who face the same prices may have different degrees of addiction if they have different experiences. Temporary events can permanently 'hook' a rational person to an addictive good; for example, a person may become permanently addicted to heroin because of peer pressure as a teenager. A person can acquire sufficient consumption capital to remain hooked when the temporary stress subsides.

Quitting

A rational person will end an addiction if events lower demand for the addictive good or the stock of consumption capital decreases; they may decide to put an abrupt end to addiction by going 'cold turkey' because they are aware that there will be more gain in the long term despite short-term 'pain' or loss of utility; and may postpone terminating the addiction as they look for ways to reduce sizeable short-term utility loss from stopping abruptly. For example, to stop smoking, a person may try a smoking clinic, chewing gum, and exercising until they find a successful method to reduce the short-term utility loss from quitting. Therefore, behaving rationally can still lead to failure. In general a person will decide to stop being an addict when the long term benefits outweigh the costs in the short-term.

Bingeing

Bingeing, such as overeating, may seem to be a prototypical irrational behaviour but the model can account for this. The presence of two consumption capital stocks can be used to explain binge behaviour. For example, to get cycles of overeating, one capital stock called eating capital must be complementary with eating and have a higher depreciation rate, while the other stock called weight must be substitutable. If a person with low weight and eating capital became addicted to eating, as eating increases over time, eating capital would rise more rapidly than weight because it has a higher depreciation rate. Ultimately, eating would begin to fall because weight would continue to rise as the negative utility of a high body weight was greater than the utility from further eating. Lower food consumption then depreciates the stock of eating capital relative to weight, and the reduced level of eating capital keeps eating down even after weight has begun to fall. Eating picks up again only when weight has reached a sufficiently low level. The increase in eating then raises eating capital starting the whole cycle again. The cycles can either be damp or explosive (or constant) depending upon whether the steady state is stable or unstable. Binges do not reflect inconsistent behaviour that arises from struggles for control. Rather, they are seen as the outcomes of consistent maximisation over time that recognises the effects of current increased eating on both future weight and the desire to eat more in the future.

Contributing Theories:

None of the theories included within this book were identified as contributing to the development of the Rational Addiction Model.

Taken from:

Becker, G.S. & Murphy, K.M. (1988). A theory of rational addiction. *Journal of Political Economy*, 96(4), 675-700.

52. Reflective Impulsive Model (Strack & Deutsch)

Constructs
- Perception
- Elements
- Relations between elements
- Impulsive system
    - o Experiential state of awareness
    - o Spreading activation
    - o Elements
    - o Relations between elements
    - o Associative clusters
    - o Motivational orientation
        - ☐ Approach
        - ☐ Avoidance
- Reflective system
    - o Noetic state of awareness
    - o Relational schema
    - o Truth values
    - o Syllogistic rules
    - o Noetic decisions
    - o Propositional representations
    - o Propositional categorisations
    - o Behavioural decision
        - ☐ Goal
    - o Intending
- Arousal
- Behavioural schemata
- Behaviour

Brief Summary

The Reflective-Impulsive Model is a dual-process model that explains behaviour as a function of two different, interacting, cognitive processes: the reflective system and the impulsive system. The reflective system involves reasoning and decision-making whilst the impulsive system directs behaviour based on associations between stimuli and behavioural schemata.

Description

The Reflective-Impulsive Model describes two cognitive processes, the **reflective system** and the **impulsive system**, which interact and are concurrently active, competing for control of **behaviour**. The model also accounts for motivational influences and the processes that link judgements generated by the two processing systems to behaviour. It is presented in ten 'theses' that describe the different components within it, including how they interact to serve as determinants of behaviour.

Thesis 1: Basic Assumption

Social behaviour occurs as a result of the reflective system and/or the impulsive system. In the reflective system, behaviour is determined by a decision process, whereby knowledge about potential behavioural consequences is evaluated before a preference is formed for a single behavioural option. If a decision regarding a preferred behaviour is made through this process, relevant **behavioural schemata** are activated via a mechanism of **intending**. This mechanism terminates once the behaviour is performed or the decision-related **goal** has been satisfied.

In the impulsive system, perceptual input or reflective processes activate behavioural schemata through **spreading activation**. Behaviour can occur in the absence of conscious intentions of goals.

The activation of behavioural schemata in the impulsive system may be moderated by deprivation of basic needs (e.g. hunger) or motivational orientations.

Thesis 2: Parallel Operation

Both processing systems operate in parallel; however, the systems do not operate equally. Information is always processed by the impulsive system whereas the reflective system may not be engaged in processing at all times. The extent to which information influences behaviour is determined by prior stimulation of structures representing information in the impulsive system. The intensity of a stimulus, and the amount of attention directed toward it, determine whether it is also processed by the reflective system.

Thesis 3: Capacity

The reflective system has a high threshold for processing incoming information. Therefore, information processed via the reflective system demands high cognitive capacity and requires greater attention resource than that processed via the impulsive system. Very high or very low levels of arousal, as well as distraction will interfere with the operation of this system. Processing using the impulsive system requires little or no cognitive capacity, has a low threshold for processing incoming information, and is very fast. Thus, this system directs behaviour in less optimal conditions that require greater cognitive capacity and attention.

Arousal is an important factor in determining whether or not the reflective processing system will be used. The reflective system operates best at moderate levels of arousal, as high levels of arousal facilitate frequently occurring, dominant responses (i.e. what a person is normally inclined to do) and low levels of arousal weaken reflective processes and self-control.

Thesis 4: Relations between Elements

Different types of relations connect **elements** in the two systems. In the impulsive system, elements are connected by associative links, forming a network. Patterns of activation within this **associative store** represent knowledge. The associative links vary in strength, and the strength of each link is relatively stable and modifiable only through learning. Activation of an element spreads to other elements depending on the strength of the links. Links are created or strengthened when stimuli are presented close together (temporally or spatially), creating associations between environmental aspects and motor, cognitive or affective reactions. Associative links can also be formed as a result of reflective processing. **Propositional representations** in the reflective system activate corresponding elements in the impulsive system. In this way, associative links can be formed between elements that do not occur closely together in reality, if these **propositional categorisations** are frequently made in the reflective system. Links between elements result in **associative clusters** of elements that represent knowledge (e.g. seeing features of an elderly person (e.g. grey hair) may activate a cluster of elements such as 'bald', 'slow', 'elderly', etc. Associative clusters can be arranged hierarchically and represent either concrete or abstract concepts or schemata.

In contrast to the impulsive system, knowledge is generated in the reflective system by assigning perceptual input to a semantic category. Knowledge in this system is reflected by elements which are connected by **relational schema**, with each relation being assigned a **truth value**. Representations in the reflective system can be generated or changed flexibly, and are formed by retrieving elements and relations from the impulsive system. In the reflective system, semantic knowledge is generated by assigning a truth value to these elements and the **relations between elements**. Following formation of these representations, **syllogistic rules** (defined as rules that dictate the transfer of truth from a premise to a conclusion) are applied to draw inferences that go beyond the available information (e.g. if a person is perceived as elderly then categorical knowledge is used to make the inference that they are wise).

A **noetic state of awareness**, defined as the knowledge something is or is not the case, exists alongside reflective processes. An **experiential state of awareness**, defined as a particular feeling (e.g. a feeling of knowing) may also be present. **Noetic decisions** are made in the reflective system, drawing upon syllogistic rules and evaluations of utility based upon judgements or memories of utility from past experience. Decisions may also be subject to influences from the impulsive system in cases where an experiential state of awareness is present. If feelings are propositionally categorised and contextually qualified then they may enter the reflective system and either facilitate or inhibit reflective processes.

Thesis 5: Execution of Behaviour

Behaviour is determined by a common pathway activated by input from the reflective and impulsive systems. This 'pathway' consists of behavioural schemata, which can be more or less abstract. Behavioural schemata are defined as associative clusters which are representations of co-occurring motor representations and their related conditions and consequences. Multiple schemata can be activated at one time, but an activation threshold must be reached before a behaviour is carried out. For instance, sensory perception of food might lead the impulsive system to activate an eating schema whilst the reflective system activates the decision not to eat. If schemata in different systems are activated concurrently, the chosen behaviour will be determined by conditions relating to a person's cognitive capacity and attention (e.g. if little attentional capacity is available, behaviour will be driven by the impulsive system).

Thesis 6: Precursors of Behaviour

Each system directs behaviour in different way. In the impulsive system, behaviour is directed through the activation of elements associated with behavioural schemata, with **perception** of a relevant stimulus being linked directly to behaviour. In the reflective system, behaviour is directed by decision-making processes. **Behavioural decisions** are based on a feasibility assessment of a behaviour and the desirability of its possible outcomes. The reflective system is influenced by impulsive processes as the accessibility of elements in the impulsive system may prompt reflective processing. A decision may not automatically lead to behaviour, but may result in a spread of activation to multiple elements or behavioural schemata in the impulsive system. This can occur either because conflicting behavioural schemata have been activated, or because the decision is to be executed at a later point in time.

Thesis 7: Intending

A gap (e.g. temporally) can occur between a decision and its consequent action. This may be because other conditions need to be met prior to action (e.g. the activation of behavioural schemata). If a gap occurs, constant activation of the reflective system would be needed to guarantee reflectively-directed action and this would require large amounts of cognitive effort. The gap is referred to as 'intending' and is described as a process which automatically reactivates a behavioural decision and ends when the decision-directed action has been completed or the decision-related goal has been satisfied. Intending is also hypothesised to be relevant when barriers to the goal of a decision are encountered. Barriers are overcome by the reflective system generating new means-end relationships and a new process of intending (i.e. a new behavioural decision is reactivated to achieve the decision-directed action).

Thesis 8: Motivational Orientation

Information processing in the impulsive system is influenced by a person's **motivational orientation**, which may be either **approach** or **avoidance** reactions. In 'approach', a person is prepared to decrease the distance between themselves and an aspect of the environment (through physical movement, consumption, imagination or instrumental action). In 'avoidance', a person is motivated to increase this distance or remove the particular aspect of the environment. Motivational orientation is itself determined by information processing, perceived approach or avoidance, affectual experiences or engagement in approach or avoidance behaviours.

Thesis 9: Compatibility

Information processing, affect and behaviour are influenced by compatible motivational orientations. An approach orientation prompts processing of positive information, the experiencing of positive affect and the enacting of approach behaviour. In contrast, an avoidance orientation prompts processing of negative information, the experiencing of negative affect and the enacting of avoidance behaviour.

Thesis 10: Homeostatic Dysregulation

In situations where basic needs are deprived, behavioural schemata that have previously and frequently resulted in needs satisfaction will be activated. Needs-related objects (i.e. objects related to the satisfaction of needs) will be experienced more positively under deprivation, whilst needs-irrelevant objects will be devalued.

The influence of needs deprivation can thus direct motivational orientation and evaluative associations.

A diagram of the Reflective-Impulsive Model can be found on p.239 of Strack & Deutsch (2004).

Contributing Theories:

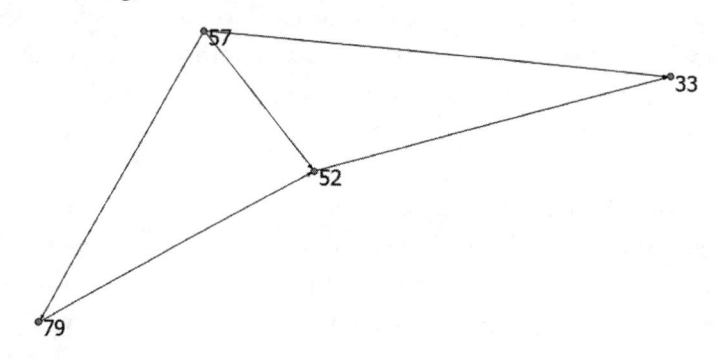

As outlined in the network diagram, the following theories included within this book were identified as contributing to the development of the Reflective Impulsive Model:

57. Self-Efficacy Theory

79. Theory of Planned Behaviour

Taken from:

Strack, F. & Deutsch, R. (2004). Reflective and Impulsive Determinants of Social Behaviour. *Personality and Social Psychology Review*, 8(3), 220-247.

53. Regulatory Fit Theory (Higgins)

Constructs
- Goal pursuit
- Motivational orientation
    o Promotion focus
    o Prevention focus
- Goal means
    o Eagerness
    o Vigilance
- Regulatory fit
- Value
    o Value from fit
- Prospective evaluations
- Retrospective evaluations
- Motivation
- Strength of engagement

Brief Summary

Regulatory Fit Theory states that if a person's motivational orientation (i.e. the attitudes or beliefs that are directing goal pursuit) is congruent with the methods they are using to achieve the goal, they will be more motivated in their efforts towards goal achievement and assign more value to goal pursuit than if they are incongruent.

Description

According to Regulatory Fit Theory, **goal pursuit** begins with a particular **motivational orientation** (i.e. the specific concerns and interests of a person that have motivated them to pursue the goal). The methods that a person uses to achieve a goal are termed '**goal means**'. During the process of goal pursuit, people anticipate and/

or experience desirable or undesirable outcomes of goal means (e.g. as a result of goal achievement or failure). People assign **value** to goal means based on the extent to which they are believed to contribute to goal attainment.

If a person's motivational orientation is congruent with their goal means, they will experience '**regulatory fit**'. This regulatory fit increases their **strength of engagement** in goal pursuit means by making them 'feel right' about their goal means. Regulatory fit functions by increasing the value of goal means (termed **value from fit**) above and beyond the value generated by their contribution to goal attainment.

Five hypotheses arise from this central proposal. First, people will have a preference for goal means that give higher regulatory fit. Secondly, people's **motivation** during goal pursuit will be higher when regulatory fit is higher. Thirdly, when regulatory fit is higher people's **prospective evaluations** of choices will be more positive (for desirable choices) or more negative (for undesirable choices) than if regulatory fit was lower. Fourthly, when regulatory fit is higher people's **retrospective evaluations** of their choices will be more positive. Fifthly and finally, people will assign higher value to entities or goal pursuits that were chosen with high regulatory fit.

Motivational Orientations and Goal Means

There are two distinct types of motivational orientation: **promotion focus** and **prevention focus**. A 'promotion focus' orientation is defined as a motivational orientation which is concerned with the presence or absence of positive outcomes, whilst a 'prevention focus' orientation is defined as a motivational orientation which is concerned with the presence or absence of negative outcomes. There are also two related types of goal-pursuit means: **eagerness means** and **vigilance means**. Eagerness means are those which ensure 'hits' (i.e. looking for means of advancement) and minimise the chances of errors of omission (i.e. not closing off possibilities), and have good regulatory fit with a promotion focus orientation. Vigilance means are those which ensure the correct rejection of options (i.e. carefulness) and ensure against errors of commission (i.e. avoidance of mistakes), and have good regulatory fit with a prevention focus orientation. Whilst these two types of motivational orientation and goal means are central to the theory the theory can be applied to any type of motivational orientation which has an ideal means of goals pursuit that promotes regulatory fit.

Contributing Theories:

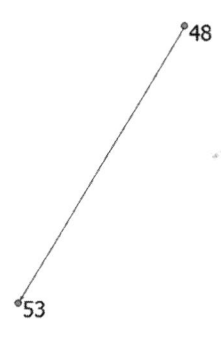

As outlined in the network diagram, the following theories included within this book were identified as contributing to the development of the Regulatory Fit Theory:

48. Prospect Theory

Taken from:

Higgins, T.E. (2000). Making a Good Decision: Value from Fit. *American Psychologist*, 55(11), 1217-1230.

Supplemented by:

Higgins, T.E. (2005). Value from Regulatory Fit. *Current Directions in Psychological Science*, 14(4), 209-213.

54. Relapse Prevention Model (Marlatt & Gordon)

Constructs

- Perceived control
- High risk situations
    - Negative emotional states
    - Interpersonal conflict
    - Social pressure
- Coping response
- Self-efficacy
- Positive expectancies
- Lapse
- Abstinence violation effect
    - Commitment
    - Duration of abstinence
    - Cognitive dissonance
    - Personal attribution
- Covert Antecedents
    - Unexpected high risk situations
    - Planned relapse
- Probability of relapse

Brief Summary

The Relapse Prevention Model provides a theoretical account of factors that increase or decrease the risk of relapse during a period of abstinence from an addictive substance or behaviour, focusing on factors determining how people will react to high-risk situations for relapse. It proposes explanations for the 'abstinence violation effect' in which lapses commonly lead to full relapse.

Description

The Relapse Prevention Model focuses on the maintenance of abstinence from excessive or addictive behaviours. It proposes different classifications of factors that contribute to the probability of relapse (failure to modify behaviour), and aims to provide a framework for relapse prevention.

People maintaining abstinence experience a sense of **perceived control** over their addictive behaviour, which becomes greater the longer that abstinence is maintained. Perceived control is maintained until a person is faced with a **high risk situation** which threatens perceptions of control and may trigger a lapse and increase the risk of relapse. There are three categories of high-risk situations; **negative emotional states** (e.g., anger, anxiety, depression), **interpersonal conflict** (on-going or recent conflict in an interpersonal relationship such as marriage or friendship) and **social pressure** (verbal persuasion or being with others who are performing the behaviour).

Factors that lower the **probability of relapse** in a high-risk situation include using effective **coping responses** (e.g. assertiveness in coping with social pressure) and perceptions of **self-efficacy** (i.e. a person's beliefs about their ability to cope). These factors are closely related, with the perceived control that is linked to periods of abstinence bolstering coping self-efficacy and thus reducing the risk of relapse. However, if a person is unable to cope with a high risk situation their sense of self-efficacy is weakened. The risk of relapse is further increased by **positive expectancies** about the effects of engaging in the addictive behaviour (e.g. stress reduction from having an alcoholic drink). If an inability to cope coincides with positive expectancies, the risk of an initial **lapse** is high.

Whether a lapse will develop into a full relapse is determined by the **abstinence violation effect** which is an 'all-or-nothing' perspective whereby a lapse is seen as having violated abstinence, with no route back. This effect occurs when a person is committed to an extended or indefinite period of abstinence. Higher **commitment** leads to greater intensity of the abstinence violation effect, as does a longer duration of abstinence. The **abstinence violation effect** is characterised by **cognitive dissonance** (feelings of conflict and guilt) and **personal attribution** (i.e. a person blaming themselves as the cause of the relapse).

There may also be **covert antecedents** to relapse. Whilst the focus of the model is on people who unexpectedly encounter high risk situations, some people may covertly **plan relapse** by making choices that lead them to a high-risk situation.

A diagram of the relapse process in the Relapse Prevention Model can be found on p.38 of Marlatt, G.A. & Gordon, J.R. (1985). *Relapse Prevention: Maintenance Strategies in the Treatment of Addictive Behaviours.* New York: Guilford.

Contributing Theories:

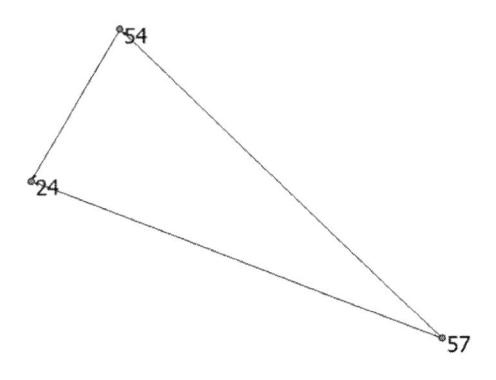

As outlined in the network diagram, the following theory included within this book was identified as contributing to the development of the Relapse Prevention Model:

57. Self-Efficacy Theory

Taken from:

Marlatt, G. A., & Gordon, W. H. (1984). Relapse prevention: Introduction and overview of the model. *British Journal of Addiction*, 79, 261-273

55. Risk as Feelings Theory (Lowenstein et al.)

Constructs

- Anticipated outcomes
- Subjective probabilities
- Other factors
- Cognitive evaluation
- Feelings
- Behaviour
- Outcomes

Brief Summary

Risk as Feelings Theory aims to explain decision-making and behaviour in risky situations, proposing that responses in risky situations are determined by the interaction between emotional reactions to a risk and cognitive evaluations of potential responses to that risk.

Description

Risk as Feelings Theory aims to provide an explanation of human decision-making under conditions of risk, and the influence of such decision-making processes upon **behaviour** and emotional outcomes. The term 'behaviour' refers to both decisions and emotion-driven responses to risk, such as panic reactions or avoidance due to phobias. Behaviour, in turn, lead to decision-making **outcomes** (including emotional outcomes).

There are two direct influences on a person's behaviour in response to risky situations: the person's emotions or **feelings** related to the risk (e.g. fear, anxiety, worry) and their **cognitive evaluation** of alternative choices. Feelings and cognitive evaluations relating to the risky situation are interrelated (i.e. cognitive evaluations influence feelings and feelings influence cognitive evaluations). Cognitive evaluations and feelings are based upon the subjective probabilities of the risky response alternatives under consideration and the desirability of the anticipated outcomes of each alternative (including anticipated emotional outcomes). However, cognitive evaluations of a risk can differ from feelings, as feelings are also determined by other factors that are not considered in a person's cognitive evaluations. These 'other factors' might include the immediacy of the risk, the salience of the risk and a person's underlying mood state at the time of decision-making.

Risk as Feelings Theory

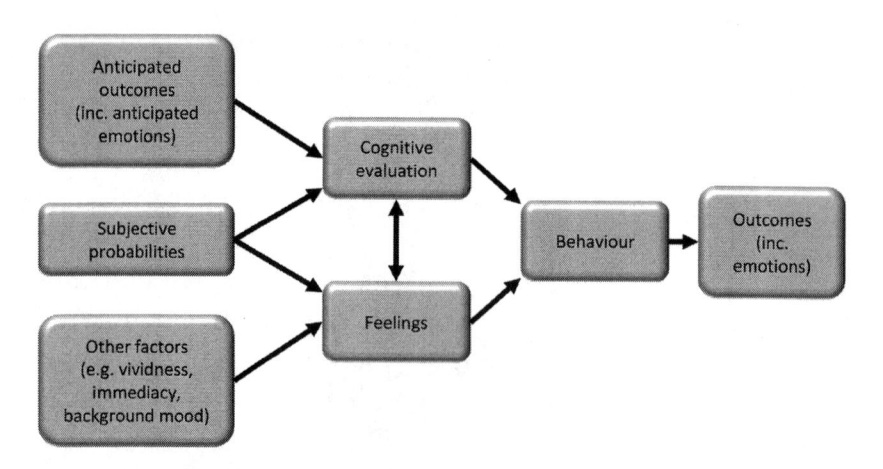

Source: Lowenstein, G.F., Weber, E.U., Hsee, C.K. & Welch, N. (2001). Risk as Feelings. *Psychological Bulletin*, 127(2), 267-286. Originally published by APA and reprinted here with permission.

Contributing Theories:

None of the theories included within this book were identified as contributing to the development of the Risk as Feelings Theory.

Taken from:

Lowenstein, G.F., Weber, E.U., Hsee, C.K. & Welch, N. (2001). Risk as Feelings. *Psychological Bulletin*, 127(2), 267-286.

56. Self-Determination Theory (Deci & Ryan)

Constructs

- Motivation
    - Intrinsic
    - Extrinsic
    - Amotivation
- Cognitive Evaluation Theory
    - Perceived locus of causality
    - Perceived competence
    - External events
        - Informational aspect
        - Controlling aspect
        - Amotivating aspect
    - Intrapersonal events
- Organismic Integration Theory
    - External regulation
    - Internalisation
        - Introjection
        - Identification
        - Integration
- Causality Orientations Theory
    - Causality orientations
        - Autonomy
        - Control
        - Impersonal
- Basic Psychological Needs Theory
    - Basic needs
        - Competence
        - Autonomy
        - Relatedness
- Goal Contents Theory
    - Goals
        - Intrinsic goals
        - Extrinsic goals

Brief Summary

Self-determination Theory is a meta-theory (comprising five mini-theories) which aims to provide a broad framework to study motivation, personality and behaviour. Central to the theory's explanation of behaviour is the distinction between intrinsic motivation (i.e. motivation due to inherent interest or enjoyment) and extrinsic motivation (i.e. motivation due to external factors or controls), and people's basic need for autonomy, competence and relatedness.

Description

Self-determination Theory is a meta-theory which aims to provide a broad framework within which human motivation, personality and behaviour can be studied. The theory comprises five mini-theories, each of which aims to explain a different aspect of motivation or personality: **Cognitive Evaluation Theory, Organismic Integration Theory** and **Causality Orientations Theory, Basic Psychological Needs Theory** and **Goal Contents Theory**. These theories are described in detail following the broader description of the theory below.

The theory states that humans are inherently active, self-motivated, curious and eager to succeed. These tendencies do not naturally develop; as people can also be alienated and mechanised, or passive and disaffected. These differences among people are primarily attributed to their fulfilment of three psychological needs for **autonomy, competence** and **relatedness** as well as to the distinction between **intrinsic motivation** and **extrinsic motivation**.

All humans have three basic needs: **competence** (i.e. the need to feel competent), **autonomy** (i.e. the need to feel volition and choice) and **relatedness** (i.e. the need to feel related to others). Social contexts that satisfy these needs promote **intrinsic motivation** to engage in behaviour (i.e. motivation due to inherent interest or enjoyment) as well as support people's developmental, psychological and behavioural well-being and health. Conversely, social contexts that undermine the satisfaction of these needs have a negative effect upon well-being and lead to other forms of motivation that may be less desirable (e.g. **extrinsic motivation**).

The type of motivation that drives a person's behaviour is more important than the amount of motivation a person possesses. Based on the amount of autonomy felt when regulating a behaviour, people's motivation can be categorised as **amotivation**, extrinsic motivation or internal motivation. Amotivation is unregulated by extrinsic or intrinsic factors and refers to a lack of intention to engage in a behaviour. Extrinsic motivation refers to motivation that is regulated by external factors or controls (i.e. low autonomy). Finally, intrinsic motivation is motivated by autonomous factors within a person (e.g. interests, values, curiosities). The more autonomous a person's motivation is, the more likely he/she is to initiate and maintain the behaviour.

Extrinsic motivation is further differentiated into four sub-types: external regulation, introjected regulation, identified regulation and integrated regulation. These sub-types lie along a continuum of internalisation in which the more internalised motivation is, the more autonomous a person is when engaging in the behaviour. External regulation motivates behaviour by controlling personally unrelated consequences (e.g. to get a reward or to avoid punishment). Introjected regulation motivates behaviour by regulating internal representations of external consequences (e.g. guilt, approval). Identified regulation occurs once a person accepts the regulation of the behaviour as his/her own. In this type of regulation, motivation occurs because the outcome of the behaviour is important to the person (e.g., engaging in physical activity because it is important to the person). Finally, integrated regulation refers to behaviour that is motivated because the behaviour is consistent with the person's sense of self (e.g. 'I run because I am a runner').

Cognitive Evaluation Theory

Cognitive Evaluation Theory describes how the external environment, in the form of the social context and interpersonal interaction, can influence intrinsic motivation and stresses the importance of autonomy and competence for intrinsic motivation. It is composed of four propositions:

1. External events that promote a more external **perceived locus of causality** for a behaviour (i.e. those that control behaviour) will undermine intrinsic motivation for that behaviour, whilst external events that promote a more internal locus of causality (i.e. those that support autonomy) will bolster intrinsic motivation. The perceived locus of causality can be seen as representative of the extent to which a person feels they are determining their own behaviour.

2. External events that increase **perceived competence** (e.g. success, positive feedback) will bolster intrinsic motivation whilst external events that decrease perceived competence (e.g. failure) will undermine intrinsic motivation. Increases in perceived self-competence will only lead to increases in intrinsic motivation if the perceived locus of causality for the behaviour is internal. Decreases in perceived competence can occur in cases of controlled behaviour, but only if a person attributes the cause of failure to themselves.

3. External events that are relevant to a behaviour can have three aspects: an **informational aspect** (events that convey

competence without being experienced as controlling), a **controlling aspect** and an **amotivating aspect** (feedback that reduces people's sense of competence leaving them with little intrinsic or extrinsic motivation). The relative salience of each of these aspects determines how external events influence intrinsic motivation. The informational aspect of an event enhances intrinsic motivation by promoting an internal perceived locus of causality and increased perceived competence. The controlling aspect undermines intrinsic motivation by promoting an external perceived locus of causality. The amotivating aspect also undermines intrinsic motivation by reducing perceived competence.

4. Intrapersonal events may also be informational, controlling or amotivating, having similar effects on intrinsic motivation as when they occur in external events.

Organismic Integration Theory

Organismic Integration Theory is concerned with extrinsic motivation, and specifically with explaining variations in felt autonomy in relation to externally motivated behaviours. Whilst extrinsic motivators may undermine intrinsic motivation (as they can be seen as controlling), extrinsically motivated people can still feel autonomous. This autonomy arises when the **external regulation** (i.e. control/extrinsic motivation) of behaviour is internalised by a person. There are three types of **internalisation**, which exist on a spectrum: **introjection**, **identification** and **integration**.

Introjection is when a person internalises an external control or regulation but does not accept it as their own, and hence still feels pressured and controlled by it. Introjection leads to implicit threats of guilt, shame and self-derogation after failure and of pride and self-aggrandisation after success. Identification is when people accept the justification for a behaviour and accept responsibility for regulating the behaviour. In cases of identification people will engage in a behaviour without feelings of pressure and control, and with feelings of autonomy. Integration is when an identification has been integrated with other aspects of a person's 'true self', so that extrinsically motivated behaviour becomes fully self-determined and autonomous.

Causality Orientations Theory

Causality Orientations Theory aims to describe individual differences in how people's behavioural regulation is influenced by the environment. People are oriented towards interpreting environmental events as informational, controlling or amotivating. A person's behaviour, cognitions and affect are influenced by their orientation, termed the causality orientation. There are three distinct types of causality orientations: autonomy, control and impersonal. People are oriented to each these orientations to varying extents. In turn, the relative strength of these orientations influences their behaviour.

People with an autonomy orientation will orient to what interests them. They tend to initiate or regulate behaviour in response to intrapersonal events or external events that are perceived to be informational (internal perceived locus of causality). In contrast, people with a control orientation will orient to social controls and rewards. They tend to initiate or regulate behaviour in response to introjected regulation or external events that are perceived to be controlling (external perceived locus of causality). Finally, people with an impersonal orientation will focus on their lack of personal control or competence. They perceive themselves to be incompetent and function erratically and non-intentionally. Impersonally oriented people believe that behaviour and outcomes are unrelated, feel incapable of mastering external forces and are unable to manage the internal forces of drives and emotions.

Basic Psychological Needs Theory

Basic Psychological Needs Theory is concerned with the connection between basic needs and wellness. All humans have the **basic needs** for **competence** (i.e. the need to feel competent), **autonomy** (i.e. the need to feel autonomous) and **relatedness** (i.e. the need to feel related to others. Social contexts can either satisfy or undermine these needs. Social contexts that help to satisfy basic needs promote better motivation, support people's inherent activeness and promote better developmental, psychological and behavioural well-being and health. Conversely, social contexts that undermine needs satisfaction have a negative effect upon well-being and lead to worse forms of motivation (e.g. external motivation).

Goal Contents Theory

Goal Contents Theory is concerned with people's **goals** or desired outcomes. There are two types of goals: **extrinsic goals** and **intrinsic goals**. Extrinsic goals are defined as goals which are related to external indicators of worth (e.g. enhancing wealth, projecting an attractive image of oneself). Intrinsic goals are defined as goals that are related to the satisfaction of basic needs (e.g. building or enhancing relationships, personal growth). People with more extrinsic goals are more controlled in their efforts towards goal achievement and have lower levels of well-being. People with more intrinsic goals are more autonomous in their goal pursuit efforts and have higher levels of well-being.

Types of Motivation and Regulation in Self-Determination Theory

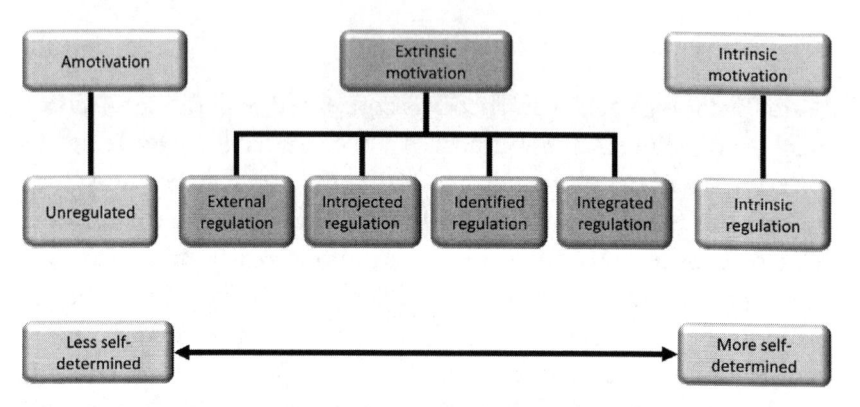

```
Amotivation        Extrinsic motivation                                    Intrinsic motivation

Unregulated   External      Introjected    Identified    Integrated        Intrinsic
              regulation    regulation     regulation    regulation        regulation

Less self-determined  <------------------------------------>  More self-determined
```

Source: Deci, E.L. & Ryan, R.M. (2008). Facilitating optimal motivation and psychological well-being aross life's domains. *Canadian Psychology*, 49(1), 14-23. Originally published by APA and reprinted here with permission. APA is not responsible for the accuracy of this translation.

Contributing Theories:

None of the theories included within this book were identified as contributing to the development of Self-Determination Theory.

Taken from:

Deci, E.L. & Ryan, R.M. (1985). *Intrinsic motivation and self-determination in human behaviour.* New York: Plenum Publishing Co.

Supplemented by:

Deci, E.L. & Ryan, R.M. (2008). Facilitating optimal motivation and psychological well-being across life's domains. *Canadian Psychology*, 49(1), 14-23.

Ryan, R.M. (2009). Self-determination Theory and Wellbeing. *Wellbeing in Developing Countries*, 1, 1-2.

57. Self-Efficacy Theory (Bandura)

Constructs

- Self-efficacy
    - o Magnitude
    - o Generality
    - o Strength
- Outcome expectancies
- Capability
- Incentives
- Sources of expectation of personal efficacy
    - o Performance accomplishments
    - o Vicarious experience
    - o Verbal persuasion
    - o Emotion arousal
- Cognitive appraisal of efficacy information

Brief Summary

Self-efficacy theory proposes that a central psychological mechanism underpinning behaviour change is people's beliefs that they are capable of that change. Perceptions of self-efficacy are based on four sources of information: personal experience of success, vicarious experience of success, verbal persuasion about capability and emotional arousal.

Description

Self-efficacy is central to explaining the mechanisms underlying behavioural change and is critical to analysing changes in fearful and avoidant behaviour. Perceived self-efficacy (also referred to as efficacy expectations) is defined as a person's belief that they are capable of carrying out a specific behaviour that will lead to desired outcomes, and is distinct from **outcome expectancies** (beliefs about whether a certain behaviour will lead to desired outcomes).

The theory was originally developed to explain changes in coping (fearful and avoidant) behaviours. Expectations of self-efficacy influence both the initiation and maintenance of behaviour. They determine whether a person will attempt to engage in behaviour (i.e. they are more likely to make an attempt if their self-efficacy is higher), their choice of behavioural setting (i.e. they are likely to avoid settings which they feel are beyond their coping abilities) and the amount of effort and persistence they will invest in the face of aversive experiences. Engaging in activities which are subjectively threatening, but objectively safe, will result in experiences that bolster self-efficacy and correct inaccurate perceptions of threat (in turn reducing avoidance of threatening circumstances).Behaviour is also seen to be dependent upon the presence of the necessary **capabilities** and **incentives** to perform the behaviour.

Dimensions of Efficacy Expectations

Self-efficacy expectations can vary across three dimensions: magnitude, generality and strength.

- **Magnitude.** Some people's self-efficacy expectations are limited to their beliefs about their ability to perform simple tasks, whereas others' extend to moderately difficult or the most difficult tasks.

- **Generality.** Self-efficacy expectations vary in the extent to which they are applicable only to behaviours in specific domains in which they have been experienced, or generalise to other behaviours.

- **Strength.** Weak self-efficacy expectations can easily be extinguished by experiences of failure. Conversely, people with strong self-efficacy expectations will continue to attempt to perform a behaviour even after a number of unsuccessful attempts.

Sources of Efficacy Expectations

Expectations of self-efficacy are formed on the basis of four sources of information: performance accomplishments, vicarious experience, verbal persuasion and emotional arousal.

- **Performance accomplishments.** Performance accomplishments are based on personal experiences of mastery, that is, prior experiences of successful performance of the behaviour. Successful attempts strengthen self-efficacy expectations whilst unsuccessful attempts weaken them, particularly if failure occurs early in the initiation of attempts. If strong self-efficacy expectations are developed through repeated successes, the detrimental influence of occasional failures is likely to be lessened. Once strong self-efficacy expectations have been developed, expectations are likely to generalise to other situations where low self-efficacy expectations have previously been a barrier to initiating behaviour.

- **Vicarious experience.** Self-efficacy expectations may also be based upon vicarious experiences of mastery, that is, observation of others successfully performing the behaviour in question, or engaging in threatening activities without the expected adverse consequences occurring. Vicarious experiences can generate the belief that with greater effort, they too will improve in performance. As the influence of vicarious experience upon self-efficacy expectations relies upon inferences about ability based on social comparison, it is a less dependable source of self-efficacy and therefore weaker and less stable than those derived from performance accomplishments.

- **Verbal persuasion.** People may, through suggestion, be persuaded into the belief that they are capable of successfully coping with circumstances with which they have failed to cope in the past. As this source does not include any direct experience of success, self-efficacy expectations developed through verbal persuasion are likely to be weaker than those derived from performance accomplishments. In addition, self-efficacy expectations generated through verbal persuasion can easily be extinguished through unsuccessful coping attempts, particularly in people who have experience failure many times before.

- **Emotional arousal.** Situations which are stressful or demanding commonly elicit emotional arousal which, in certain circumstances, may provide a person with information about their ability to cope. Physiological arousal is one source of information which people rely on to judge their state of anxiety and their vulnerability and stress. Because high arousal usually undermines successful performance of behaviours, people are more likely to have high self-efficacy expectations when they are not experiencing such arousal.

Cognitive Processing of Efficacy Information

The impact of information on self-efficacy depends on how it is **cognitively appraised**. Appraisal is influenced by social, situational and temporal factors. For example, success is more likely to increase self-efficacy if it is cognitively appraised as being due to skill than if it is thought to be a matter of chance. Success with minimal effort may reinforce a strong sense of self-efficacy but success that has been hard-won may imply low ability and so not alter one's sense of self-efficacy.

Sources of Self-Efficacy and Suggested Modes of Induction

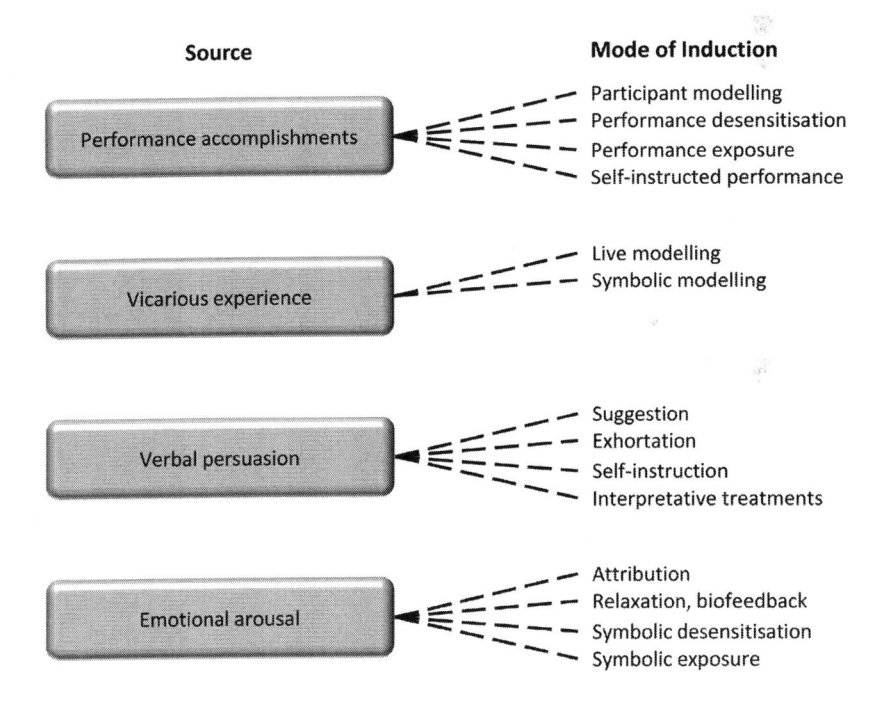

Source	Mode of Induction
Performance accomplishments	Participant modelling Performance desensitisation Performance exposure Self-instructed performance
Vicarious experience	Live modelling Symbolic modelling
Verbal persuasion	Suggestion Exhortation Self-instruction Interpretative treatments
Emotional arousal	Attribution Relaxation, biofeedback Symbolic desensitisation Symbolic exposure

Source: Bandura, A. (1977). Self-efficacy: Toward a Unifying Theory of Behavioural Change. *Psychological Review*, 84, 191-215. Originally published by APA and reprinted here with permission.

Contributing Theories:

None of the theories included within this book were identified as contributing to the development of Self-Determination Theory.

Taken from:

Bandura, A. (1977). Self-efficacy: Toward a Unifying Theory of Behavioural Change. *Psychological Review*, 84, 191-215.

58. Self-Regulation Theory (Kanfer & Gaelick)

Constructs
- Sources of control
    o Immediate environment
    o Biological system
    o Cues
- Automatic processing
- Controlled processing
- Self-regulation/self-regulatory processes
- Stages of the self-regulation process
    o Self-monitoring
    o Self-evaluation
        ☐ Standards
    o Self-reinforcement
- Attributional processes
    o Perceptions of control
    o Evaluation in respect to goals
    o Internal attribution
    o External attribution

Brief Summary

Self-Regulation Theory outlines the cognitive processes by which people regulate or control their own behaviour. The theory proposes that self-regulation depends upon people monitoring their own behaviour and comparing it to a desired or acceptable standard, with the outcome of this comparison determining the behavioural outcome of these self-regulatory processes.

Description

Self-Regulation Theory proposes that behaviour is determined by three **sources of control**: a person's **immediate environment**, their **biological system** and **cues** (arising from the person's cognitions and goals). These three factors interact to determine behaviour, with the relative importance of each changing at different times and in different contexts (e.g. eating behaviour might be primarily controlled by the biological system at one point, but at another, environmental factors such as the sight or smell of food might become important). According to the theory, adequate self-regulation can reduce the influence of fluctuations in biological and environmental factors upon behaviour, allowing for a more consistent pursuit of personally set goals over time and across contexts.

The theory is based upon the assumption that everyday behaviour consists of chains of behavioural responses, where each response is cued by the preceding response until an activity (e.g. driving to work) is completed. Such behavioural sequences relate to a mode of cognitive processing termed **automatic processing**. **Self-regulation** processes apply to other cases – such as where learned behaviour chains are not available, are interrupted or become ineffective, or where choices between alternative responses need to be made. These self-regulation processes involve a qualitatively different mode of cognitive processing: **controlled processing**. Controlled processing requires continuous decision-making between response alternatives and attentional focus.

The self-regulation process first involves a **self-monitoring** stage, in which a person closely and deliberately monitors their own behaviour. Through past experience, people will develop expectations about acceptable behaviour within the relevant domain (e.g. a person self-monitoring their alcohol consumption will have expectations about acceptable levels of alcohol consumption). These expectations form **standards** by which a person can judge their own behaviour. In a second stage, which is termed the **self-evaluation** stage, a person makes comparisons between the information about their own behaviour gathered during the self-monitoring stage and their standards for that behaviour. If self-monitoring has been insufficient or inaccurate, or if standards are unrealistic or poorly defined, effective self-regulation will be undermined at this stage. The third stage of **self-reinforcement** involves a person's reactions to the information gained during the self-evaluation stage, specifically their cognitive and emotional reactions of satisfaction or dissatisfaction.

The third stage serves a motivational purpose. If a person notices no discrepancy between the standard and their own behaviour (or if their behaviour exceeds the standard), they will not be motivated to change their behaviour. However, if their behaviour falls short of the standard, the resultant dissatisfaction will result in attempts to change behaviour. During these attempts the self-regulation process is repeated until the standard is met or until efforts to change behaviour are abandoned. In cases where behaviour falls short of the standard and discrepancies are very large or are reacted to with self-punishment, the resultant emotions could lead to motivation to avoid rather than motivation to change behaviour.

Later versions of the theory also incorporate **attributional processes** into the model, which influence progression through the stages. Firstly, for self-regulatory processes to occur at all, a person must view the behaviour as being under their control (**perceptions of control**). In addition, people evaluate their behaviour in respect to the short- and long-term goals (**evaluation in respect to goals**), and self-regulatory processes are unlikely to occur in cases where the behaviour is deemed to be trivial or irrelevant. Finally, during the self-reinforcement stage, discrepancies may either be attributed to an aspect of the person (i.e. **internal attribution**) or to an external cause (i.e. **external attribution**). Internal attributions can create stronger motivation for behaviour change, but might also undermine efforts to change if they relate to negative and unmodifiable personal characteristics.

A diagram representing Self-Regulation Theory can be found on p.290 of Kanfer & Gaelick (1991).

Contributing Theories:

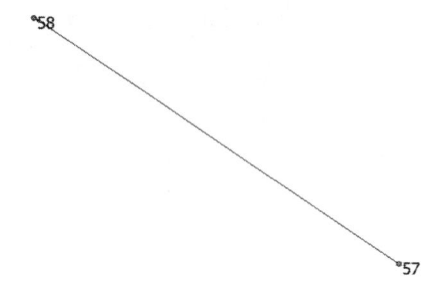

As outlined in the network diagram, the following theory included within this book was identified as contributing to the development of Self-Regulation Theory:

57. Self-Efficacy Theory

Taken from:

Kanfer, F.H. & Gaelick, L. (1991). Self-management methods. In F.H. Kanfer & A.P. Goldstein (Eds.). *Helping people change: A textbook of methods* (pp. 305-360). New York: Pergamon Press.

59. Six Staged Model of Communication Effects (Vaughan & Everett)

Constructs

- Pre-contemplation
    - Comprehension
        - Message is recognised and understood
    - Identification
        - Message is perceived as relevant
- Contemplation
    - Persuasion
    - Pros and cons of behaviour change
    - Self-efficacy
    - Parasocial interaction
- Preparation
    - Intention
- Intention
- Validation
- Action
    - Availability and accessibility of necessary services
- Maintenance
    - Social support
- Role-modelling

Brief Summary

The Six Staged Model of Communication Effects is a synthesis of four existing theories (the hierarchy of effects model, the stages of change model, social learning theory and diffusion of innovations theory). The model hypothesises that mass media messages influence behaviour through identification with media characters who serve as role models, and through interpersonal communication.

Description

The Six Staged Model of Communication Effects describes the internal cognitive processes that a person goes through in response to mass media communications, as well as responses in the external environment such as communication with others. The model proposes that people go through six steps in the process of behaviour change: **pre-contemplation, contemplation, preparation, validation, action** and **maintenance**.

- **Pre-contemplation:** People at this stage do not know about the behaviour, or regard it as irrelevant to them. Exposure to communications about the behaviour at this stage may be processed cognitively or affectively. Cognitive processing may result in **comprehension** of the message and subsequently the **message being recognised and understood**. Affective processing involves **identification with homophilious** (i.e. similar to oneself) **characters** in a mass media campaign, such that the **message is perceived as relevant**.

- **Contemplation:** People proceed to this stage if they recognise and understand a message, and perceive it as relevant to themselves. They consider the **pros and cons of behaviour change**, as they may be aware of the relevance and benefits but also believe misinformation about side-effects and have low self-efficacy (i.e. perceptions of their ability) in relation to adopting the behaviour. Thus, **persuasion** of the benefits of the behaviour (e.g. messages that emphasise the trustworthiness family planning) and **self-efficacy** enhancing messages (e.g. modelling successful adoption of the behaviour) are needed for progression. In addition, '**parasocial interaction**' often occurs at this stage; this may take the form of identification with a media message through strong identification with a media character, or it may involve a person seeking advice from their peers about the potential behaviour change.

- **Preparation:** People at this stage have formed an **intention** to pursue the behaviour change. They believe in the benefits of the change and have high self-efficacy relating to the behaviour change. Some people might adopt the new behaviour at this stage while for others communication and agreement with another person (e.g. partner) may be necessary. Media messages may be influential here by providing models of interpersonal communication.

- **Validation:** In this stage, people have discussed the behaviour with the relevant other at least once but have not sought professional advice on the matter or adopted the behaviour. Interpersonal communication is seen as central to this stage, and as communication levels increase, people's perceptions of the relevant other's opinions on the matter become more accurate.

- **Action:** In this stage, a person takes action by seeking professional help for the provision of information and the necessary for carrying out the behaviour change. For instance, in the context of family planning this would involve contacting a family planning service. The **availability and accessibility of necessary services** is a key factor at this stage. Communication messages may play a role in this stage by provide models of communication with relevant professionals.

- **Maintenance:** This stage involves the maintenance of a consistent change in behaviour and the recognition of the benefits of doing so. **Social support** in maintaining the change may also be an important influence at this stage. Again, media messages may play a role in this stage by providing models of people who are satisfied with their adoption of the behaviour.

From the 'contemplation' stage onwards the influence of **role-modelling** provided by characters in the media is an important factor in facilitating progression though the stages.

A diagram of the Six-Staged Model of Communication Effects can be found on p.208 of Vaughan & Everett (2000).

Contributing Theories:

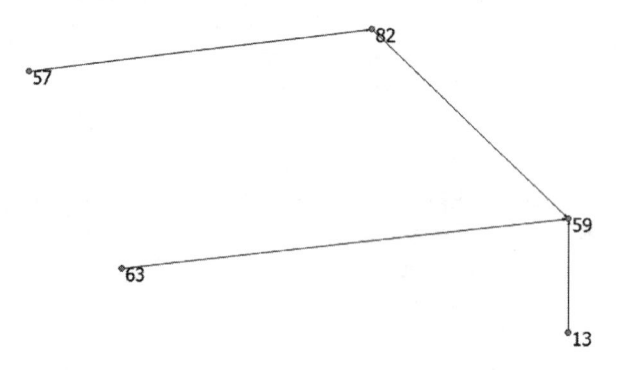

As outlined in the network diagram, the following theories included within this book were identified as contributing to the development of the Six-Staged Model of Communication Effects:

13. Diffusion of Innovations

63. Social Cognitive Theory

82. Transtheoretical Model of Behaviour Change

Taken from:

Vaughan, P.W., & Everett, E.M. (2000). A Staged Model of Communication Effects: Evidence from an Entertainment-Education Radio Soap Opera in Tanzania. *Journal of Health Communication,* 5(3), 203-227.

60. Social Action Theory (Ewart)

Constructs

- Action state dimension
    - Health habits
        - Action-outcome feedback loop
        - Action scripts
    - Change mechanisms
        - Goals
        - Expectations
        - Strategies
        - Capabilities
    - Action contexts
        - Physical
        - Social
        - Biological
        - Mood/arousal
    - Social interdependence
        - Social closeness
            - Interlinked scripts
            - Shared goals
- Process dimension
    - Problem solving
    - Motivational processes
        - Outcome expectancies
        - Self-efficacy
        - Goal structures
            - Personal projects
            - Self-directive goals
            - Self-standards

- o   Generative capabilities
    - ☐ Declarative knowledge schemas
    - ☐ Procedural schemas
        - • Cognitive control schemas
- o   Social interaction processes
    - ☐ Conjoint competence

- Contextual dimension
- o   Settings
    - ☐ Physical
    - ☐ Social
    - ☐ Tasks
- o   Relationship systems
- o   Organisational systems
- o   Temperament
- o   Biological conditions

Brief Summary

Social Action Theory aims to provide a framework for guiding efforts to promote behaviour change at the population level. The theory emphasises the influence of social and environmental factors upon behaviour, and also outlines cognitive processes that are proposed to be instrumental in behaviour change.

Description

Social Action Theory provides a framework which can be used to identify methods of promoting self-regulation to facilitate health behaviour change. The theory aims to guide health promotion efforts at the population, rather than individual, level. It comprises an **action state dimension**, a **process dimension** and a **contextual dimension**. In the 'action state dimension', self-regulation is viewed as a desired action state, and the role of social context in the maintenance of health routine or health habits is emphasised. The 'process dimension' includes a collection of interrelated change mechanisms, and specifies causal links between individual change processes and interpersonal environments. The 'contextual dimension' outlines the role of environmental and social influences in either facilitating or hindering individual change.

Action State Dimension

Self-regulation is seen as a desired 'action state', the goal of which is to create **health habits. Health habits** are health-protective behavioural routines or automatic action sequences that are directed by an **action-outcome feedback loop**. They are defined as scripted behaviour chains or **'action scripts'**, where one action within a sequence reinforces the previous action and guides the next. Thus, actions are directed by their outcomes, with action consequences being monitored and subsequent behaviour being directed by (or adjusted on the basis of) these consequences. In the action state dimension, the generation of desired action-outcome feedback loops is dependent upon the activation of social-cognitive **change mechanisms**, such as **goals**, **expectations**, **strategies** and **capabilities**. These mechanisms are in turn either facilitated or hindered by **action contexts** (i.e. the context in which action takes place), including the **physical, social, biological** and **mood/arousal** context that a person is in.

The action state dimension incorporates the concept of **social interdependence**: people's action scripts are interlinked, meaning that a person in a relationship has the potential to influence another's action sequences and thus their likelihood of goal attainment. These **interlinked scripts** can facilitate the attainment of multiple goals (e.g. sharing a meal can both satisfy hunger and provide entertainment). The closeness of social relationships can be defined as the number of interlinked scripts and **shared goals** in a social relationship. The greater the **social closeness**, the greater the potential for the disruption of action sequences and goal attainment. Thus, successful health behaviour change may be dependent upon disruptive interlinked scripts being unlinked.

Process Dimension

There are several processes by which action scripts are created or modified (i.e. by which people can transition to a new action state, thus changing their behaviour). **Problem-solving** strategies provide guides for action in different circumstances, varying in complexity from 'if-then' rules to much more complex collections of thoughts, feelings and behaviours. Problem-solving strategies are generated by the **motivational processes** of **outcome expectancies**, **self-efficacy** and **goal structures**. 'Outcome expectancies' are beliefs about whether or not an action will lead to valued outcomes (e.g. beliefs about whether a behaviour will be pleasurable or will lead to improvements in health or appearance). Outcome expectancies influence decisions about whether or not to adopt a health-enhancing behaviour. 'Self-efficacy' is a person's beliefs about whether or not they are capable of performing a behaviour. Problem-solving strategies will not be generated unless a person believes themselves to be capable of the behaviour, regardless of their underlying desire to engage in the behaviour.

Health habits exist in larger clusters of action scripts which relate to the achievement of a superordinate goals, or '**personal projects**' (e.g. to achieve a certain social standing, to acquire financial wealth). These personal projects influence behaviour by directing the generation of **self-directive goals** (i.e. behavioural intentions). Thus, if health behaviour change is viewed as beneficial to a personal project, a person will more easily adopt it. People also develop self-standards against which they judge their efforts towards goal attainment, with achievement stimulating further effort. Self-directive goals and **self-standards** interact with self-efficacy. Self-efficacy influences the selection of strategies for action, whilst goals and self-standards affect levels of self-efficacy.

Cognitive schemas are instrumental in the processes of problem solving, goal formation, self-efficacy appraisal and forming outcome expectations. Schemas are sets of knowledge that either represent facts or beliefs about the world and about oneself (**declarative knowledge schemas**) or the skills and routines for performing tasks (**procedural schemas**). Taken together, a person's cognitive schemas represent their **generative capabilities**. A particular type of procedural schema, **cognitive control schema**, influences behavioural choices by increasing temptation avoidance-related self-efficacy. In addition, declarative knowledge schemas influence motivation to self-regulate. For instance, cognitive representations of illness may influence perceptions of physical symptoms, and thus affect the accuracy of perceptions of personal risk.

A person's social environment also determines their ability to make motivational appraisals and formulate strategies for action through **social interaction processes**. **Conjoint competence**, defined as the ability of people in a social relationship to collaborate in problem solving, can either facilitate or hinder a person's ability to make a change in their behaviour.

Contextual Dimension

The contextual dimension explains how environmental factors (e.g. societal and organisational factors) can either disrupt or maintain a person's action state by influencing self-change processes. There are five main environmental factors that influence behaviour: **settings**, **relationship systems**, **organisational systems**, **temperament** and **biological conditions**. Settings may be **physical** (i.e. the physical features of a person's environment, **social** (i.e. other people within the proximal environment) or **tasks** (i.e. the tasks that a person routinely performs within their environment). Settings influence both problem solving strategies and goals by determining the availability of resources such as time, money and accessibility to healthy foods or exercise facilities. 'Relationship systems' (i.e. social relationships) influence behaviour in a multitude of ways. For instance, the cooperation of a spouse can facilitate adherence to a healthy diet, advice from friends might include the suggestion of effective problem-solving strategies and social obligations might present a barrier to behaviour change. 'Organisational systems' are the organisational structure at the governmental, economic, educational and healthcare levels of a person's environment, and can affect a person's environmental settings, access to resources and exposure to health communications.

A person's temperament and biological condition interact with physical settings and relationship systems, ultimately influencing their generative capabilities and goals. For instance, the environment in which a person grows up may determine their cognitive development. Similarly, the innate temperament with which a person is born might influence their choice of social relationships, which might in turn affect their health-related goals or expectations. These social and physical environmental contexts interact to determine mood/arousal states (i.e. positive or negative affect). Mood and arousal levels influence self-regulatory processes in a number of ways. For instance, they may influence people's self-control ability or their ability to appraise behavioural consequences.

Social Action Theory

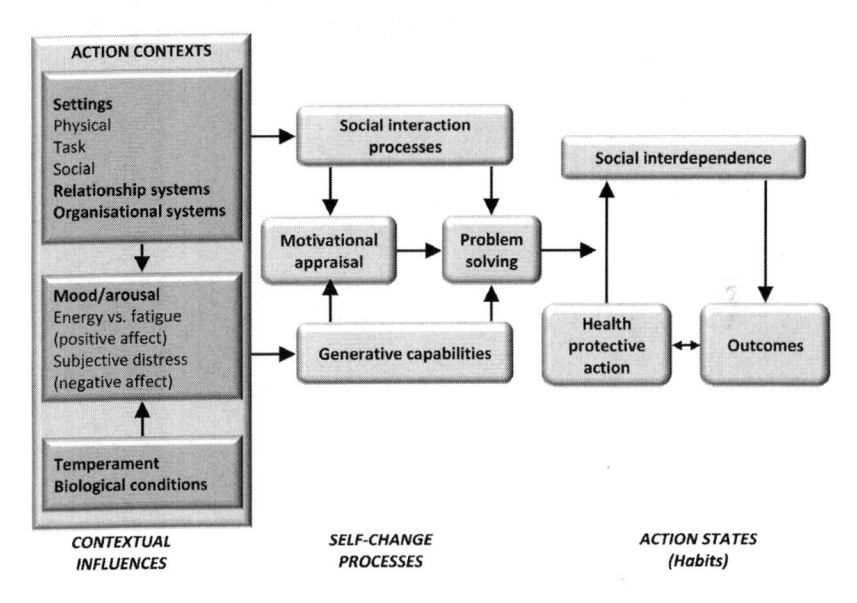

Source: Ewart, C.K. (1991). Social Action Theory for a Public Health Psychology. *American Psychologist*, 46 (9), 931-946. Originally published by APA and reprinted here with permission.

Contributing Theories:

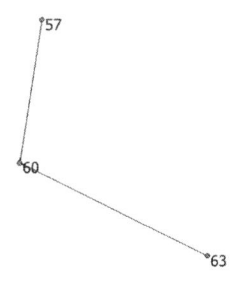

As outlined in the network diagram, the following theories included within this book were identified as contributing to the development of Social Action Theory:

57. Self-Efficacy Theory

63. Social Cognitive Theory

Taken from:

Ewart, C.K. (1991). Social Action Theory for a Public Health Psychology. *American Psychologist*, 46(9), 931-946.

61. Social Action Theory (Weber)

Constructs

- Social action
    - o Instrumentally rational
    - o Value-rational
    - o Affectual
    - o Traditional
- Social relationship
- Usage
- Custom
- Self-interest

Brief Summary

Social Action Theory states that whilst much action might be carried out unconsciously and distinctions between types of action may not always be clear, it is conceptually important to distinguish social action from other types of action. Social action may be oriented in one of four ways: instrumentally rational, value-rational, affectual or traditional.

Description

Social Action Theory defines 'social action' as behaviour that is meaningfully oriented towards others (as opposed to inanimate objects). Social action may be oriented in four different ways. These four types may overlap and are not exhaustive.

1. **Instrumentally rational** action is determined by expectations about the behaviour of objects and other

human beings. In this case the various means and end results of actions are rationally weighed and considered.

2. **Value-rational action** is determined by a belief in the value of the action for its own sake and independent of any consideration of its success. The value might be ethical, aesthetic or religious, or it could be any cause or duty. The action would be pursued regardless of any possible costs to the person involved. This type of action is always irrational.

3. **Affectual action** is determined by the person's emotional and feeling states. In some cases it may not be possible to consider it as meaningfully oriented action but in others it may be a conscious release of emotional tension.

4. **Traditional action** is determined by habit and constitutes the greater part of everyday actions. Again, it is not always meaningfully oriented; however habitual action can be conducted with a degree of self-consciousness.

Social action involves **social relationships**. These may be cooperative or uncooperative. They may consist of conflict, attraction, hostility, friendship, love, loyalty, economic exchange and so on. They may be brief or long-lasting, formal or informal.

Certain courses of social action are repeated by a single person or multiple people. If an action is repeated regularly it is termed '**usage**'. Usage may include fashion or convention, both of which are oriented towards social prestige. If usage is based upon long-standing practice it is called '**custom**'. Custom includes norms and conformity. Customs are not required legally but are conducted on the basis of free will and are often in the interests of those involved. Those who share similar instrumentally oriented expectations may be said to act out of '**self-interest**'. In this case the interests of others are not taken into account. This may arouse antagonism which in the end, may damage self-interest.

Contributing Theories:

Social Action Theory was originally published in 1922 and is the oldest theory within this book. Therefore, none of the theories included within this book were identified as contributing to the development of Social Action Theory.

Taken from:

Weber, M. (1978). Economy and Society: an outline of interpretive sociology. California: University of California.

62. Social Change Theory (Thompson & Kinne)

Constructs

- Norms
- External environment
    - Key events
    - Secular trends
    - Policies
    - Economic conditions
    - Technology
- Community system
    - Social movements
    - Community development
    - Vested interests
- Locality development
- Community organisation
    - Organisation development
    - Leadership
    - Diffusion
- Collective action
- Role models
- Social environment
- Behaviour change

Brief Summary

Social Change Theory proposes that the external environment influences community goals, norms, values and organisations which influence social norms (shared rules and expectations) regarding health behaviours, which bring about behavioural change at an individual level.

Description

Social Change Theory aims to describe how social norms that lead to unhealthy behaviours can be replaced with social norms that support healthier behaviours. The theory assumes that health improvements are best achieved by altering community, rather than individual, norms. In the theory, **'norms'** are defined as shared rules and expectations and 'communities' are regarded as systems that share values and institutions and that provide the context for health-related activities. Communities comprise political, economic, health, education, communication, religious, recreational and social welfare sub-systems, as well as voluntary groups and social movement groups.

This **community system** is generally stable, with consensus regarding goals, norms and values. However, stimuli from the **external environment** (in the form of **key events**, **secular trends**, **policies**, **economic conditions** and **technologies**) can influence norms and values within the community system. For example, governmental policy to reduce smoking in public places has an effect on community systems. **Vested interests** (e.g. tobacco companies) aim to preserve the status quo but **social movements** (e.g. employees who campaign for smoke-free areas at work) can arise to counter these and **community developments** may occur with the aim of changing community behaviours. External forces (e.g. government policies) may use **locality development** or social planning theories to bring about change.

At the subsystem level various **community organisations** work together to achieve change. Additional policies may be imposed that are compatible with the goals of the project (e.g. community restrictions on places where smoking is allowed). Some organisations take on **leadership** roles. Change is spread to other groups within the community through a process of **organisational**

development and **diffusion** via social networks. People are exposed to these changing norms, which may be reinforced by influential **role models**. As things progress, **collective action** and changes in the **social environment** eventually bring about new norms (i.e. smoking is no longer considered socially acceptable in public spaces) and widespread individual **behaviour change** is then likely to occur (i.e. fewer people start smoking and more people stop).

Contributing Theories:

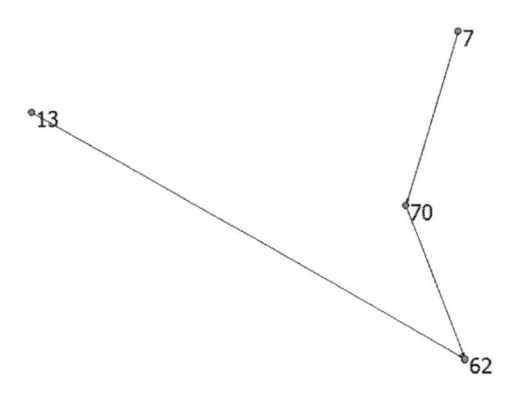

As outlined in the network diagram, the following theories included within this book were identified as contributing to the development of Social Change Theory:

13. Diffusion of Innovations

70. Social Learning Theory

Taken from:

Thompson, B. & Kinne, S. (1990). Social change theory: applications to community health. In N. Bracht (Ed.), *Health Promotion at the Community Level*. Newbury Park: Sage Publications.

63. Social Cognitive Theory (Bandura)

Constructs

- Triadic reciprocality
    - Behaviour
    - Personal and cognitive factors
    - Environment
- Basic capabilities
    - Symbolising capability
    - Forethought capability
    - Vicarious capability
    - Self-regulatory capability
    - Self-reflective capability
        - [ ] Perceived self-efficacy

Brief Summary

Social Cognitive Theory aims to provide a framework for the study and understanding of human thought and behaviour. The central proposal of the theory is that behaviour, the environment and personal factors all interact to determine each other. In addition, the theory proposes that human functioning can be best understood in terms of five basic capabilities for symbolic thought, forethought, observational learning, self-regulation and self-reflection.

Description

Social Cognitive Theory is a theoretical framework that aims to guide the study of human action, thought and motivation. At the core of the theory is the causal model of **triadic reciprocality**; the proposition that the **environment**, **behaviour**, and **personal and cognitive factors** all interact as determinants of each other. To explain behaviour, thought and motivation, human functioning is described in terms of a number of **basic capabilities**. These basic capabilities are termed **symbolising capability, forethought capability, vicarious capability, self-regulatory capability** and **self-reflective capability**.

Symbolising Capability

The capacity of humans to use symbols is referred to as the 'symbolising capability'. Symbols are used for transforming experiences into mental models that can be used to guide future behaviour and for ascribing meaning to experiences. For instance, symbols can be used to plan courses of action by cognitively evaluating anticipated outcomes of different modes of action.

Forethought Capability

The 'forethought capability' refers to the ability to regulate behaviour on the basis of the future. This may occur through setting goals, planning courses of action to achieve an imagined future and the motivation and guidance of action on the basis of anticipated outcomes. The capacity for forethought-directed action is heavily dependent upon the symbolising capacity, as cognitive representations of future events act as motivators or guides for action.

Vicarious Capability

The 'vicarious capability' refers to the ability to learn through observation (i.e. by modelling others' behaviour, attitudes, etc.). Whilst learning through action can occur, learning by imitation is more effective for enhancing the rate of learning. In addition, some learning can only occur vicariously (e.g. language, novel patterns of behaviour that can only be communicated socially).

Self-Regulatory Capability

The 'self-regulatory capability' refers to people's ability to motivate or regulate their own behaviour on the basis of their personal standards and evaluations of their behaviour. Specifically, self-regulation is defined as the identification of discrepancies between actual behaviour and personal standards and the subsequent adjustments to behaviour. Self-regulation may also involve modifications to the external environment through organising environmental conditions that facilitate or reinforce behaviour.

Self-Reflective Capability

The capacity for self-reflection is seen as uniquely human, and it enables people to analyse their own experiences, thoughts and knowledge. The self-reflective capability functions to generate generic knowledge through reflection on personal experiences and knowledge. The thoughts that are generated, modified or verified through self-reflection guide actions and determine anticipations. Outcomes of this are involved in further self-reflection to evaluate the adequacy of the preceding thoughts, and to modify them accordingly. These processes usually generate 'truthful' thought, but may cause erroneous thinking in some cases. For instance, some behaviours that arise from erroneous thinking may result in social consequences that confirm that thinking.

One particular type of self-reflective thought is the most influential upon behaviour: people's judgements of their ability to cope effectively in different circumstances (i.e. perceived self-efficacy). Perceptions of self-efficacy influence people's choices of action, the effort and perseverance they invest in action and the anxiety or confidence with which they approach actions. These actions that are influenced by perceptions of self-efficacy result in either successes or failures, which will in turn be reflected upon to inform future judgements of self-efficacy.

Contributing Theories:

None of the theories included within this book were identified as contributing to the development of Social Cognitive Theory.

Taken from:

Bandura, A. (1986). *Social Foundations of Thought and Action: A Social Cognitive Theory*. New Jersey, US: Prentice-Hall.

64. Social Consensus Model of Health Education (Romer & Hornik)

Constructs

- Social consensus
    o Social knowledge
    o Social beliefs
    o Social meanings
    o Social norms
- Consensual beliefs
- Stereotypes
- Education
- Individual knowledge
- Individual beliefs
- Individual attitudes
- Personal relevance
- Behaviour

Brief Summary

The Social Consensus Model proposes that health education aimed at individuals alone is insufficient as it fails to target potentially inaccurate but socially-supported beliefs and norms. According to the model, health education at the broader societal level is needed to ensure that the behaviour is adopted and maintained over time.

Description

The Social Consensus Model is a model of health education that has a particular focus on limiting the spread of HIV among young people and acknowledges that health education alone will not lead to behaviour change. It suggests that the gap often found between knowledge and practice may be reduced by increasing social consensus.

There are two major assumptions underlying the Social Consensus model. First, that knowledge of a health threat raises social issues that require further resolution before action can be taken. For example, people need to consider the relevance of the threat to them and the desirability of their response to it. Second, that the social environment can influence behaviour independently of education.

Behaviour is influenced by two sets of factors. First, **individual knowledge**, **individual beliefs** and **individual attitudes** have a direct influence on behaviour. Second, **social knowledge, beliefs, meanings and norms** have (1) a direct influence on behaviour and (2) an indirect influence on behaviour, mediated by their influence upon individual knowledge, beliefs and attitudes. Both individual knowledge, beliefs and attitudes and social knowledge, beliefs, meanings and norms are influenced by education.

Social consensus refers to the consensus of **knowledge, beliefs**, **social meanings** and **social norms** that exist within social environments. 'Social meanings' include the images and interpretations that social groups assign to behaviour, while 'social norms' refer to the social expectations defining appropriate behaviour. The social environment also transmits **consensual beliefs** and **stereotypes**, which can influence people and may present obstacles to behaviour change. **Education** can be undermined if these social beliefs and stereotypes are in conflict with factual knowledge. These socially-supported beliefs, norms and meanings present major impediments to behaviour change. Thus, education may need to be directed to entire communities rather than selected individuals or sub-groups because this is more likely to have an impact on the social consensus.

Health threats raise social issues, including the issue of how to respond to threat in ways considered acceptable within a person's social environment. Unless the social consensus is addressed, educational efforts aimed at individual people may be undermined. For example, even though a teenager may have taken on board the health education message that condoms protect against HIV, they may still fail to use a condom because doing so presents an image of sex as planned and unspontaneous.

Awareness of the seriousness of a health threat and of its **personal relevance** needs to be conveyed at a community level for it to be effective at the individual-level, because if only certain groups are seen as susceptible to the threat the perception of personal relevance will be diminished. The social consensus regarding appropriate behaviour requires continuous reinforcement if behaviour change is to be maintained so that large-scale, mass media programmes may be most effective in achieving this.

A diagram of the Social Consensus Model of Health Education can be found on p.288 of Romer & Hornik (1992).

Contributing Theories:

None of the theories included within this book were identified as contributing to the development of the Social Consensus Model of Health Education.

Taken from:

Romer, D. & Hornik. R. (1992). HIV education for youth: The importance of social consensus in behaviour change. *AIDS Care*, 4(3), 285-307.

65. Social Development Model (Hawkins & Weis)

Constructs

- Units of socialisation
    - Families
    - Schools
    - Peers
- Opportunities for involvement
- Skills for involvement
- Reinforcement for involvement
- Involvement
- Social bonding
    - Commitment
    - Attachment
    - Belief
- Association with non-delinquent peers
- Non-delinquent behaviour

Brief Summary

The Social Development Model aims to provide an explanation of how delinquency and crime among young people can be prevented. The core tenet of the theory is that social bonding within units of socialisation such as family, peers and school is the most influential factor in the prevention of delinquent behaviour.

Description

The Social Development Model of delinquency prevention integrates theories that address the roles of control and social learning on delinquent behaviour. In the process of social development, behaviour is influenced by three key **units of socialisation: families**, **schools** and **peers**. These influence behaviour sequentially, both directly and indirectly. There are three types of process variables that operate within each unit: **opportunities for involvement**, **skills for involvement** and **reinforcement for involvement** (i.e. having the opportunities and skills to interact with conventional others and receiving reinforcement for such interactions). These variables determine whether a person's **involvement** in that unit will result in the development of a **social bond** with the unit. A 'social bond' comprises (1) a **commitment** to conventional society, (2) an **attachment** to conventional society and (3) a **belief** in conventional society. The term 'conventional' can be defined as 'non-delinquent'.

All three process variables are prerequisites for involvement and adequate social bonding within a socialisation unit. Opportunities for involvement are a necessary precursor to the development of a social bond, but are not sufficient for such a bond to develop. Opportunities for involvement promote the development of attachment and commitment to conventional others and conventional rules of behaviour. However, social bonding will only occur if **involvement** is positively evaluated by the person (i.e. it is perceived as rewarding). Two factors determine whether or not involvement is positively evaluated: a person's skills for involvement and external reinforcements for the desired behaviour (i.e. conventional, non-delinquent behaviour). This development of a social bond reduces the likelihood that a young person will **associate with delinquent peers**, both directly and indirectly (i.e.

through the influence on peer associations), thus promoting **non-delinquent behaviour.**

A diagram of the Social Consensus Model of Health Education can be found on p.79 of Hawkins & Weis (1985).

Contributing Theories:

None of the theories included within this book were identified as contributing to the development of Social Development Model.

Taken from:

Hawkins, J.D. & Weis, J.G. (1985). The social development model: an integrated approach to delinquency prevention. *Journal of Primary Prevention, 6*(2), 73-97.

66. Social Ecological Model of Behaviour Change (Panter-Brick et al.)

Constructs

- Attitudes
    - Behavioural beliefs and their evaluative aspects
- Social norms
    - Normative beliefs and motivation to comply
- Self-efficacy
    - Efficacy beliefs
- Intention to change
- Trigger for change
- Culturally acceptable intervention
- Culturally compelling intervention
- Social ecology
    - Enabling factors
        - Skills
        - Ability
    - Local and external investments
        - Political commitments
        - Financial commitments
        - Community priorities
        - Organisational support
    - Constraints on agency
        - Time
        - Economic
        - Social
        - Physical
- Behaviour change
- Health impact
- Sustainability
- Feedback loop

Brief Summary

The Social Ecological Model of Behaviour Change emphasises the importance of embedding interventions in the social and ecological settings that contextualise human behaviour provides a theoretical account of the determinants of behaviour change and provides a framework for the design and evaluation of behaviour change interventions.

Description

The Social Ecological Model of Behaviour Change aims to provide a framework for designing behaviour change interventions that take into account social and physical settings, and external factors that shape human agency (i.e. ability to act). It rests on the assumption that the design of **culturally acceptable interventions** should focus upon the primary determinants of **intentions to change** behaviour. These **attitudes** towards the behaviour (beliefs about how favourable or unfavourable the behaviour is), **social norms** (beliefs about what others do and what others think one should do) and **self-efficacy** (a person's beliefs about their ability to perform the behaviour) which are, in turn, functions of underlying beliefs. Attitudes are a function of **behavioural beliefs and their evaluative aspects** (i.e. beliefs about and evaluations of the possible outcomes of the behaviour). Social norms are a function of **normative beliefs and motivation to comply** (a person's beliefs about what important others think they should do, and their motivation to comply with those wishes). Self-efficacy is a function of **efficacy beliefs** (a person's belief about whether they have the skills and abilities to perform the behaviour, even in the face of barriers). High self-efficacy, positive attitudes and pro-behaviour change norms are proposed to lead to strong intentions to change.

For intentions to change to be translated into actual behaviour change, interventions must be embedded in the social and cultural contexts in which they take place (i.e. **social ecology**). The social ecology includes **enabling factors** for behaviour change (i.e. the necessary **skills** and **abilities**), **local and external investment** in behaviour change and **constraints on agency**. Local and external investments include **political commitments, financial commitments, community priorities** and **organisational support**. Proposed constraints on agency include **time constraints, economic constraints, social constraints** and **physical constraints**. Further, there must also be a **trigger for change** in the form of a compelling message (i.e. an intervention). According to the model, the shift from intentions to action also represents the transition from a culturally acceptable intervention to a **culturally compelling intervention**.

For behaviour change interventions to be considered effective, proof of **health impact** (a function of behaviour change) is required. Health impact can be evaluated through both objective measurement and cultural perceptions, and is proposed to feed into a **feedback loop** by which health impact moderates attitudes, social norms and self-efficacy, and each of their underlying beliefs. Evaluations of the **sustainability** of the link between behaviour change and health impact also feed into this feedback loop.

A diagram of the Social Ecological Model of Behaviour Change can be found on p.2813 of Panter-Brick, Clarke, Lomas, Pinder & Lindsay (2006).

Contributing Theories:

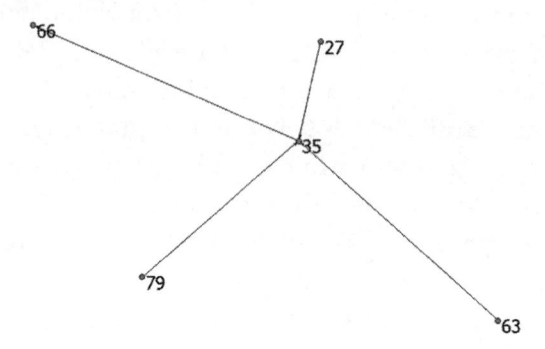

As outlined in the network diagram, the following theory included within this book was identified as contributing to the development of the Social Ecological Model of Behaviour Change:

35. Integrative Model of Behavioural Prediction

Taken from:

Panter-Brick, C., Clarke, S.E., Lomas, H., Pinder, M. & Lindsay, S.W. (2006). Culturally compelling strategies for behaviour change: a social ecology model and case study in malaria prevention. *Social Science & Medicine*, 62(2), 2810-2825.

67. Social Ecological Model of Walking (Alfonzo)

Constructs
- Hierarchy of walking needs
    o Pleasurability
    o Comfort
    o Safety
    o Accessibility
    o Feasibility
- Affordances
- Life-cycle circumstances
    o Individual level
    o Group level
    o Regional level
- Outcomes
    o Dichotomous
        □ No walking
    o Duration
        □ Brief walk
        □ Longer walk
    o Type
        □ Destination walking
        □ Strolling walking
        □ Combination walking

Brief Summary

The Social-Ecological Model of Walking proposes a model of the decision-making process underlying walking behaviour, with fulfilment of a hierarchy of walking needs being requisite antecedents to walking. This hierarchy is placed within a social-ecological framework, which outlines the factors that determine whether fulfilment of needs will translate into walking behaviour.

Description

The Social-Ecological Model of Walking proposes that people's decision to walk is affected by individual, group, regional, and physical-environmental factors. Some of these factors are more influential than others during the decision-making process. A **hierarchy of walking needs** represent the context in which the decision-making process that determines walking occurs.

Hierarchy of Walking Needs

Within the hierarchy are five levels of walking needs: the most fundamental is **feasibility** (personal ability or limits), then **accessibility, safety, comfort,** and **pleasurability** being the highest-order need. A person would not usually consider a higher-order need if a more basic need was not already met. For instance, even in a very pleasurable environment for walking a person would be unlikely to consider walking if safety needs were not met. However, lower-order needs do not have to be fully satisfied for consideration of the next level of needs to occur. People do not always consider the levels within the hierarchy in the order above – a decision to walk may be motivated by several needs at once, and in cases where a particular need is continually deprived, that need may not be considered at all. The evaluation of needs may be a subconscious process – people may be consciously unaware of their needs evaluations.

Fulfilment of all five needs is not necessary to motivate walking, and the choice to walk can occur at any level in the hierarchy. Furthermore, even fulfilment of all five needs would not necessarily lead to walking, as additional factors are instrumental in the decision-making process.

The Social-Ecological Framework

The hierarchy of walking needs arranges variables relating to the urban form in which walking decision-making takes place into those that are more or less fundamental in the decision-making process. The variables within the hierarchy are antecedents to behaviour, being either present or absent in the context in which decision-making takes place. However, it is the affordance of needs that is the most proximal determinant of behaviour. **Affordances** are defined as the environment properties that allow the behaviour to occur (i.e. fulfil walking needs). For walking behaviour to be carried out, these affordances must both exist and be perceived by the person. The perception of affordances may differ across individuals, as it is influenced by a person's perceptions, habits and motivations. Thus, perceived affordances mediate the relationship between the hierarchy of needs and walking behaviour.

However, perceived affordances are not a direct determinant of walking decisions. '**Life-cycle circumstances**' moderate the relationship between the hierarchy of needs and walking behaviour. Life-cycle circumstances refer to people's unique characteristics; and include **individual-level** attributes (e.g. physiological factors, psychological characteristics, demographic characteristics), **group-level** factors (e.g. cultural factors) and **regional-level** characteristics of the setting in which walking is to take place (e.g. climate, topography). These factors determine how many levels of the needs hierarchy need to be fulfilled for walking to take place. For instance, if a person has positive attitudes towards walking and is committed to improving their health, only the most basic needs in the hierarchy need to be met for walking to take place. Conversely, a person with less positive attitudes and lower levels of commitment would require the fulfilment of higher-order needs to make the decision to walk. In a similar manner, group-level characteristics such as culture might determine how many needs must be fulfilled for walking to take place if the culture emphasises the importance of exercise, or is apathetic towards exercise. Regional-level characteristics could exert their influence by possessing conditions that act to increase or decrease a person's baseline motivation for walking (e.g. a warm climate might increase motivation and a cold climate might decrease motivation). Thus, life-cycle circumstances act as moderators of the relationship between the hierarchy of needs and walking behaviour by influencing a person's baseline level of motivation for walking, which is inversely related to the level of needs that are required to be met.

Finally, there are different categories of walking **outcome**, which are based on walking-related decisions. These decisions include the **dichotomous** decision of whether or not to walk, decisions about the **duration** of the walk and decisions about the **type** of walk to have (or the purpose of the walk). The outcome categories defined are: **no walking, brief walk, longer walk, destination walking, strolling walking** and **combination walking.** Fewer needs may require fulfilment for certain walking outcomes (e.g. more needs may require fulfilment for a longer walk), and some needs in the hierarchy may be more salient or necessary dependent upon the type (or purpose of a walk).

A diagram of the Social Ecological Model of Walking can be found on p.820 of Alfonzo (2005).

Contributing Theories:

None of the theories included within this book were identified as contributing to the development of Social Ecological Model of Walking.

Taken from:

Alfonzo, M.A. (2005). To walk or not to walk? The hierarchy of walking needs. *Environment and Behaviour*, 37(6), 808-836.

68. Social Identity Theory (Tajfel & Turner)

Constructs

- Groups
    - o In-groups
    - o Out-groups
- Intergroup behaviour
- Social categorisation
- Self-reference
- Social identity
- Self-esteem
- Intergroup comparison
- Intergroup differentiation

Brief Summary

Social Identity Theory aims to explain intergroup behaviour and intergroup conflict. Behaviour among social groups is related to the desire of group members to differentiate themselves positively from other groups and to form positive evaluations of their own group.

Description

Social Identity Theory is a theory of **intergroup behaviour** (i.e. behaviour by one or more individuals towards one or more others that is based upon the perception that they belong in a different social category to those others). A **group** is defined as a number of people that perceive themselves to belong to the same social category, who share emotional involvement in this social category and have a shared evaluation of the group and their membership in it.

Intergroup behaviour results from social groups striving to differentiate themselves from each other due to people's desire to positively evaluate their own group via **intergroup comparisons**. These intergroup comparisons are facilitated by **social categorisations** which are cognitive tools which serve to provide order and classification to the social environment. In turn, social categorisations facilitate **self-reference**, a process by which people's place in society can be defined. Social groups therefore give their members a **social identity**, based upon comparisons against members of other groups.

Intergroup comparison allows for **intergroup differentiation** which is influenced by three factors. Firstly, the extent to which people have internalised their group membership as part of their self-concept. Secondly, the extent to which the social situation allows for the evaluation of relevant attributes (as not all between-group differences have evaluative significance). Thirdly, in-groups do not compare themselves to all out-groups, but only against out-groups that are perceived as relevant (with judgements of relevance being based upon factors such as similarity and proximity).

The relationship between intergroup comparison and intergroup behaviour is further articulated by several theoretical assumptions and principles which are outlined below.

Theoretical Assumptions

There are three general assumptions in Social Identity Theory:

1. People are motivated to preserve or increase their **self-esteem**.

2. Social categories and membership of social groups are positively or negatively valued. A person's social identity is positive or negative according to the overall value weighting across the social groups to which they belong.

3. A person evaluates their own group (the **in-group**) against other groups (**out-groups**) through social comparisons of positively or negatively valued characteristics. A positive discrepancy between a person's own group and others will be met with high regard and a negative discrepancy will be met with low regard.

Theoretical Principles

There are three theoretical principles that aim to explain intergroup behaviour:

1. People are motivated to preserve or achieve a positive social identity.

2. Positive social identity is generated by comparative evaluations of the in-group that result in a positive discrepancy between group characteristics.

3. A negative self-identity will either result in people attempting to leave their own group for a group that is more positively distinctive, or in people striving to make their own group more positively distinctive.

Contributing Theories:

None of the theories included within this book were identified as contributing to the development of Social Identity Theory.

Taken from:

Tajfel, H. & Turner, J. (1986). The Social Identity Theory of Intergroup Behaviour. In S. Worchel & W. G. Austin (Eds.), *Psychology of Intergroup Relations* (2nd ed., pp. 7-24). Chicago: Nelson-Hall

69. Social Influence Model of Consumer Participation (Dholakia et al.)

Constructs
- Value perceptions or motives (individual level variables)
    o Self-referent values
        □ Purposive value
        □ Self-discovery
    o Group-referent values
        □ Maintaining interpersonal interconnectivity
        □ Social enhancement
    o Entertainment value
- Social influence variables (group level variables)
    o Social identity
        □ Cognitive
        □ Affective
        □ Evaluative
    o Group norms
        □ Mutual agreement
        □ Mutual accommodation
- Decision making and participation
    o Desires
    o We-intentions
    o Participation behaviour
- Network-based virtual communities
- Small-group-based virtual communities

Brief Summary

The Social Influence Model of Consumer Participation aims to explain why consumers participate in two different kinds of virtual community: network-based and small-group-based. It identifies individual motives and desires and social identity and group norms as explanatory factors.

Description

The Social Influence Model of Consumer Participation consists of three main groups of variables: **value perceptions or motives** (individual level variables), **social influence** (group-level variables) and **decision making and participation**. Some individual level variables are proposed to influence group level variables and both are seen to influence participation in virtual communities, through the mediating factor of desires. The model generates sixteen hypotheses regarding these relationships.

Value Perceptions or Motives

Value perceptions can be seen as individual motives for participating in virtual communities. They include **purposive value** (the benefit of achieving an instrumental or informational goal), **self-discovery** (the personal understanding gained through interacting with others), **maintaining interpersonal interconnectivity** (the value obtained from a web of support and contact with others), **social enhancement** (the approval and improved social status gained as a result of contributing to the online community) and **entertainment value** (fun and relaxation). Purposive value and self-discovery are categorised as **self-referent values**, while maintaining interpersonal interconnectivity and social enhancement are categorised as **group-referent values**. The stronger these value perceptions (individual motives) are, the stronger the sense of identification with the virtual community and the stronger the commitment to group norms.

Social Influence

Social influence variables that affect participation in virtual communities are proposed to include social identity and group norms. **Social identity** refers to a person's sense of identification with, and membership of, the virtual community. Social identity is made up of **cognitive, affective** and **evaluative** components, which refer (respectively) to self-awareness in categorising oneself as a member of the group, a sense of attachment and involvement in the group and an appraisal of self-worth based on membership of the group. **Group norms** are defined as the goals, values, beliefs and conventions of the group's members. The stronger the understanding of and commitment to group norms, the stronger the identification with the virtual group will be.

Group norms implicitly create both agreement about how to engage in online activity and a willingness to accommodate others in online interactions. The stronger the understanding of and commitment to group norms, the greater is the **mutual agreement** to participate in the virtual group and the greater is the willingness to **mutually accommodate** others to allow participation. Strong mutual agreement and accommodation both lead to stronger desires to participate in the online communities.

Decision Making and Participation

'Decision making and participation' variables include **desires**, **'we-intentions'** and **participation behaviour**. Desires are considered to mediate the individual and social influence variables by transforming the many antecedent variables into a motivation to act. A stronger sense of social identity, or identification with the group, leads to stronger desires to participate in the virtual group.

A 'we-intention' is defined as a person's commitment to engage in joint action with others. Stronger desires, stronger commitment to group norms and a stronger sense of identification with the group are all proposed to lead to higher levels of intention to participate in the virtual group. Higher levels of intentions to participate in the group lead to greater levels of participation in the virtual group.

Finally, the model distinguishes between two different kinds of online community. **Network-based virtual communities** are defined as those structured around a specialist or common focus, such as a gardening bulletin board. These require only minimal levels of engagement. **Small-group-based virtual communities** are those with shared goals, whose members engage in higher levels of group interaction and form a dense web of relationships which they aim to maintain.

Network-based virtual community members have self-referent values, so the impact of these is stronger than for small-group-based members. Small-group-based community members have group-referent values, so the impact of these is stronger than for network-based members. The impact of self-referent values on the social influence variables (i.e. sense of identification with the group and commitment to group norms) will be stronger for network-based members than for small-group-based members, while the impact of group-referent values on the social influence variables will be stronger for small-group-based members than for network-based members.

A diagram of the Social Influence Model of Community Participation can be found on p.243 of Dholakia, Bagozzi, Klein & Pearo (2004).

Contributing Theories:

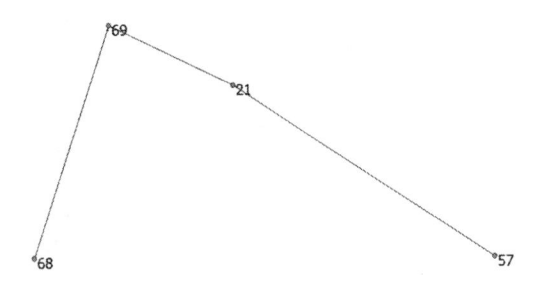

As outlined in the network diagram, the following theories included within this book were identified as contributing to the development of the Social Influence Model of Consumer Participation:

21. Goal Directed Theory

68. Social Identity Theory

Taken from:

Dholakia, U.M., Bagozzi, R.P., Klein, L. & Pearo, A. (2004). A social influence model of consumer participation in network- and small-group-based virtual communities. *International Journal of Research in Marketing*, 21(3), 241–263.

70. Social Learning Theory (Miller & Dollard)

Constructs

- Drive
    - Innate drives
    - Acquired drives
- Cue
- Response
- Reward
    - Innate rewards
    - Acquired rewards
- Extinction
- Spontaneous recovery
- Generalisation
- Discrimination
- Gradient of reward
- Anticipatory response
- Imitation
    - Same behaviour
    - Matched-dependent behaviour
    - Copying

Brief Summary

Miller and Dollard's Social Learning Theory primarily aims to explain how people learn through the imitation of others and outlines four factors that are instrumental to learning (drive, cue, response and reward).

Description

Miller and Dollard's Social Learning Theory aims to explain how imitative learning takes place, with four factors instrumental to the learning process: drive, cue, response and reward.

Drive

Drive is the motivation or desire to act or respond, and is a stimulus that triggers action. **Innate drives** provide the majority of motivation for action. These include stimuli such as pain, hunger or thirst. **Acquired drives** develop on the basis of innate drives. These include stimuli such as fear (based on pain) and appetite (based on hunger) and may be based on multiple innate and acquired drives, such as the desire for money (based on hunger, cold, anxiety, etc.).

Cue

Whilst a drive motivates a person to act, a cue determines the action that will be made, and when and where it will be made. Cues include environmental stimuli such as a school bell indicating that class is over or traffic lights indicated whether to stop or proceed. Thus, stimuli can be either drives or cues. Whether or not stimuli serve as drives depends on their strength. For instance, a weak sound does not stimulate action and ending the sound would hold little reward. However, a very loud sound might stimulate action to escape from or cease that sound, the outcome of which would be rewarding. Similarly, whether or not stimuli serve as cues depends upon their distinctiveness. For instance, differences in the tone of voice used by adults can elicit different learned responses from children. Cues direct the motivation to act arising from drives towards the correct response. For instance, if a hungry person sees a restaurant sign, they will follow that sign.

Response

The response to a certain cue, in the presence of a certain drive, must be learned. This learning process occurs when the correct response to a specific cue is performed for the first time, and is rewarded (e.g. by satiation of the drive). Certain responses are easier to learn than others due to the frequency at which they occur, which increases the likelihood that the response will be performed in the presence of the cue prior to learning. Prior to learning; responses can be arranged according to their likelihood of occurrence in an initial or **innate hierarchy**. As a result of learning the rewarded response will become more likely, resulting in a new hierarchy called the **resultant hierarchy**. Correct responses can be identified either through trial-and-error of randomly occurring responses, or may be guided to a degree by verbal instruction, imitation or prior related learning.

Reward

Rewards strengthen the tendency for a person to make certain responses to certain cues in the presence of drives. If a person is rewarded for their response to a certain cue, they will be more likely to repeat that response in the presence of that cue. If they are not rewarded, they will be less likely to. Rewards can also be seen as reductions in drives (e.g. lessened hunger). There are both innate rewards (e.g. reductions in drives such as hunger and pain) and acquired rewards (e.g. reductions in drives such as anxiety; the receipt of money).

Details of the Learning Process

Characteristics of the learning process are:

- **Extinction.** Reward is not only instrumental to the learning of appropriate responses to cues but also to the maintenance of that response. If learned responses repeatedly go without reward, then the tendency for that response to be performed will progressively decrease. This decrease in tendency is termed 'extinction'. The stronger the tendency towards a response, the more resistant it will be to extinction.

- **Spontaneous recovery.** Over time, the effects of extinction are likely to subside. Spontaneous recovery refers to the tendency towards recovery of an extinguished response, such that some time after extinction occurs, a person may attempt that response again. Thus, extinction does not 'destroy' learned responses, but rather inhibits them.

- **Generalisation.** 'Generalisation' refers to the process by which the effects of learning in one situation are transferred to another. If an appropriate response to one cue (or set of cues) is learned through reward, there will be a tendency towards that response in the presence of a similar cue (or set of cues). The greater the similarity between cues, the greater the amount of generalisation.

- **Discrimination.** If a generalised response is performed and not rewarded, then the tendency for that response to be used in the presence of that specific set of cues will be diminished. Thus, people will learn to discriminate between appropriate responses to similar but different cues depending on whether a generalised response is rewarded or not.

- **Gradient of reward.** The greater the temporal proximity between response and rewards, the more effective that rewards will be. For instance, if a person makes a number of responses to a cue and a reward occurs following the last response, their tendency towards using that response in the presence of that cue will be strengthened to a greater extent than their tendency towards the other responses. As a sequence of responses may be necessary to gain reward, the 'gradient of reward' also explains how people may learn to shorten that sequence such that only necessary responses within that sequence are performed.

- **Anticipatory response.** Anticipatory responses are related to generalisation and the gradient of reward. Within a response series, responses that are temporally more proximal to a reward will, wherever possible, become earlier in the sequence than they were originally. Through this process, unnecessary responses in the sequence can be removed by being 'crowded out'. For instance, if a child touched a hot stove, the pain will elicit a response of withdrawing the hand, which is rewarded by a reduction in pain. In subsequent instances, the child may stop short at reaching out to the stove and withdrawing their hand before touching it (i.e. the withdrawal has moved up in the sequence).

Imitation

There are three types of **imitation: same behaviour, matched-dependent behaviour** and **copying**. 'Same behaviour' refers to instances in which two people have the same response to the same cue, and are stimulated to do so independently. For instance, two people might board the same train because they both read the departures board detailing its destination.

'Matched-dependent behaviour' occurs when one person is older, more intelligent or more skilled than another. For instance, children match their behaviour with adults and people who are less skilled at a task will match their behaviour with those who are more skilled at a task. In cases such as this, the 'leader' of the pair is operating under the influence of drives, and responding to learned cues for reward. The 'follower', however, has not learned to respond to the same cue but rather has learned to respond to the actions of the leader, or to imitate. Thus, their response is matched to that of the leader but is dependent upon cues from the leader.

'Copying' involves one person learning to model his behaviour on that of another. For learning to be effective, the person must be able assess the similarities and differences between their own behaviour and the leader's. Learning to copy often occurs in the presence of a third individual who rewards the follower for similarities and punishes them for differences. Ultimately, learning to copy results in a person being capable of independently identifying and responding to cues of similarity or difference.

Contributing Theories:

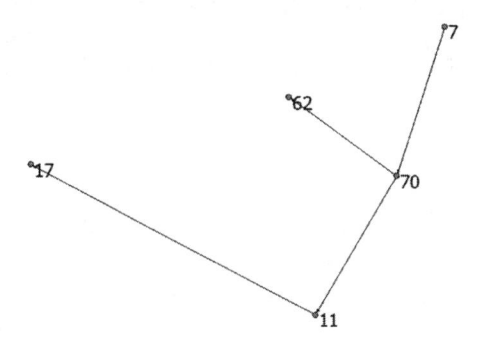

As outlined in the network diagram, the following theory included within this book was identified as contributing to the development of the Social Learning Theory:

7. Classical Conditioning

Taken from:

Miller, N.E. & Dollard, J. (1945). *Social Learning and Imitation*. London, UK: Kegan Paul.

71. Social Norms Theory (Perkins & Berkowitz)

Constructs

- Actual norms
- Perceived norms
- Misperceptions
    - o   Pluralistic ignorance
    - o   False consensus
    - o   False uniqueness
- Injunctive norms
- Descriptive norms

Brief Summary

Social Norms Theory is a theory of human behaviour, which proposes that behaviour is influenced by inaccurate perceptions of the thoughts and behaviours of other people within their social group.

Description

Social Norms Theory proposes that human behaviour is influenced by inaccurate perceptions of the thoughts and behaviours of other people within a social group (i.e. norms). For instance, a person might overestimate the alcohol consumption of their peers which would lead to increased alcohol consumption by that person. Similarly, underestimations of the attitudes or behaviours of others in relation to a particular behaviour discourage engagement in that behaviour. Put simply, people adjust their behaviour to be in line with their subjective perceptions of the norm. The discrepancy between **perceived norms** and **actual norms** is termed a '**misperception**'. It is the misperception which influences behaviour.

Misperceptions

There are three types of misperception: **pluralistic ignorance, false consensus** and **false uniqueness**. Pluralistic ignorance is the most common type of misperception and occurs when the majority of members of a group believe that the majority of their peers think or act differently to themselves (i.e. the majority falsely believe themselves to be in the minority). For instance, if a majority of group members engaged in regular exercise but *believed* that the majority of the group were relatively sedentary, these people would adjust their behaviour to become more sedentary.

'False consensus' refers to instances in which a person inaccurately believes that the majority of other members of their group act and think in the same way that they do, when in fact that person is in the minority. For instance, a person who is very sedentary might falsely believe that the majority of their peers are also sedentary, and leave their behaviour unchanged. The false consensus misperception serves the function of rationalising maladaptive behaviour and facilitating denial that behaviour is problematic (i.e. self-serving bias).

'False uniqueness' refers to a person incorrectly believing that their thoughts or behaviours are more unique than those of their peers. This type of misperception may influence behaviour by causing people to withdraw from the social group that they incorrectly believe to have different norms.

Types of Norms

There are two main types of norm: **injunctive norms** and **descriptive norms**. Injunctive norms refer to attitudes, beliefs and morals (i.e. what people think is 'right' to do). Descriptive norms refer to behaviour (i.e. what people actually do).

Contributing Theories:

None of the theories included within this book were identified as contributing to the development of the Social Norms Theory.

Taken from:

Perkins, H.W. & Berkowitz, A.D. (1986). Perceiving the Community Norms of Alcohol Use Among Students: Some Research Implications for Campus Alcohol Education Programming. *International Journal of the Addictions*, 21, 961-976.

Supplemented by:

Berkowitz, A. D. (2004). The Social Norms Approach: Theory, Research, and Annotated Bibliography. Higher Education Centre for Alcohol and Other Drug Prevention [On-line]. Available at: http://www.edc.org/hec

72. Systems Model of Health Behaviour Change (Kersell & Milsum)

Constructs

- External antecedent condition:
    - Parental and hereditary/genetic process
        - Basic physiological makeup, birthdate, sex etc.
        - Family structure
        - Physiological makeup
    - Socio-cultural environmental milieu
        - Health environmental factors
        - Social cultural influences

- Personal antecedent condition:
    - Personal demographic dynamics
        - Personal demographic characteristics
    - Personal socialization process
        - Social influences
    - Personal health dynamics
        - Health status

- Socio-psychological condition
    - Perception of self
        - Attitudinal variables
    - Perception of social influences
        - Motivation to comply (with social influence)

- Perception of health status
  - Health beliefs
- Perception of environmental factors
  - Beliefs about incentives/barriers for health behaviour

- Behavioural condition
  - Intention formation process
    - Health intention
  - Behavioural repertoire
  - Skills/behaviours
  - Behaviour change/maintenance
    - Health behaviours

- Feedback

Brief Summary

The Systems Model of Health Behaviour Change integrates social, environmental, psychological and physiological factors into a theoretical account of the health behaviour change process (and its antecedents), with a view to providing a framework for the development of health education curricula.

Description

The Systems Model of Health Behaviour Change recognises that behaviour change depends on multiple factors and integrates social, environmental, psychological and physiological factors into a theory of health behaviour change. It aims to be applicable to the prevention, cessation or maintenance of health-related behaviours, although for different circumstances (e.g. adoption of health-promoting behaviours versus cessation of health-damaging behaviours) different aspects of the model are particularly relevant. Processes for behaviour change are presented across four levels lying along a proximal-distal continuum of behaviour change processes. The levels are **external antecedent condition, personal antecedent condition, socio-psychological condition** and **behavioural condition**. The behaviour change processes that arise in each level feed into the next most proximal level.

External Antecedent Condition

The initial level of the model comprises 'external antecedent conditions', which involve two processes: the **parental and hereditary/genetic process** and the **socio-cultural environmental milieu**. The 'parental and hereditary/genetic process' encompasses three sets of factors: a person's **birthdate, sex and basic psychological makeup**, a person's **family structure** (e.g. size and composition of family) and factors related to a person's **physiological makeup** (e.g. cardiovascular and musculoskeletal function). The 'socio-cultural environmental milieu' includes **health environmental factors** (e.g. pollution) and **social cultural influences** (e.g. social norms of the general population, the healthcare system).

Personal Antecedent Condition

The behaviour change processes within the 'personal antecedent condition' level arise from the processes in the previous level, and include **personal demographic dynamics, personal socialization process** and **personal health dynamics**. The 'personal demographic dynamics' process is influenced by a person's birthdate, sex and basic psychological make-up, and determines **personal demographic characteristics** such as educational achievement, occupation, income and geographic location. The 'personal socialisation process' is influenced by a person's family structure and by socio-cultural influences. This process teaches people their role within the family and within society, resulting in **social influences** on behaviour such as peer pressure and parental modelling. The 'personal health dynamics' process is influenced by the 'socio-cultural environmental milieu', a person's physiological make-up and a person's actual **health behaviours** (e.g. smoking), and determines **health status**.

Socio-Psychological Condition

The behaviour-change processes that arise in the 'socio-psychological condition' level are: **perception of the self, perception of social influences, perception of health status, and perception of environmental factors.** The 'perception of the self' process is influenced by personal demographic dynamics, a person's perception of social influences and feedback from their **behavioural repertoire**. The 'perception of the self' process encompasses the development self-concept, self-image, personal values and personality, and determines attitudinal variables such as their attitudes, values, self-concept, self-esteem, motivation and self-efficacy.

The 'perception of social influences' process is influenced by social influences, a person's perception of self, and a person's perception of their health status. A person's perception of social influences determines their **motivation to comply with social influences**.

The 'perception of their health status' process is influenced by a person's objective health status and their perceptions of social influences and environmental factors. This process results in a person's **health beliefs** about their susceptibility and vulnerability to a variety of potential health problems.

The 'perception of environmental factors' process is influenced by health environmental factors and a person's perception of their health status. This process determines people's **beliefs about the incentives or barriers for health behaviour** (e.g. availability of programs).

Behavioural Condition

At the final level, attitudinal and belief variables that arise from the 'socio-psychological condition' level processes influence the **intention formation process** which results in a **health intention**. Depending upon whether a person's **behavioural repertoire** includes **skills or behaviours** to change, their health intentions may or may not lead to **behaviour change or maintenance**.

Feedback

Additionally, a **feedback** loop is involved in the behaviour change process, whereby behaviour change or maintenance influences the behavioural repertoire, 'personal health dynamics' and the 'socio-cultural environmental milieu'.

A diagram of the Systems Model of Health Behaviour Change can be found on p.122 of Kersell & Milsum (1985).

Contributing Theories:

None of the theories included within this book were identified as contributing to the development of Systems Model of Health Behaviour Change.

Taken from:

Kersell, M.W. & Milsum, J.H. (1985). A systems model of health behaviour change. *Behavioural Science*, 30, 119-126.

73. Technology Acceptance Model 1, 2 & 3 (Davis; Venkatesh & Davis; Venkatesh & Bala)

Constructs

- Perceived usefulness
- Perceived ease of use
- Intention
- Usage (behaviour)
- Subjective norm
    - o   Internalisation
    - o   Identification
- Image
- Voluntariness
    - o   Compliance
- Job relevance
- Output quality
- Result demonstrability
- Experience
- Anchors
    - o   Computer self-efficacy
    - o   Perceptions of external control
    - o   Computer anxiety
    - o   Computer playfulness
- Adjustments
    - o   Perceived enjoyment
    - o   Objective usability

Brief Summary

The Technology Acceptance Model describes the factors that influence the acceptance and usage of technology, and the mechanisms underlying these influences. Central to the model is the proposal that technology acceptance/usage is primarily determined by two factors: perceptions of 'ease of use', and perceptions of usefulness.

Description

The Technology Acceptance Model seeks to explain the acceptance and usage of information technology and stems from the Theory of Reasoned Action which states that behaviour is primarily determined by intentions to carry out that behaviour, which is in turn determined by the subjective norm regarding the behaviour and attitudes towards the behaviour. In its original formulation, the Technology Acceptance Model replaces the distal determinants in the Theory of Reasoned Action with two variables which deal specifically with technology acceptance, 'ease of use' and 'usefulness'. Since the original proposal of the model, two expansions of the model have been proposed which add further constructs (and relationships between constructs) to the model.

Original Model

Intentions to use a technology (and subsequently actual usage **behaviour**) are determined by two variables: **perceived ease of use** and **perceived usefulness**. 'Perceived ease of use' is defined as a person's beliefs about the level of effort required to use the technology, whilst 'perceived usefulness' is defined as a person's beliefs about whether or not using the technology will enhance their performance. Perceived ease of use is an antecedent to perceived usefulness (i.e. the two variables are not parallel determinants of intentions), as it is necessary to see a technology as easy to use to perceive it as useful.

The Second Version of the Technology Acceptance Model

This introduces a number of additional social and cognitive constructs that influence usage of information technology (i.e. behaviour), perceived ease of use and perceived usefulness. There are three distinct social influences on the acceptance (or rejection) of a technology: **subjective norm**, **voluntariness** and **image**. 'Image' is the degree to which a person perceives that use of a technology enhances one's status among one's social group, and influences. Image has a positive influence on the perceived usefulness of a technology. Subjective norm is a person's perception of important others' beliefs about whether they should or should not perform the behaviour, and has a direct positive influence on behaviour, perceived usefulness and image.

Voluntariness, defined as the extent to which a person perceives that the usage of a technology is mandatory, moderates the influence of subjective norms upon intentions. Subjective norms have a direct influence upon intentions when a behaviour is perceived to be mandatory, and no effect upon intentions when a behaviour is perceived to be voluntary. Subjective norms can influence intentions indirectly through three other mechanisms: **compliance**, (when a behaviour is performed in order to achieve a goal or avoid a punishment), **internalisation** (incorporation of important others' belief about the behaviour into one's own belief system) and **identification** (a person believes that performing a behaviour will elevate their social status). Subjective norms influence perceived usefulness through the internalisation mechanism, and image through the identification mechanism.

There are four distinct cognitive instrumental determinants of perceived usefulness: **job relevance**, **output quality**, **result demonstrability** and **perceived ease of use** (retained from the original model). 'Job relevance' is defined as a person's perception of how applicable a technology is to their job. 'Output quality' refers to perceptions of how well a technology performs job-relevant tasks. 'Result demonstrability' is defined as the extent to which the results of using the technology are tangible, allowing for the attribution of improved job performance to technology use. According to the model, people's judgements about the perceived usefulness of a technology are based upon cognitive comparisons between what a technology does and what they need to do in their job. These four cognitive constructs have a direct, positive influence upon perceived usefulness.

Experience moderates the influence of subjective norms on intentions and perceived usefulness. As people become more experienced with a new system the effect of subjective norms on intentions is weakened.

The Third Version of the Technology Acceptance Model

This retains the structure and constructs of the second version but adds predictors of 'perceived ease of use'. Perceptions of ease of use are based on **anchors**, defined as people's general beliefs about technology and technology use. These anchors are **computer self-efficacy** (a person's perception of whether they are capable of performing a task using the technology), **computer anxiety** (the level of apprehension or fear felt when faced with the possibility of using technology), **computer playfulness** (the level of cognitive spontaneity in interactions with technology) and **perceptions of external control** (beliefs about whether external resources are available to support technology usage). The first three anchors are individual differences, whilst the latter is a factor that facilitates behaviour.

Once a person has had experience with a new technology, **adjustments** further influence perceptions of ease of use. Two adjustments are proposed: **perceived enjoyment** (the extent to which using the technology is perceived as enjoyable in its own right, regardless of job performance consequences) and **objective usability** (a comparison of technologies based on the actual [as opposed to perceived] amount of effort needed to perform a task). Experience in using a technology determines the level of influence that the determinants of perceived ease of use have. For instance, with increasing experience of the system, self-efficacy and perceptions of external control will maintain a strong influence on perceptions of ease of use. In contrast, the influences of computer playfulness and computer anxiety will weaken with increasing experience. In addition, greater experience will strengthen the effects of perceived enjoyment and objective usability upon perceived ease of use. Experience also moderates the influence of perceived ease of use upon perceived usefulness (with the influence becoming stronger as experience increases), the influence of computer anxiety on perceived ease of use (with the influence becoming weaker at greater levels of experience) and the influence of perceived ease of use upon intentions to use (with the influence becoming weaker as experience increases).

The antecedents of perceived ease of use do not affect perceived usefulness, and the antecedents of perceived usefulness do not influence perceived ease of use.

Diagrams of the second and third versions of the Technology Acceptance Model can be found on p.188 of Venkatesh & Davis (2000) and p.280 of Venkatesh & Bala (2008), respectively.

Contributing Theories:

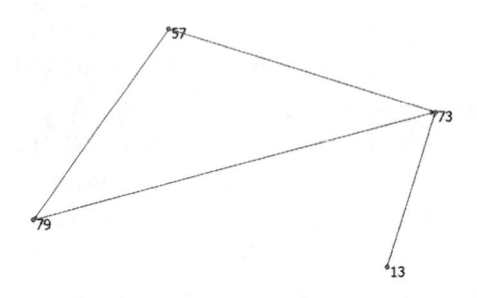

As outlined in the network diagram, the following theories included within this book were identified as contributing to the development of the Technology Acceptance Model:

13. Diffusion of Innovations

57. Self-Efficacy Theory

79. Theory of Planned Behaviour

Taken from:

Davis, F.D. (1989). Perceived Usefulness, Perceived Ease of Use, and User Acceptance of Information Technology. *MIS Quarterly*, 13(3), 319-340.

Venkatesh, V. & Davis, F. D. (2000). A Theoretical Extension of the Technology Acceptance Model: Four Longitudinal Field Studies. *Management Science*, 46(2), 186–204.

Venkatesh, V. & Bala, H. (2008). Technology Acceptance Model 3 and a Research Agenda on Interventions. *Decision Sciences*, 39(2), 273–315.

74. Temporal Self-Regulation Theory (Hall & Fong)

Constructs

- Motivational sphere
    - o Connectedness beliefs
    - o Temporal valuations
        - □ Value
        - □ Perceived temporal proximity
    - o Intentions
- Ambient temporal contingencies
    - o Behavioural pre-potency
    - o Self-regulatory capacity
        - □ Self-efficacy
    - o Observed behaviour

Brief Summary

Temporal Self-Regulation Theory is a framework for understanding human behaviour that can be viewed as irrational. The model emphasises the role of the temporal proximity and value of anticipated benefits, and the costs and outcomes of behaviours, in influencing whether behaviour is determined by rational decision-making processes or by self-regulatory ability and/or behavioural pre-potency (i.e. likelihood the behaviour will be performed).

Description

Temporal Self-Regulation Theory aims to provide an explanation for maladaptive or 'self-defeating' health-related behaviours. The capacity to perform a behaviour is seen as the result of a complex interaction between biological, cognitive and social factors. Determinants of behaviour are organised into two categories: those in the **motivational sphere** and those relating to **ambient temporal contingencies**.

Motivational Sphere

Motivation (behavioural intentions) to carry out a specific behaviour is a function of two main factors: **connectedness beliefs** and **temporal valuations**. 'Connectedness beliefs' are defined as beliefs about the connectedness of the behaviour to later outcomes, or perceptions of the likelihood of expected outcomes of the behaviour. 'Temporal valuations' are the values attached to certain outcomes, and incorporate the temporal distribution of outcomes. For instance, the benefits of stopping drinking alcohol may be apparent almost immediately, whilst the benefits of exercising once a week may not be realised until weeks or months later. Therefore, temporal valuations are a function of not only the **value** attached to an outcome, but also the **perceived temporal proximity** of the outcome (the greater the proximity, the higher the valuation).

Ambient Temporal Contingencies (Social and Physical Environment)

Variations in the strength of the relationship between **intentions** and **observed behaviour** occur as a result of the moderating influence of two factors: **behavioural pre-potency** and **self-regulatory capacity**. Behavioural pre-potency is defined as a reflection of the frequency of past performance of the behaviour and/or the presence of internal drive states or environmental cues to action. Thus, behavioural pre-potency refers to the likelihood that a behaviour will be performed. Self-regulatory capacity is defined as any state- or trait-like factors that influence a person's ability to make efforts to regulate their behaviour (e.g. energy levels, executive functioning).

The amount of influence these moderating factors have upon behaviour is dependent upon 'ambient temporal contingencies' (i.e. the costs and benefits of a specific behaviour, and their level of immediacy, in a given context). Their influence grows stronger when the temporal disjunction between positive and negative contingencies grows greater (e.g. when benefits are much more immediate than costs). Behavioural pre-potency and self-regulatory capacity also have direct effects upon behaviour. For instance, if past performance of the behaviour has been frequent and there are cues to the behaviour in the environment, the behaviour is likely to occur even if intentions are not present (i.e. habitual behaviour). Low self-regulatory capacity can have a direct influence on the likelihood of behaviours in the absence of any related intentions, depending upon immediate contingencies.

In cases where there is no temporal disjunction between costs and benefits (i.e. the immediacy of both is equal), self-regulatory capacity and behavioural pre-potency would have zero moderating influence upon the intention-behaviour relationship. Thus, behaviour in cases such as this is determined solely by the influence of connectedness beliefs and temporal valuations upon intentions.

Behaviour can, in turn, modify connectedness beliefs, temporal valuations, self-regulatory capacity and behavioural pre-potency via feedback loops. For example, those who experience positive outcomes may come to believe that the maintenance of a behaviour is worth it (change their temporal valuation), so that when they consider performing the behaviour in the future, intentions are strengthened. **Self-efficacy** is a person's perception of their likelihood of successful self-regulation in the future, based upon past experience. Thus, self-efficacy is represented in the feedback loop from behaviour to self-regulatory capacity, and by the direct and moderating influences of self-regulatory capacity upon behaviour.

A diagram of Temporal Self-Regulation Theory can be found on p.14 of Hall & Fong (2007).

Contributing Theories:

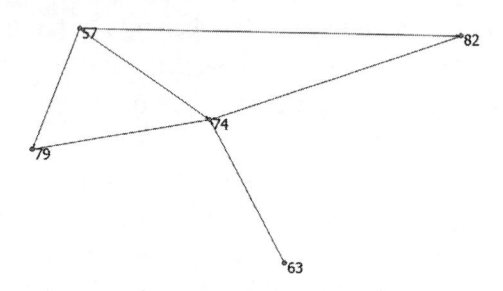

As outlined in the network diagram, the following theories included within this book were identified as contributing to the development of the Temporal Self-Regulation Theory:

57. Self-Efficacy Theory

63. Social Cognitive Theory

79. Theory of Planned Behaviour

82. Transtheoretical Model of Behaviour Change

Taken from:

Hall, P.A. & Fong, G.T. (2007). Temporal self-regulation theory: A model for individual health behaviour. *Health Psychology Review*, 1(1), 6-52.

75. Terror Management Theory (Greenberg et al.)

Constructs

- Terror/anxiety
- Need for self-esteem
- Cultural worldview/cultural drama
    o Self-esteem
        ☐ Faith in the cultural drama
        ☐ Sense of value within the cultural drama
- Social behaviour

Brief Summary

Terror Management Theory aims to explain why humans have a need for self-esteem and how that need influences their behaviour. Self-esteem acts as a buffer against our inherent terror of inevitable mortality. The majority of social behaviour is aimed towards maintaining individual self-esteem.

Description

Terror Management Theory is built around the idea that people's behaviour is influenced by their need for **self-esteem**. People's constant **need for self-esteem** leads them to behave in a manner that allows them to maintain their personal sense of value.

The human capacity for symbolic, temporal and self-reflective thought provides people with the ability to question their existence and causes them to become aware of their own inevitable mortality. If incapable of suppressing thoughts of their own death or of the futility of existence, humans would be constantly paralysed by **terror** or **anxiety**. Humans have defended themselves from this terror by developing **cultural worldviews** (also referred to as

cultural dramas) that impart a sense of meaning, predictability and immortality to life.

The cultural worldview within which a person exists forms the basis for their self-esteem. People have a constant need for self-esteem that influences their behaviour. Humans learn during childhood development that being 'good' leads to warmth and care from their parents and being 'bad' leads to potential loss of care and protection, and possible 'annihilation' by parents. As a result, a positive self-concept becomes associated with feelings of security and a negative self-concept becomes associated with feelings of existential terror and anxiety. Thus, people must behave in ways that allow them to believe that they are valuable (i.e. have self-esteem) to minimise feelings of terror and anxiety. As people develop into adults, their self-esteem is no longer generated by being valued by their parents but rather by being valued by the culture in which they exist.

There are two essential components of self-esteem: having **faith in the cultural drama/worldview** and having a **sense of value within the cultural drama**. Self-esteem is threatened by events that threaten the validity of people's cultural worldview, or that suggest shortcomings. Thus a large proportion of people's **social behaviour** is directed towards protection of their self-esteem by sustaining faith in the cultural drama and maintaining their sense of value within the cultural drama.

The existence of an 'out-group' with an alternate cultural worldview can threaten a person, as this threatens the validity of their own worldview. They may therefore defend themselves against threats to the validity of their cultural worldview by displaying negative attitudes and behaviours towards 'out-group' members. People may strive to maintain a sense of personal value within the cultural drama by behaving in ways that fulfil the roles expected of them by their culture, and may protect their sense of value against threat through self-presentation (i.e. trying to maintain a public image of being a 'good' or valuable person according to the cultural worldview).

Contributing Theories:

None of the theories included within this book were identified as contributing to the development of Terror Management Theory.

Taken from:

Greenberg, J., Pyszczynski, T. & Solomon, S. (1986). The Cause and Consequences of a Need for Self-Esteem: A Terror Management Theory. In R.F. Baumeister (Ed.), *Public Self and Private Self* (pp. 189-212). SpringerLink.

76. Terror Management Health Model (Goldenberg & Arndt)

Constructs

- Health-related scenarios or threats
- Conscious death thought activation
- Non-conscious death thought activation
- Moderating variables related to death/health threat
- Threat-avoidance outcomes
- Health behaviour-oriented outcomes
- Relevance of behaviour for meaning and self-esteem
- Relevance of behaviour for threat of creatureliness
- Health-defeating outcomes
- Health-facilitating outcomes
- Avoidance of body-oriented health behaviour

Brief Summary

The Terror Management Health Model postulates that conscious and non-conscious thoughts about mortality play an important role in determining the factors that motivate decisions about health and health behaviour.

Description

The Terror Management Health Model integrates Terror Management Theory with several behaviour change models including the Health Belief Model and the Theory of Reasoned Action. The model brings together health-related and self-oriented motivations to explain health behaviour. Central to the model is the idea that conscious and non-conscious thought about death influence the types of motivation that influence health-related decisions and behaviours.

Terror Management Theory predicts that when people are reminded of their own mortality they aim to reduce their anxiety. They can do this through proximal responses such as repressing death-related thoughts or through distal responses such as distancing themselves from the anxious thoughts. Belief in an afterlife is an example of the latter.

In the context of **health-related scenarios or threats**, people become aware of their mortality by experiencing either **conscious death thought activation** or **non-conscious death thought activation**. If conscious thoughts of death are activated, people will be motivated to remove them due to the high anxiety they cause. Removal of concerns about death may be achieved by either threat avoidance (e.g. suppression of death-related thoughts) or through health-related behaviour (e.g. stopping smoking). If either of these responses is successful, this reduces the need for the alternate response (e.g. thought suppression is successful, so health behaviours are not modified). **Moderating variables** relevant to the association between death and the health threat determine which one of these responses occurs. An example is efficacy beliefs (i.e. beliefs about one's ability to carry out a behaviour, and the effectiveness of that behaviour in achieving the desired outcome) related to potential coping behaviours.

However, if a health threat or health-related scenario triggers non-conscious death thoughts, health-related decisions are based on the relevance of health behaviours to a person's **self-esteem** and sense of **meaning**. The outcome may be either **health-defeating** or **health-facilitating**, depending upon how the behaviour might impact a person's self-esteem and worldview. The behavioural outcome is additionally influenced by the 'threat **of creatureliness**' presented by the behaviour, and a person's sensitivity to such a threat. 'Creatureliness' is defined as 'a reminder of physicality' and has the potential to undermine symbolic defences (such as a belief in an afterlife, as creatureliness reminds people that they are mortal animals). If people are sensitive to threats of creatureliness, they may **avoid body-oriented health behaviours** to prevent discomfort.

The Terror Management Health Model

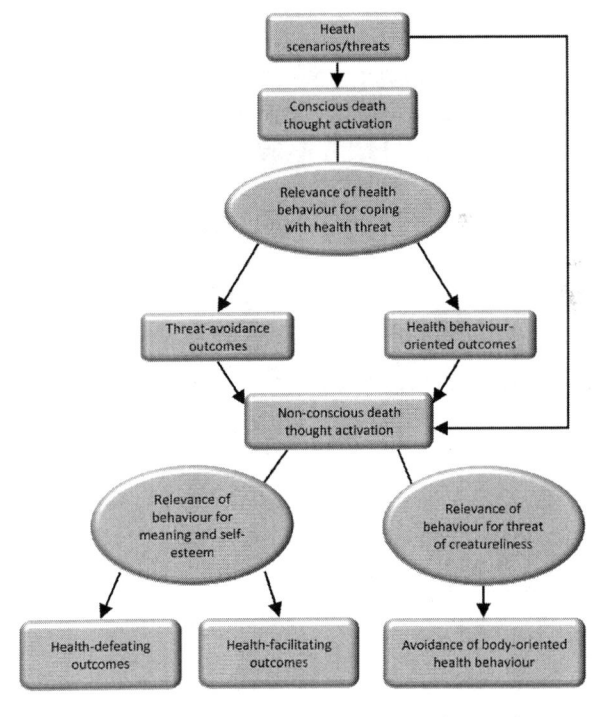

```
Heath scenarios/threats
        ↓
Conscious death thought activation
        ↓
Relevance of health behaviour for coping with health threat
        ↓                    ↓
Threat-avoidance        Health behaviour-
outcomes                oriented outcomes
        ↓                    ↓
Non-conscious death thought activation
        ↓                    ↓
Relevance of            Relevance of
behaviour for           behaviour for threat
meaning and self-       of creatureliness
esteem
    ↓       ↓               ↓
Health-defeating  Health-facilitating  Avoidance of body-oriented
outcomes          outcomes             health behaviour
```

Source: Goldenberg, J.L., & Arndt, J. (2008). The implications of death for health: A terror management health model for behavioural health promotion. *Psychological Review*, 115, 1032-1053. Originally published by APA and reprinted here with permission.

Contributing Theories:

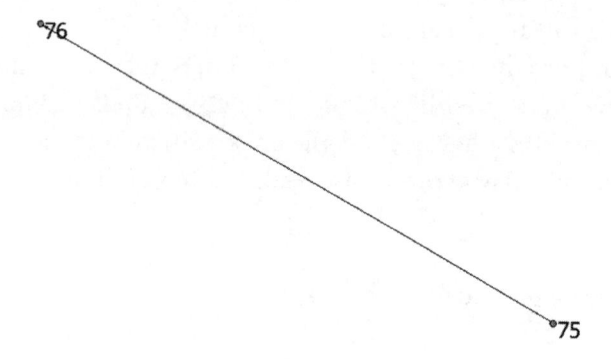

•76
•75

As outlined in the network diagram, the following theory included within this book was identified as contributing to the development of the Terror Management Health Model:

75. Terror Management Theory

Taken from:

Goldenberg, J.L., & Arndt, J. (2008). The implications of death for health: A terror management health model for behavioural health promotion. *Psychological Review*, 115, 1032-1053.

77. Theory of Interpersonal Behaviour (Triandis)

Constructs

- Acts
- Goals
- Behavioural intentions
    - Specific
    - General
- Self-image
- Affect
- Perceived consequences
- Value of the consequences
- Habit
- Facilitating conditions
- Social factors
    - Norms
    - Roles
    - General behavioural intentions
    - Rules of behaviour
    - Contractual arrangements
    - Self-monitoring
    - Self-concept
- Cues associated with the behaviour
- Affect associated with the behaviour

Brief Summary

The Theory of Interpersonal Behaviour aims to explain and predict the likelihood of people engaging in social behaviours or 'acts'. According to the theory, the probability of a behaviour being carried out is determined primarily by habit strength, behavioural intentions and the presence of facilitative conditions.

Description

The Theory of Interpersonal Behaviour aims to explain and predict the likelihood of people engaging in social behaviours or 'acts'. Acts are combinations of physical movements that are socially recognised as actions or behaviours. Acts vary in many ways, such as how commonly they occur, how long they last, their intensity and their probability of occurring. Acts are generally combined into patterns which represent **goals** and **behavioural intentions**. A goal is the outcome of a combination or sequence of a number of acts, whereas a behavioural intention is the thought process which is the direct antecedent of an act. Behavioural intentions can be reflective of **general** intentions (e.g. to show concern) or specific intentions that correspond directly to acts (e.g. to call a friend).

To explain and predict the likelihood of people engaging in acts, the theory is divided into two components. The first describes the factors or combinations of factors that determine the likelihood of an act being carried out. The second describes the factors that determine behavioural intentions.

Determinants of the Probability of an Act

The probability of an act being carried out is determined by three factors: (1) strength of **habit** for carrying out the act (reflected by the number of times a person has previously performed that act), (2) strength of behavioural intention to carry out the act and (3) whether or not **conditions that facilitate** performance of the act are present. Each of these factors may be more strongly predictive of some acts than they are of others, more strongly predictive for some people than for others and/or more strongly predictive in some circumstances than in others.

The probability of an act being carried out is proportional to the strength of habit and to the strength of intention. It can be determined by multiplying the sum of 'habit' and 'intention' by a person's ability to carry out the act. Thus, habit strength and intention strength are irrelevant if someone does not have the ability to carry out the act: in such cases the probability of an act would be nil. The weighting of the influences of habits and intentions upon the probability of an act (i.e. how strongly predictive they are in a specific circumstance, in a specific individual, etc.) reflect the extent to which an act is deliberate or automatic. Individual arousal also affects the probability of an act. When a person is highly aroused (e.g. in situations of threat, anxiety or uncertainty), the performance of behaviours that are determined by habit improves whilst the performance of novel behaviours (i.e. determined by intentions) deteriorates. Thus, the relative weighting of habits and intentions can vary from moment to moment.

Determinants of Behavioural Intentions

Behavioural intentions are a function of **social factors.** Social factors include the norms, roles and general behavioural intentions that are generated from interpersonal relationships. Social factors also include **rules of behaviour**, **contractual arrangements**, **self-monitoring** and **self-concept**. Rules of behaviour determine how a person behaves in specific social situations (e.g. introductions, parties, weddings). 'Contractual arrangements' are specific arrangements made between individuals (e.g. to meet in a specific location at a specific time). Contractual arrangements can become goals, which then guide a series of behavioural intentions. Self-monitoring is a process involving self-observation and self-control, to maintain situation-appropriate behaviour. It is guided by situational cues. Finally, self-concept refers to the traits and behaviours that a person attributes to themselves (i.e. the 'type' of person they think they are). People are most likely to adopt behavioural intentions that are in line with their self-concept. The model does not state how these factors combine to form social factors. It is hypothesised that they have an additive relationship with social factors, but the authors emphasise that further research is needed.

In addition to social factors, behavioural intentions are also a function of a person's **affect** associated with the behaviour. Affect refers to the positive or negative emotions felt by a person when thinking about a behaviour. These affects develop because **cues associated with the behaviour** (including cognitive representations of that behaviour, or intentions) become associated with pleasant or unpleasant outcomes.

Finally, behavioural intentions are a function of the **value of the perceived consequences**. 'Perceived consequences' are a person's subjective perceptions of the consequences that are likely to arise from a behaviour. Accordingly, the **value of the perceived consequences** refers to a person's positive or negative feelings about the consequences of a behaviour is generated by the frequency with which a behaviour leads to certain consequences, and the value of those consequences. The more frequently a behaviour and consequence co-occur, the stronger the link between them. The value of the perceived consequences is the sum of the subjective probability that a particular behaviour will lead to a particular consequence and the value of that consequence.

In total, behavioural intentions are a function of social factors, affect associated with the behaviour, and the value of the perceived consequences. The relative weightings of each of these determine the extent to which they affect the formation of behavioural intentions.

Contributing Theories:

None of the theories included within this book were identified as contributing to the development of the Theory of Interpersonal Behaviour.

Taken from:

Triandis, H.C. (1977). Interpersonal behaviour. Monterey, CA, US: Brooks/Cole Publishing Company.

78. Theory of Normative Social Behaviour (Rimal & Real)

Constructs

- Descriptive norms
- Behaviour
- Normative mechanisms
    - o Injunctive norms
        - ☐ Social approval
    - o Outcome expectations
        - ☐ Benefits to oneself
        - ☐ Benefits to others
        - ☐ Anticipatory socialization
    - o Group identity
        - ☐ Similarity
        - ☐ Aspiration

Brief Summary

The Theory of Normative Social Behaviour aims to provide a theoretical account of the mechanisms by which normative beliefs influence behaviour, developed with a specific focus upon alcohol consumption. It proposes that normative beliefs influence behaviour through the mechanisms of social approval, group identity and beliefs about the benefits of the behaviour.

Description

The Theory of Normative Social Behaviour provides an explanation of the mechanisms by which normative beliefs (i.e. perceptions of the prevalence of a behaviour and beliefs about whether a behaviour is considered socially acceptable by important others) influence alcohol consumption **behaviour** (particularly in college/university students). The theory distinguishes between two types of norms: **descriptive norms** and **injunctive norms**. Descriptive norms refer to beliefs about the prevalence of a behaviour (e.g. beliefs about how much alcohol university students drink), whilst injunctive norms refer to people's perceptions of what important others expect them to do or approve of. Injunctive norms are a function of perceptions about **social approval**.

Other normative beliefs include **outcome expectations** and **group identity**. There are three types of outcome expectations: **benefits to oneself** (beliefs about whether engaging in the behaviour will be beneficial), **benefits to others** (beliefs about whether others engaging in the behaviour would benefit from doing so) and **anticipatory socialisation** (beliefs that alcohol is a social lubricant). Group identity has two components: how much **similarity** a person feels they have to a certain group and a person's **aspirations** to emulate others in a group.

Descriptive norms have a direct influence on behaviour. However, the strength of that influence is moderated by the other **normative mechanisms** of injunctive norms, outcome expectations and group identity. For example, the influence of descriptive norms upon alcohol consumption becomes stronger as pro-alcohol consumption injunctive norms/outcome expectations/group identity become greater.

A diagram of the Theory of Normative Social Behaviour can be found on p.392 of Rimal & Real (2005).

Contributing Theories:

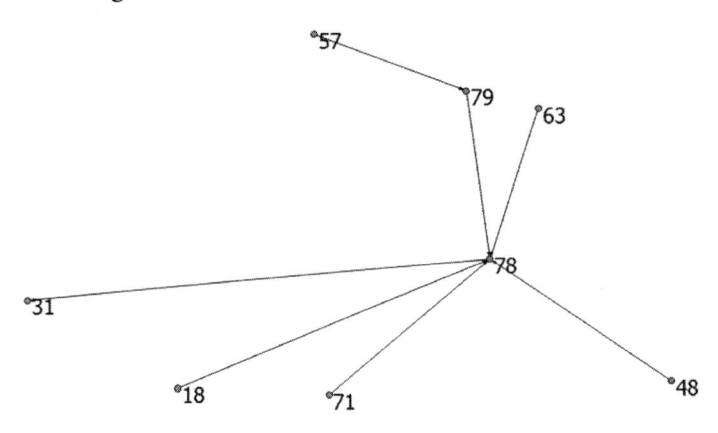

As outlined in the network diagram, the following theories included within this book were identified as contributing to the development of the Theory of Normative Social Behaviour:

18. Focus Theory of Normative Conduct

48. Prospect Theory

63. Social Cognitive Theory

71. Social Norms Theory

79. Theory of Planned Behaviour

Taken from:

Rimal, R.N. & Real, K. (2005). How Behaviours are Influenced by Perceived Norms: A Test of the Theory of Normative Social Behaviour. *Communication Research*, 32(3), 389-414.

79. Theory of Planned Behaviour (Ajzen)

Constructs

- Attitude
    - o Behavioural beliefs
- Subjective norms
    - o Normative beliefs
- Perceived behavioural control
    - o Control beliefs
- Intention
- Behaviour

Brief Summary

The Theory of Planned Behaviour is a model of purposeful human behaviour. Intentions are the direct precursors of behaviour and are, in turn, determined by attitudes towards the behaviour, subjective norms and perceived behavioural control. Attitudes are determined by behavioural beliefs, subjective norms by normative beliefs and perceived behavioural control by control beliefs.

Description

The Theory of Planned Behaviour is an extension of an earlier theory, the Theory of Reasoned Action. It was developed in order to improve the Theory of Reasoned Action's predictive power, as the earlier model was unable to account for behaviours not under volitional control. To accommodate this, 'perceived behavioural control' was added to the model. The key determinants of behaviour are attitudes, subjective norms, perceived behavioural control and behavioural intentions.

Attitude is defined as a person's attitude towards trying to perform the behaviour, and is seen to be a function of their **behavioural beliefs** (the degree to which the person has a favourable or unfavourable evaluation of the behaviour) relating to the possible outcomes of trying to perform the behaviour.

The **subjective norm** is defined as a person's perceptions of whether important others believe that they should perform the behaviour. Subjective norm is a function of **normative beliefs.** The earliest description of the model defined subjective norms as a function of perceptions of important others' approval of the behaviour, and perceptions of important others' beliefs that trying the behaviour will succeed. However, later descriptions of the model define subjective norms as a function of a person's perceptions of important others' approval of the behaviour and the person's motivation to comply with important others.

Perceived behavioural control is defined as the extent to which a person feels able to perform the behaviour. It is a function of **control beliefs**: beliefs about the presence or absence of factors that can either facilitate of impede performance.

Behavioural **intention** refers to the motivation to perform the behaviour, and encapsulates a person's willingness to try to perform a behaviour or how much effort they plan to put into performing the behaviour. **Behaviour** is a person's manifest, observable response in a given situation.

Intentions are directly determined by attitudes, subjective norm and perceived behavioural control. Whilst attitudes and subjective norms do not directly influence behaviour, perceived behavioural control and intentions are both direct determinants of behaviour.

A diagram of the Theory of Planned Behaviour can be found on p.182 of Ajzen (1991).

Contributing Theories:

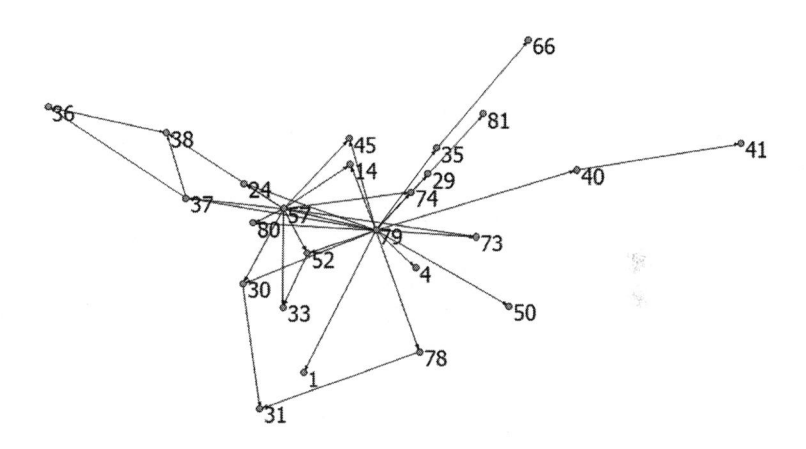

As outlined in the network diagram, the following theory included within this book was identified as contributing to the development of the Theory of Planned Behaviour:

57. Self-Efficacy Theory

Taken from:

Ajzen, I. (1985). From Intentions to Actions: A Theory of Planned Behaviour. In J. Kuhl & J. Beckman (Eds.). Action Control: From Cognition to Behaviour (pp. 11-39). Germany: Springer-Verlag.

Supplemented by:

Ajzen, I. (1991). The Theory of Planned Behaviour. *Organisational Behaviour and Human Decision Processes*, 50, 179-211.

80. Theory of Triadic Influence (Flay & Petraitis)

Constructs
- Streams of influence
    o Attitudinal influences
        □ Cultural environment
            • Health related knowledge
            • Health related values
            • Expectations about consequences
            • Evaluations of consequences
    o Social influences
        □ Immediate social context
            • Social learning
            • Social bonding
            • Perceived norms
            • Motivation to comply
    o Intrapersonal influences
        □ Biology/personality
            • Sense of self
            • Social competence
            • Skills
            • Self determination
- Attitudes
- Social normative beliefs
- Self-efficacy
- Tiers of influence
    o Ultimate causes
    o Social personal nexus
    o Expectancy-value
    o Cognitive
    o Decisions
- Experience
- Feedback
- Health-related behaviour

Brief Summary

The Theory of Triadic Influence is a synthesis of several micro-level theories of health behaviour in which three streams of influence (attitudinal, social and intrapersonal) flow through five levels of causation to explain health-related behaviour (ultimate causes, social personal nexus, expectancy-value, cognitive, decisions).

Description

The Theory of Triadic Influence outlines three '**streams of influence**' that are proposed to determine health-related cognitions and behaviour. These are **attitudinal influences**, **social influences** and **intrapersonal influences**. Attitudinal influences are seen to originate in a person's broader **cultural environment**, social influences in their **immediate social context** and intrapersonal in **biology and personality** factors. These influences may operate independently, additively or interactively.

Attitudinal Influences

Attitudinal influences arise from the provision of information by schools, mass media, religion and other people. People assimilate this information about health and health-related behaviour, which shapes their **health-related knowledge** and **health-related values**. These, together with **expectations about the consequences** of a health-related behaviour and **evaluations of the consequences**, shape **attitudes** to health-related behaviour which in turn contribute to decisions about engaging in health related behaviour.

Social Influences

A person's health-related behaviour and their perception of norms concerning various health-related behaviours may be influenced by the attitudes, values and behaviours of others with whom they share close **social bonds** through **social learning**. Together, **perceived norms** and the **motivation to comply** with others' beliefs determine a person's **social normative beliefs** (a sense of what is normal and socially acceptable), which in turn influence decisions about whether or not to adopt particular health-related behaviours.

Intrapersonal Influences

Intrapersonal influences originate both in an individual's biology and personality. Intrapersonal influences include a person's ability to control their behaviour, which has an impact on their **sense of self** and **social competence**. These influence a person's sense of **self-determination** and their health-related **skills**, which then shape their health-related **self-efficacy** (i.e. their sense that they have the skills and will to take charge of their health). People with a stronger sense of self-efficacy are more likely to decide to adopt behaviours that lead to health.

Tiers of Causes

Each stream of influence flows through five tiers before impacting on behaviour. The first and most important tier comprises the **ultimate causes** of behaviour: the sociocultural environment (attitudinal stream), the social setting (social stream) and biological/genetic and personality factors (intrapersonal stream). The second tier is termed the **social-personal nexus** tier, and is where knowledge/values, social bonding/learning and sense of self/social competence are formed. This flows down to the third tier (**expectancy-value** tier), where variables from the social-personal nexus tier are proposed to become specific to the health-behaviour in question (forming expectancies, evaluations, motivation to comply, perceived norms, self-determination and social skills). All the streams of influence then flow into the fourth tier (the **cognitive** tier), where attitudes, social normative beliefs and self-efficacy beliefs are formed. Together, these variables determine health related decisions/intentions in the fifth tier, termed the **decisions** tier.

Experience of engaging in the **health-related behaviour** will influence future behaviour via a process of **feedback**. For instance, behaviour that gains approval from others is more likely to be repeated.

A diagram of the Theory of Triadic Influence can be found on p.24 of Flay & Petraitis (1994).

ABC OF BEHAVIOUR CHANGE THEORIES

Contributing Theories:

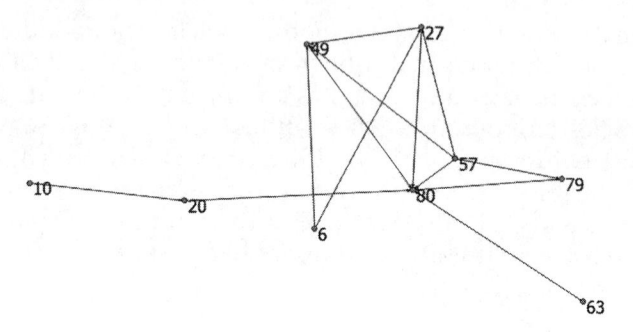

As outlined in the network diagram, the following theories included within this book were identified as contributing to the development of the Theory of Triadic Influence:

20. General Theory of Deviant Behaviour

27. Health Belief Model

49. Protection Motivation Theory

57. Self-Efficacy Theory

63. Social Cognitive Theory

79. Theory of Planned Behaviour

Taken from:

Flay, B.R. & Petraitis, J. (1994). The Theory of Triadic Influence: A New Theory of Health Behaviour with Implications for Preventive Interventions. *Advances in Medical Sociology*, 4, 19-44.

81. Transcontextual Model of Motivation (Hagger et al.)

Constructs

- Perceived autonomy support
- Autonomous motivation/locus of causality
    - External regulation
    - Introjected regulation
    - Identified regulation
    - Intrinsic motivation
- Attitudes
- Subjective norms
- Perceived behavioural control
- Intentions
- Behaviour

Brief Summary

The Transcontextual Model of Motivation provides a theoretical explanation of how perceived support for behavioural autonomy and motivational orientations in educational contexts can influence motivation and behaviour in other contexts.

Description

The Transcontextual Model of Motivation integrates Self-Determination Theory and the Theory of Planned Behaviour. It aims to explain the psychological processes involved in the influence of motivation and support for autonomy within educational contexts upon motivation and behaviour in extramural (i.e. outside education) contexts. The theory was originally developed to explain how motivational factors related to physical activity education determine motivational factors related to leisure-time activity and actual physical activity behaviour in young people. Later, it was extended to a more general focus on motivation in educational and extramural contexts.

Perceived autonomy support in the educational context (e.g. students' perceptions of how autonomy-supportive the motivational climate in their education context is) influences students' perceived **locus of causality (autonomous motivation)** in relation to behaviours carried out within an educational context. This 'locus of causality' is made up of **external regulation, introjected regulation, identified regulation** and **intrinsic motivation**, which represent points on a continuum of intrinsically to extrinsically determined behaviour. Intrinsically motivated behaviours are those that are engaged in for enjoyment or interest alone, with no external reinforcement or pressure. 'Identified regulation' refers to behaviours that are not necessarily enjoyed but are valued positively. 'Introjected regulation' refers to behaviours carried out because of a perceived external pressure to do so. Finally, externally regulated behaviours are those carried out because significant others force their enactment. An environment that is not autonomy-supportive (e.g. provision of controlling of performance-related feedback) is detrimental to intrinsic motivation.

The perceived loci of causality in an educational context has a strong influence on perceived **loci of causality** in extramural contexts (e.g. high intrinsic motivation in an education context will lead to high intrinsic motivation in an extramural context). The effect of perceived autonomy support in educational contexts upon locus of causality in extramural contexts can be fully explained by its influence on locus of causality in educational contexts. A more recent version of the model adds that **perceived autonomy support** in extramural contexts (e.g. perceptions of how autonomy-supportive parents and peers are) will influence the perceived locus of causality factors in the extramural context.

Perceived locus of causality factors in extramural contexts influences **intentions** to engage in the relevant behaviour. However, their influence on intentions is indirect and mediated by **attitudes** (beliefs about/evaluations of a behaviour), **subjective norms** (social pressure to engage in a behaviour from significant others) and **perceived behavioural control** (a person's beliefs about their ability to carry out a behaviour). Specifically, intrinsic motivation and identified regulation positively influence attitudes and perceived behavioural control, and external regulation and introjected regulation positively influence subjective norms. Intentions thus develop as a function of attitudes, subjective norms and perceived behavioural control, and are the primary determinant of **behaviour**.

The Transcontextual Model Applied to Physical Activity

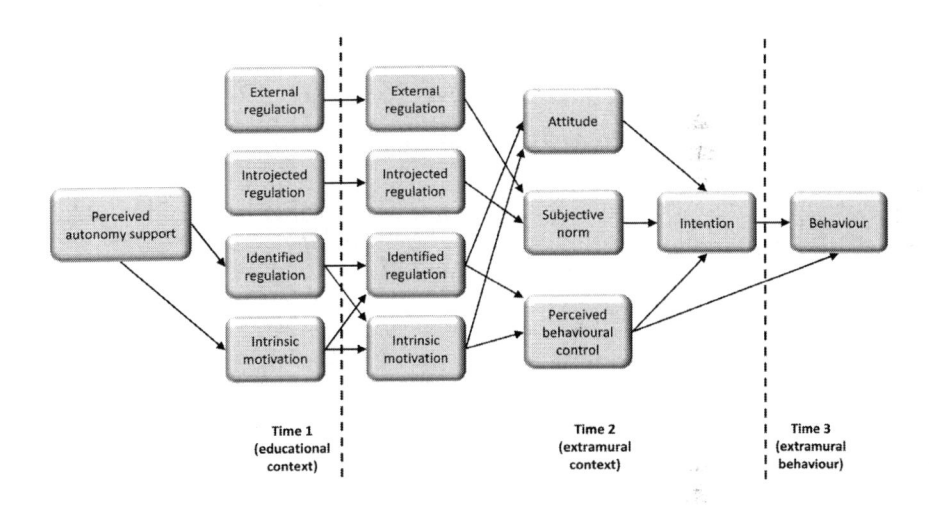

Source: Adapted from Hagger, M.S., Chatzisarantis, N.L.D., Culverhouse, T. & Biddle, S.J.H. (2003). The Processes by Which Perceived Autonomy Support in Physical Education Promotes Leisure-Time Physical Activity Intentions and Behaviour: A Trans-Contextual Model. *Journal of Educational Psychology*, 95(4), 784-795. Originally published by APA and reprinted here with permission.

Contributing Theories:

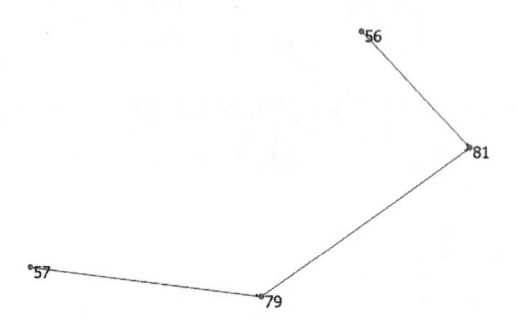

•56
•81
•57
•79

As outlined in the network diagram, the following theories included within this book were identified as contributing to the development of the Technology Acceptance Model:

56. Self-Determination Theory

79. Theory of Planned Behaviour

Taken from:

Hagger, M.S., Chatzisarantis, N.L.D., Culverhouse, T. & Biddle, S.J.H. (2003). The Processes by Which Perceived Autonomy Support in Physical Education Promotes Leisure-Time Physical Activity Intentions and Behaviour: A Trans-Contextual Model. *Journal of Educational Psychology*, 95(4), 784-795.

Supplemented by:

Hagger, M.S. & Chatzisarantis, N.L.D. (2007). The Trans-Contextual Model of Motivation. In M.S. Hagger & N.L.D. Chatzisarantis (Eds.), *Intrinsic Motivation and Self-Determination in Exercise and Sport* (pp. 53-70). Leeds, UK: Human Kinetics Europe Ltd.

Hagger, M.S. & Chatzisarantis, N.L.D. (2012). Transferring motivation from educational to extramural contexts: a review of the trans-contextual model. *European Journal of Psychology and Education*, 27, 195-212.

82. Transtheoretical Model of Behaviour Change (Prochaska & DiClemente)

Constructs

- Stages of Change
  - o Precontemplation
  - o Contemplation
  - o Preparation
  - o Action
  - o Maintenance
- Processes of Change
  - o Consciousness raising
  - o Dramatic relief
  - o Self-reevaluation
  - o Environmental reevaluation
  - o Social liberation
  - o Self-liberation
  - o Stimulus control
  - o Helping relationships
  - o Counter conditioning
  - o Reinforcement management
- Decisional balance
- Self-efficacy
- Temptation

Brief Summary

The Transtheoretical Model proposes that behaviour change occurs in five sequential stages from precontemplation (not planning to change within the next 6 months), contemplations (thinking about changing within 6 months but within the next month), preparation (taking steps towards changing within the next month), action (attempting the change), and maintenance (having changed for at least 6 months). It identifies processes of change that lead to transition between the stages and proposes different processes linked to different stage transitions.

Description

Stages of Change

Behaviour change involves progress in five sequential stages of motivation/readiness to change: **precontemplation**, **contemplation**, **preparation**, **action** and **maintenance**. Whilst the model states that progress through the stages is sequential (i.e. stages are not skipped), moving backward to a previous stage is possible.

- **Precontemplation:** People in this stage are not seriously considering behaviour change in the foreseeable future (i.e., within the next six months and may be unaware of any need to change. Alternatively, they may be aware but be unwilling to think about change, be defensive or resistant to pressures to change or lack confidence in their ability to change.

- **Contemplation:** People in this stage are aware that there is a problem and are seriously considering behaviour change within the next six months but are not yet committed to act. They are more responsive to information and feedback about their behaviour than those in the previous stage. However, people may be ambivalent about the costs and benefits of change and may remain in this stage for a long time (years).

- **Preparation:** People in this stage are ready for action and seriously intend to change within the next month. They have already taken some preparatory action such as making reductions to a problem behaviour or 'trying' novel healthy behaviours (for example, reducing the number of cigarettes smoked per day). They have typically made unsuccessful behaviour change attempts in the previous 12 months and behaviour change does not reach the level of effective (i.e. health-promoting) action.

- **Action:** People in this stage have made significant overt effort to change their behaviours and have met a behaviour-specific criterion (e.g. not smoking for 24 hours or more). This stage lasts around six months before progression to the next.

- **Maintenance:** People in this stage have been able to sustain behaviour change for more than six months and are working to prevent relapse. They are typically more confident that they will continue and maintain health behaviour change and less likely to relapse than people in the action stage.

Spiral Pattern of Change

Progress through these stages may not be linear because most people relapse and do not achieve their aims on the first attempt. Most people are likely to progress through the stages up to action and relapse, regressing to precontemplation, contemplation or preparation. However, in order not to regress to an earlier stage, people need to learn from their experiences before they can progress through the stages again.

Processes of Change

There are ten 'processes of change' that facilitate or stimulate movement from stage to stage. Different processes are important in facilitating movement between different stages, with experiential processes being used more in the contemplation and preparation stages and behavioural processes being used more in the action and maintenance stages. These processes are:

- **Consciousness raising.** Increasing awareness about the problem and improving the accuracy of information processing about the problem and about the self (e.g. seeking information, observations, interpretations). This process is a mediator between the precontemplation stage and the contemplation stage.

- **Dramatic relief.** Experiencing and releasing feelings about the problem and the solution (e.g. expressing and feeling upset at risk information). This process is a mediator between the precontemplation stage and the contemplation stage.

- **Environmental reevaluation.** Cognitive and affective assessments of how a personal behaviour might have an impact on the social environment (e.g. thinking the world would be a better place if everyone stopped smoking). This process is a mediator between the precontemplation and the contemplation stage.

- **Self-reevaluation.** A person's cognitive and affective assessments of their self-image in relation to the problem behaviour (e.g. thinking that stopping smoking is part of being a responsible person). This process is a mediator between the contemplation stage and the preparation stage.

- **Self-liberation.** A person's belief in their ability to change a particular behaviour and their commitment to act on that belief. This process is a mediator between the preparation stage and the action stage.

- **Helping relationships.** Relationships characterised by openness, trust and empathy, which are supportive in regards to the problem behaviour and health behaviour change. This process is a mediator between the action stage and the maintenance stage.

- **Counter conditioning.** The adoption of healthier behaviours as substitutes for problem behaviours. This process is a mediator between the action stage and the maintenance stage.

- **Stimulus control.** When a person makes changes to their environment so that cues for problem behaviours are reduced and cues for healthier behaviours increased. This process is a mediator between the action stage and the maintenance stage.

- **Reinforcement management.** This occurs when a person is rewarded (by themselves or by others) for engaging in healthy behaviours, or conversely when they are punished for not engaging in healthy behaviours. This process is a mediator between the action stage and the maintenance stage.

- **Social liberation.** Noticing social, policy or environmental changes that facilitate health behaviour change (e.g. noticing that society has changed in ways that may smoking cessation easier).

Intervening Variables

There are two additional variables that influence movement from stage to stage: **decisional balance** and **self-efficacy**. Decisional balance is influential in the decision to move toward action, and is defined as an evaluation of the pros (advantages and positive aspects) and cons (disadvantages or negative aspects) of behaviour change. If the balance of pros and cons is such that there are more pros than cons then change is more likely. In contrast if there are more cons than pros, there is a barrier to change. The balance between pros and cons differs from stage to stage, with pros beginning to outweigh cons early in the contemplation stage.

Self-efficacy is defined as a person's beliefs about their ability to carry out a behaviour in any given situation. Self-efficacy relates to both behaviour change and to **temptations** to carry out the problem behaviour. Self-efficacy influences the use of processes of change during the different stages whilst temptation influences relapse. High temptation levels and low self-efficacy are characteristic of the precontemplation stage, with this gap narrowing during the contemplation and preparation stages. Early in the action stage, self-efficacy and temptation levels are in balance, with self-efficacy rising and temptation falling over time.

Movement through the Stages of Change with Cycles of Relapse

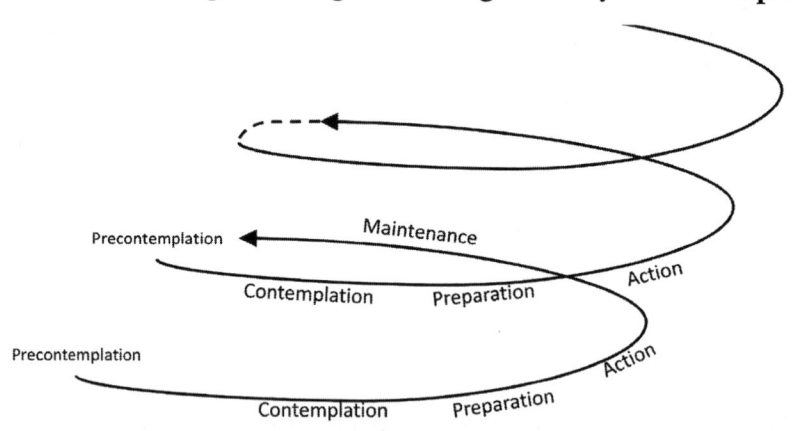

Source: Prochaska, J. O., DiClemente, C. C., & Norcross, J. C. (1992). In search of how people change: Applications to addictive behaviour. *American Psychologist*, 47, 1102-1114. Originally published by APA and reprinted here with permission.

Contributing Theories:

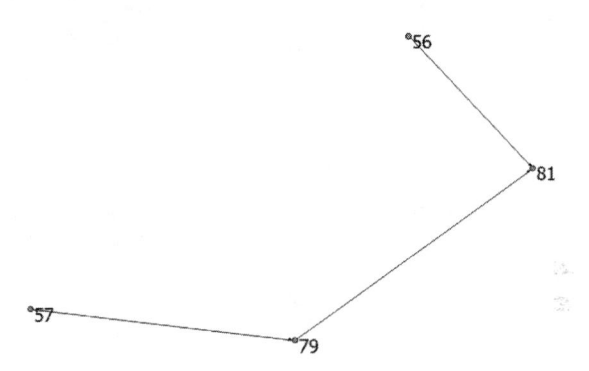

°56
　　　°81
°57
　　°79

As outlined in the network diagram, the following theory included within this book was identified as contributing to the development of the Transtheoretical Model of Behaviour Change:

57. Self-Efficacy Theory

Taken from:

Prochaska, J.O. & DiClemente, C.C. (1982). Transtheoretical therapy: Toward a more integrative model of change. *Psychotherapy: Theory, Research and Practice*, 19(3), 276-288.

Prochaska, J.O., DiClemente, C.C., & Norcross, J.C. (1992). In search of how people change: Applications to addictive behaviour. *American Psychologist*, 47, 1102-1114.

Supplemented by:

Prochaska, J. O., Redding, C.A., Harlow, L.L., Rossi, J.S. & Velicer, W.F. (1994). The Transtheoretical Model of Change and HIV Prevention: A Review. *Journal of Consulting and Clinical Psychology*, 21, 471-486.

83. Value Belief Norm Theory (Stern et al.)

Constructs

- Personal values
    - Altruistic values
    - Egoistic values
    - Traditional values
    - Openness to change values
- New ecological paradigm
- Awareness of consequences
- Ascription of responsibility
- Personal moral norms
- Environmental activism
- Environmental citizenship
- Policy support
- Private-sphere behaviours

Brief Summary

Value Belief Norm Theory aims to explain support for social movements, particularly pro-environmental movements. People who accept the values of a movement and hold a belief that things they value are endangered (and that their actions can mitigate that danger) will experience a sense of responsibility to act in support of that movement.

Description

Value Belief Norm Theory aims to explain environmentalism and conservation behaviour. It proposes a casual chain of values, beliefs and norms that lead to support for a social movement (specifically environmentalism). According to the model, each variable in the chain affects the next, and may affect variables more than one level down the 'chain'. There are five levels in the causal chain which progress from relatively stable, core elements of people's personality and beliefs to more focused beliefs (e.g. about human-environment interactions, their consequences and personal responsibility for minimising negative consequences). These five levels are termed **'personal values'**, **'new ecological paradigm'**, **'awareness of consequences'**, **'ascription of responsibility to self'** and **'personal moral norms'**.

Personal Values

Pro-environmental behaviour is linked to four distinct types of personal values: **altruistic values, egoistic values, traditional values** and **openness to change values**. Altruistic values are particularly important in influencing pro-environmental behaviours, whilst egoistic and traditional values have a negative influence on environmentalism.

New Ecological Paradigm

In the next step of the causal chain, personal values are followed by the 'new ecological paradigm'. This is defined as a person's 'worldview' – more specifically a view that human actions can have significant effects upon the environment and biosphere – and acceptance of this worldview is related to pro-environmental behaviour.

Awareness of Consequences

Acceptance of the 'new ecological paradigm' is followed by 'awareness of consequences' (i.e. the belief that environmental conditions can impact upon humans, other species and the biosphere) and pro-environmental behaviour is dependent upon a person holding this belief.

Ascription of Responsibility to Self

The fourth step of the causal chain is 'ascription of responsibility to self' (i.e. a person's belief that their actions could prevent the consequences realised in the previous step) and pro-environmental behaviour is dependent upon this belief being present.

Personal Moral Norms

Pro-environmental 'personal moral norms' are activated in people who hold an awareness of the consequences of environmental conditions and accept that their actions can reduce those consequences. Personal moral norms are defined as the perception that one is personally obligated to act. Activation of these norms leads to pro-environmental behaviours that are supportive of a social movement. Four distinct types of behaviours are identified in the theory: environmental activism (e.g. participation in demonstrations, involvement in social movement organisations), environmental citizenship (e.g. contributing funds to movement organisations, contacting political officials), policy support (e.g. support and acceptance of relevant policies such as mandatory recycling) and private-sphere behaviours (e.g. making reductions in energy use).

A diagram of Value Belief Norm Theory can be found on p.84 of Stern, Dietz, Abel, Guagnano & Kalof (1999).

Contributing Theories:

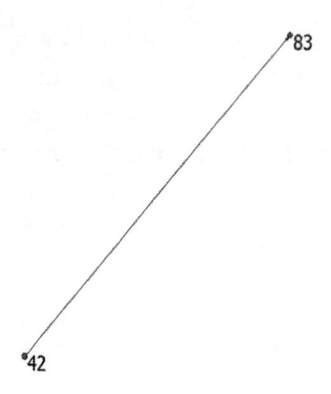

As outlined in the network diagram, the following theory included within this book was identified as contributing to the development of Value Belief Norm Theory:

42. Norm Activation Theory

Taken from:

Stern, P.C., Dietz, T. Abel, T., Guagnano, G.A. & Kalof, L. (1999). A Value-Belief-Norm Theory of Support for Social Movements: The Case of Environmentalism. *Research in Human Ecology*, 6(2), 81-97.

Chapter 5 Use of theory for intervention development: looking to the future

The project that led to this book set out to harness knowledge and expertise across four academic disciplines (psychology, sociology, anthropology and economics) to identify theories of behaviour change that have potential to inform the development of effective interventions. Even using strict selection criteria, we identified a large number of theories (83). This final chapter reflects on the main conclusions arising from this exercise, discusses its limitations and considers how theory development and use can be improved.

Current state of theories

Insights from the theories

It is apparent that the theories reviewed capture a large number of important and useful insights into behaviour and how it can be changed.

A common insight is the importance of considering motivation, ability and the facilities and barriers arising from the physical and social environment as top level factors that need to be considered (e.g. the COM-B model, the Needs-Opportunities-Abilities Model, and the Motivation-Opportunities-Abilities Model).

When it comes to motivation, reflective choice processes are mostly captured by variants of Subjective Expected Utility theory. Under this model we weigh up the costs and benefits of different courses of action according to the desirability or otherwise of a given outcome following a course of action weighted by how likely we think that outcome is to occur. Prospect Theory adds crucial insights to this formula by noting the biases that operate to make us act differently when the same information is presented in different ways. The Theory of Planned Behaviour treats as separate the perceived ability to enact a behaviour and perceived evaluation by others if we engage in a behaviour. It is interesting that other decision theory approaches such as Multi-Attribute Utility Theory and Production Rules did not feature in most of the theories covered by the review. These also provide important insights into choice processes and would be worth further attention.

Many theories recognise the importance of emotions, habits and imitation as part of the motivational system and therefore key drivers of behaviour. Affective Events theory applies this to performance at work. Risk as Feelings Theory considers how thoughts and feelings interact to generate behaviour. Operant and Classical conditioning theories clearly provide a strong foundation for theories involving habit learning and generation of emotional responses, although their influence was not generally made explicit. It is noteworthy that biological drives appear not to have been considered in most theories.

When it comes to capability, a common insight arising from the theories was the importance of self-regulatory skills and capacity. This was most evident in broadly based theories such as Social Cognitive Theory and the I-Change Model. Social skills were also noted as important for certain kinds of behaviour, for example HIV risk behaviours.

The role of the environment was widely recognised, with some theories focusing primarily on it and others integrating it with intra-personal factors. The concept of social norms was brought in in slightly different ways by many theories and in some cases differentiations were made between different types of social norm.

Several theories proposed that behaviour change involves going through a series of stages. The most commonly used of these is the Transtheoretical Model. The extent to which the process of change is best thought of in this way or as fluid and dynamic has been the subject of debate and reviews of interventions based on stage-based models have not found these to offer an advantage over other models.

One attraction of stage-based approaches is that they offer a basis for tailoring interventions. For example, it seems logical that individuals who are not considering changing their behaviour would be most influenced by motivational types of intervention while those who were in the process of changing might benefit more from interventions focusing on self-regulatory skills and capacity. Those who had already changed may benefit most from interventions focusing on vigilance to prevent lapses. The Relapse Prevention Model takes this further in proposing insights into how lapses can be prevented from turning into full blown relapse. More dynamic and fluid models such as PRIME Theory still offer the potential for tailoring on these factors, but also take account of evidence that a wide variety of change trajectories need to be accommodated. For example, it has been noted that approximately half of attempts to quit smoking appear to happen without pre-planning and these are at least as likely to be successful as those that are planned. It has also been noted that offering support for quitting smoking to all smokers, regardless of their putative stage of change, can result in a higher proportion stopping than seeking to move smokers in pre-contemplation forward by a stage. Given the popularity of stage-based theories in intervention design, it will be important to examine further how best to characterise the change process and tailor interventions accordingly.

Several of the theories are explicitly synthetic or integrative, seeking to capture all the important concepts involved in understanding behaviour, or at least providing a peg-board on to which concepts contained within specific theories can be hung. The CEOS Model, PRIME Theory and the I-Change Model are three such attempts. The CEOS Model and PRIME Theory both make a strong statement about how reflective, thoughtful analysis and emotional, habitual and instinctive processes combine to generate behaviour. They follow the ancient metaphor of the rider and the elephant in which the rider (our self-conscious reflective selves) does not have direct control over our behaviour, but has to communicate with and influence the elephant (our emotional, instinctive and habitual selves) in order to do so. At the same time, the elephant is influencing the rider, for example in leading us to believe things that we want to believe. This is distinct from the Reflective Impulsive Model which proposes that these two interacting systems operate in parallel. It is not clear at this stage how this hierarchical versus parallel distinction for 'reflective' and 'automatic' processes in the control of behaviour can be operationalised for the purposes of testing. This is an area that merits further investigation.

These integrative theories were developed explicitly to bring together diverse theories and observations about behaviour. PRIME Theory had its origins in the field of addiction while the CEOS focuses on hard-to-maintain behaviours. With such a wide body of theory covered by the present review, the task of assessing how far these or other theories truly have the capacity to embrace the full range of insights offered by more specific behaviour change theories has become tractable. This is something that we intend to pursue over the coming months and years.

Perhaps the most striking impression to emerge from the theories reviewed in this book is the wealth of insights they provide. This strongly supports the view presented at the beginning of this book that intervention designers should canvass widely from these theories for ideas to bring into their interventions. As we have noted, we are only at the beginning of developing systems for efficient searching of the theories and selection of constructs. But at the very least intervention designers can now more easily identify what is on offer.

Although, the story to emerge from this review of theories is generally very positive, the review did identify a number of issues that the field needs to address to make progress. We now turn to these.

Reporting of theories

The process of identifying and characterising theories of behaviour change was hampered by inadequate reporting of the theories, even to the extent that it was often difficult to judge whether propositions were or were not part of the theories being proposed. Definitions of constructs were often not clear or not provided, and construct terminology was not consistent, with different terms used interchangeably for the same construct in the same theory. Specification of relationships between constructs was often limited to lines in a diagram without clear indication of what those lines meant. When theory proponents presented or critiqued alternative theories, they often failed to indicate whether or how their proposed theory was informed by this existing work.

There is a clear need for a consistent language that can be used to describe theories. This language should use a consistent terminology for key constructs and relationships between these. This terminology should make clear whether constructs are intended to be interpreted as events or processes that can be mapped on to the real world, or are abstractions that have no physical manifestation linked to structures and events in time and space. They should also make clear where and why constructs have been modified from ones that have been proposed in other theories.

Theory overlap

Although we identified a very large number of different construct labels, 1659 in total, many of these appeared to be alternative labels for essentially the same construct. However, due to a lack of precise definitions, there was insufficient information to group the constructs with confidence. Similarly, there was considerable overlap in the use of constructs between theories.

Focus on cognition and static structures

We found that the most widely used theories emphasised reflective cognitive processes such as intention, attitudes and beliefs, and those that take account of the more automatic processes of habit, emotions, drives and impulses have not achieved such traction. The most popular theories also seemed to take relatively little account of context, and yet there are clearly major insights to be gleaned from those that do.

It is also of note that the most widely used theories are statistical and static, in the sense that the paths of influence represent co-variance in populations between measured constructs. Only a few of the theories explicitly invoked a dynamic structure with change over time being directly modelled. Dialectical relationships, such as synergistic influences and transformation of quantitative into qualitative changes are extremely difficult to model but work is starting to develop on this with dynamic systems models and agent based models.

Focus on current behaviour rather than generating behaviour change

While, as a whole, the theories identified a wide range of explanatory factors, with some notable exceptions (e.g. the Transtheoretical Model, CEOS Theory and PRIME Theory,), few theories specify explicitly how to bring about change. Most accounted for variation in patterns of behaviour within populations rather than explaining how behaviour changes within individuals over time. In the future, it would worth theories paying greater attention to explicit modelling of change processes.

Theory modifications

Since evidence does not stand still, one would not expect theory to do so. Some theories within the compendium were updated by authors, reflecting authors' evolving thoughts or new constructs and relationships within the theory, informed by the emergence of new evidence that either supported or refuted parts of the initial theory. However, this occurred in only a small minority of cases. Where there was evidence of theory development, there was little evidence that this informed theories more broadly.

Some theories represented small changes to previous theories, but the authors considered the changes sufficient to warrant labelling the theory 'new'. This raises the questions of what constitutes a 'new' theory and what are the advantages and disadvantages of adding theories with slight modifications on the basis of one or two studies rather than sticking with existing theories and building a weight of evidence before rejecting, refining, or developing.

On the one hand, it is undesirable for the field to be limited to theories that are not fit for purpose and constrain scientific thinking and study. On the other, the field will advance most efficiently if there is co-ordinated, systematic testing of current theories across research groups with a shared perspective about when theories should be abandoned and when and how to move from a body of empirical evidence to theory development.

Connectedness of theories

While 64% of theories within the compendium named at least one theory within this book as contributing to their development, only 22% of theories identified more than two. The theories with the highest 'out-degree' centrality scores were Social Cognitive Theory, the Health Belief Model, the Theory of Planned Behaviour and Self-Efficacy Theory with each of these theories contributing to the development of at least 10 theories within the compendium. These theories are older than others within the compendium and are among the theories most often used in health behaviour research (Painter et al., 2008) and used by physical activity and dietary interventions (Prestwich et al., 2013).

Limitations of the current review

This review had a number of important limitations that it is hoped will be addressed in future iterations. The decision to focus on theories that explicitly included behaviour led to exclusion of some major theories that have clear implications for behaviour, including a number of important theories of decision making. Also our decision to exclude theories concerned with group behaviour may be part of the explanation for the preponderance of psychological theories identified in the review, although even interventions aimed at targeting communities tend to be informed by psychological or social-psychological theories (NICE 2007; Glanz and Bishop 2010; Bonell et al 2013a; Bonell et al 2013b). This, and the decision not to include books, where sociological and anthropological theories are more likely to be found, may go some way to explaining why these types of theory are under-represented. In addition, Kelly et al (2010) found that sociological theories were missed in electronic searches, particularly if they were more than 25 years old. This had knock-on effects when it came to the network analysis in that these theories could not then be considered as having influenced theories that we did include. This was most notable for integrative theories such as CEOS Theory and PRIME Theory.

The poor theory description and lack of a standard way of describing theories was a major barrier to characterising and summarising the theories. In addition it was often suspected that theories had been influenced by previous theories but this was not made sufficiently explicit for the connection to be reliably established.

The need to summarise theories in a relatively limited space meant that we could not do full justice to the more complex theories. This was particularly evident for integrative theories.

The network analysis focused on explicit provenance relationships, that is, clear reference to a theory that informed a later theory. There are many other ontologies that could have been established, including one linking theories in terms of their constructs or the behaviours on which they focus.

It was originally intended that the theories would be evaluated in terms of a set of quality criteria. Although these criteria were established, it was not possible to apply these systematically and establish reliability for such judgements within the time frame of the project.

With these limitations in mind, the compendium achieved must be considered as a preliminary attempt and it will be essential to continue the work to improve and refine it so as to improve its usefulness.

The way forward

Updating the compendium using the website

There are several practical ways in which the work described in this book can be taken forward. One of these is for readers to use the website to propose amendments to the theory descriptions where they believe that these are inadequate or wrong. We propose to use proceeds from the sale of the book to fund updates based on these insights.

We also hope that readers will propose theories that were missed from the review but which would have met our criteria for inclusion, or new theories. Clearly it will be necessary to limit inclusion according to our criteria or a slight relaxing of the criteria, but it is very likely that there are important theories in the literature that could usefully be added.

Applying quality criteria

Having established a set of quality criteria for evaluating theories (See Chapter 1) the next step is to operationalise the criteria and establish whether they can be reliably applied to theories in this compendium. If these criteria, or ones derived from them, were found to be able to be applied reliably, the results could help inform the choice of theories for intervention design.

Developing a system for theory modification and replacement

The issue of how much, and what kind of, evidence is appropriate to trigger theory modification remains unresolved. If new theories were to be published on the basis of one or two studies that suggested an amendment to a current theory, the field would become fragmented. The complexity of behaviour change interventions means that they may function differently when delivered by different modes and in different contexts. It is often not clear whether a failure to replicate findings that have tested theoretical propositions constitutes evidence against the theory or evidence that elaborates the theory by adding moderators to tested causal relationships. The answers to questions about the implications of empirical evidence for theoretical understanding and development are likely to differ according to the type of theory and the purpose or purposes it is serving. These are fundamental questions about which cross-disciplinary discussion and consensus are urgently needed to advance theory testing and development.

Guidelines on reporting of theories

A major unexpected finding arising from this review was the inadequacy of theory descriptions in the literature. It is worth reminding ourselves what theories are and what they are for. Theories consist of one or more propositions (which can be expressed in narrative, mathematical or graphical form), which seek to explain a set of phenomena in terms of a set of constructs and the relationships between them. They are used to help provide an understanding of the phenomena within their scope, and to generate new ideas relating to the phenomena including ideas for observations about it, and predictions regarding as yet unobserved phenomena. In the behavioural and social sciences they are used in the creation of interventions to change behaviour.

Unfortunately, the value of theories is undermined by poor description. The constructs are often inadequately defined as are the relationships between them. Their provenance is often unclear and discussion of previous theories is usually limited and incomplete. It is often unclear what predictions the theory would make and how these differ from other theories. Even the scope of theories is often not described sufficiently to determine where it would and would not be expected to make predictions.

In the behavioural and social sciences, guidelines such as CONSORT have considerably improved the design and reporting of studies (Schulz, Altman, & Moher, 2010). They are clearly needed for the reporting of theories. We present here a set of proposals that might contribute to such guidelines.

To be maximally useful the guideline development process should follow the tried and tested approach used for CONSORT (Moher, Schulz, Simera, & Altman, 2010). If funding can be obtained, this will take months or years to set up and at least a year to complete. In the meantime we have used our experience in preparing this compendium to generate a set of proposals that may provide a useful *aide memoire*.

Table 5.1 presents proposals for a checklist that could be used by authors and journals in the same ways as CONSORT is currently used. It includes the item, a description of the item and an example involving a simple 'dummy' theory. Note that the theory is not being proposed as a serious theory but is just being used to illustrate how a theory description would be written.

Table 5.1 Preliminary proposals for guidelines for theory description

Item	Description	Example
Name	What is the name of the theory (including an acronym if appropriate)?	The Theory of Unplanned Behaviour (TUB)
Brief summary	What is the theory about and what are its main propositions?	This theory aims to complement the Theory of Planned Behaviour to explain behaviours that are not pre-planned. It proposes that the probability of a given unplanned behaviour (B) occurring over a given time period is proportional to strength of the impulse(s) to engage in that behaviour (I) which in turn is proportional to 1) habit strength (H), 2) emotional valence (V), and 3) facilitatory context (C).
Scope	What phenomena does the theory seek to explain?	The TUB aims to explain behaviours that are not pre-planned in the sense that they occur without or despite self-conscious analysis of the costs and benefits.
Target	Is the theory about individuals, populations, or social structures (e.g. organisations)?	The TUB is about individuals
Type	What broad type of theory is it? (statistical, realist, dynamic, narrative [2])	The TUB is a statistical theory
Rationale	Why is the theory needed and how does the theory improve on any previous theories?	The TUB is needed because, while the TPB and other social cognitive models address behaviours that are planned (as defined above), we lack a statistical theory that serves the same function for unplanned behaviours, bringing together influences from habit learning, biological drives, emotional reactions and the current social and physical environment in a way that can use survey responses to explain and predict relevant behaviours.

2 Statistical theories express the influence that constructs have on each other in terms of the probability that a construct will take on a certain value as a function of values taken by other constructs; realist theories explicitly express causal connections between constructs in a way that can in principle (though not necessarily in practice) be mapped on to physical structures and events; dynamic theories propose ways in which values of constructs change over time as a function previous values and other constructs; narrative theories express constructs and the relationships between them as linguistic propositions without specifying any particular mathematical functions.

Constructs	What are the elements of the theory, indicating in each case whether they are hypothetical constructs[3]?	Unplanned behaviour (B): A behaviour that occurs without or despite self-conscious analysis of the costs and benefits. Such behaviours can be divided into those that are 'automatic' (occurring without any conscious awareness), and 'semi-automatic' (occurring with conscious awareness but driven by emotional valence and/or habit). Impulse (I): A hypothetical construct representing the net impulse strength arising from action and inhibition tendencies. Emotional valence (V): The strength of feeling of want or need to engage in the behaviour. Want involves a feeling of anticipated pleasure or satisfaction. Need refers to a feeling of anticipated relief from mental or physical discomfort. Habit strength (H): A hypothetical construct representing the strength of stimulus-impulse association relating the behaviour to the context.
Relationships	How are the elements of the theory related to each other?	$p(B) = c_1 + f(x.I) + e_1$ $I = c_2 + y.V + z.H + w.C + e_2$ where c_1 and c_2 are constants between 0 and 1, e_1 and e_2 are error distributions, f is as logit function, and x, y, z and w are regression coefficients, B is the unplanned behaviour in question, I is impulse strength, V is emotional valence, and C is strength of facilitatory context Graphically, and less specifically, the TUB takes the following form, where arrows denote 'influence': V → I, H → I, C → I, I → B

3 Hypothetical constructs are entities, structures or processes which are invented to explain observed phenomena but which may not have a direct physical manifestation

Provenance	What theories does it draw on and how?	The TUB draws on: 1. Hull's theory of habit strength by adopting its definition of habit 2. Learning theory (operant and classical) in terms of the process by which Context elicits emotional valence and habit 3. Drive theory in terms of ways that biological drives influence emotional valence 4. PRIME Theory in terms of integrating habits, emotions, drives and context into a model of behaviour
Similarity	What theories is this theory most like?	The TUB is most like: 1. The Theory of Planned Behaviour in terms of structure
Complementarity	What theories can this one be used alongside?	The TUB can be used alongside: 1. The Theory of Planned Behaviour where it is unclear how far the behaviour of interest is governed primarily by beliefs and intentions or automatic processes 2. Self-Regulation Theory where it is unclear how far ability to achieve self-control and strategies for self-regulation as important for the behaviour in question 3. Multiple theories of emotions, drives, habits and context that could help explain or predict values of V, H and C.

Operationalisation	How, if at all, are the constructs measured or identified?	B is operationalised by observation or self-report of occurrence of the behaviour in the time period in question
		'I' may need to be inferred but could be operationalised as self-rating of strength or 'urges' to engage in the behaviour
		V is operationalised by a self-rating of strength 'want or need' to engage in the behaviour
		H is operationalised as self-rating of extent to which the behaviour occurs without any evident desire or goal in mind
		C is operationalised in terms of an aggregated score of presence in the environment of presumed facilitators and absence of presumed barriers
Hypotheses	What specific hypotheses does the theory make and how do these differ from other theories?	The theory hypothesises that the probability of unplanned behaviours will be a linear function of measures of net impulse (where this can be measured) and that this will mediate independent linear associations between measures of valence, habit strength and context.
		The theory predicts that the variance in I and B accounted for by V, H and C will be a function only of the variance in those independent variables.
Uses	What can the theory be used for?	The TUB can be used to help explain variation in a given population in incidence of a range of behaviours and aid a behavioural diagnosis that may underpin design of a behaviour change intervention. It may also be used to model the effect size of interventions that are hypothesised to influence valence, habit or context to varying degrees.

It is hoped that readers will be motivated to see to what extent they can frame existing theories in terms of this template and to use the template to construct new theories. In order to improve this template, we ask readers to feed back their experiences of using it to the authors through the website **www.behaviourchangetheories.com**.

From theory to intervention

Intervention designers who acknowledge the potential usefulness of drawing on theory are faced with a question: For target behaviour X for population Y, in context Z with constraints W on intervention delivery, which theory is likely to be most appropriate and informative? In order to answer this question, we need to unpack the "black boxes" of complex interventions which obscure their active ingredients and mechanisms of action. To do this, we need a shared language to describe and organise their inner workings.

Work has begun to do this, identifying a simple Behaviour Change Ontology linking five elements: 1) behaviours, 2) theories and constructs, 3) BC techniques, 4) modes of delivery and 5) contexts, including target population and setting (An, Michie, Larsen, & Bickmore, 2014).

Figure 5.1 A scheme for a simple behaviour change ontology

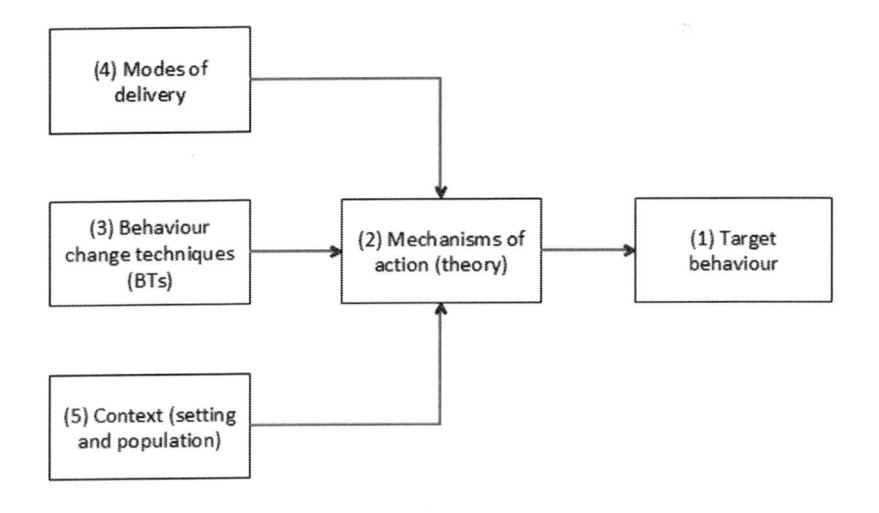

Such an ontology can address the challenges presented by complexity, concept ambiguity and knowledge fragmentation by formally and transparently organising knowledge within a domain. Work on this has been started in the case of behaviour change techniques, with the development of 93 behaviour change techniques organised into 16 groupings (Michie et al., 2013). This compendium and the Theoretical Domains Framework represent small steps towards codifying our collective knowledge about theory and component constructs. Empirical work to build on these to develop a methodology to link behaviour change techniques to theoretical constructs is ongoing (Michie, Johnston, Rothman, Kelly, & de Bruin, 2014). A behaviour change ontology will be invaluable not only for intervention design but also for using the findings from intervention evaluations to test and modify theories (Rothman, 2004).

In the absence of such an ontology, a more generic theoretical assessment using the Behaviour Change Wheel and/or Theoretical Domains Framework (Michie, Atkins, et al., 2014) can be used to identify the psychological, social and/or environmental domains to target by a behaviour change intervention. This assessment can be used to narrow the range of relevant theories, thus assisting selection to some degree, or to point to general intervention functions that are likely to be effective, that can then be translated into behaviour change techniques and supporting policies. A step-by-step guide to this approach has been written as a companion volume to this compendium (Michie, Atkins, et al., 2014).

Theory testing and application

There are imperatives other than scientific ones for developing new theories and for supporting theories despite conflicting evidence. Although most scientific advance comes about through the slow and systematic accumulation of bodies of evidence, some research cultures incentivise 'innovation' which may push researchers into declaring a new theory on a body of evidence that doesn't warrant it, for the sake of appearing 'innovative'. On the other hand, some theories may be sustained by large companies and empirically based challenge to the veracity of that theory would be seen as a threat to associated financial gain and personal prestige. In such cultures of perverse incentives, it is all the more important that a concerted and collaborative effort to develop methods for advancing theory are agreed and adhered to.

There have been important developments in study design to support theory testing. Following Weinstein's call to use experimental methods to test theory (rather than use of cross-sectional surveys to test hypothetical causal associations) (Weinstein, 2007), examples of refinements such as fractionated factorial designs (Collins, Murphy, Nair, & Strecher, 2005) and n-of-1 experiments (Johnston & Mills, 2004) have been published. Technological advances in the objective measurement of behaviour in real-time have also opened up doors for theory testing. With the means of accurately measuring behaviour through accelerometers, and a range of sensors in smartphones, clothes and objects, as people go about their everyday lives, the possibility is provided of measuring, predicting and explaining *change*.

An example of such a paradigm was a study of tens of thousands of people passing through motorway toilets, where their entrance into the toilet area and use of soap was monitored. A variety of theory-based messages were electronically displayed above the sinks, for an hour at a time, in random order 24 hours a day and the impact on ratio of toilet to soap users calculated (Judah et al., 2009).

Digital interventions, computer and smartphone-based, provide a sea-change in the possibilities of large amounts of rapidly collected, ecologically valid data for theory testing. Tens of thousands of users can provide data across many comparison conditions and these can be varied iteratively as theoretical propositions are confirmed, or contradicted. The nature of the intervention means that its fidelity is assured: usage data demonstrate what the user accessed, for how long and in what order. Thus, bodies of knowledge can systematically, efficiently and rapidly be accumulated. Combined with accurate measures of behaviour, this makes for a powerful research, and behaviour change, tool.

Final observations

This book represents the output from an ambitious project. It is clearly only a first step along the way to a true science of behaviour change involving key academic disciplines talking a common language and making use of a common corpus of evidence and theory. Arguably what we have at the moment is a form of pre-science where many of the elements that make up a science are present but they have not be integrated into a systematic method.

Even pre-science has its uses. The theories presented in this book contain a wealth of insights and it is hoped that by presenting readers with a wider range of options from which to choose when deciding what knowledge they wish to use to achieve behaviour change, better use will be made of the work of others in the field.

Taking forward this enterprise will require more than capability. It will often require the motivation to put science and its application ahead of personal standing. The imperative to make one's name by inventing a new theory will often need to be subordinated to the need for advancement and coherence in our science. We will need to be motivated to be much more respectful of what has gone before in terms of acknowledging its contribution and building on it, rather than simply starting again and duplicating much of the effort.

Advancing the field will also require opportunity. Scientists working in the field will need to be funded adequately for the developmental work and basic behavioural science from which we may later be able to create an improved technology. The current trend towards short-term funding of applied research designed to achieve a particular practical result will have to be balanced by more programmatic research designed to advance understanding. We will not reach the stars by looking for ever taller trees to climb – we will need to spend time evolving a technology that allows us to build spaceships.

References

Abraham, C., Kelly, M. P., West, R., & Michie, S. (2009). The UK National Institute for Health and Clinical Excellence public health guidance on behaviour change: a brief introduction. *Psychology, Health and Medicine, 14*(1), 1-8.

Ajzen, I. (1991). The theory of planned behaviour. *Organisational behaviour and human decision processes, 50*(2), 179-211.

Albada, A., Ausems, M. G., Bensing, J. M., & van Dulmen, S. (2009). Tailored information about cancer risk and screening: a systematic review. *Patient Education and Counseling, 77*(2), 155-171.

Albarracin, D., Gillette, J. C., Earl, A. N., Glasman, L. R., Durantini, M. R., & Ho, M. H. (2005). A test of major assumptions about behaviour change: a comprehensive look at the effects of passive and active HIV-prevention interventions since the beginning of the epidemic. *Psychological Bulletin, 131*(6), 856-897. doi: 10.1037/0033-2909.131.6.856

Amemori, M., Michie, S., Korhonen, T., Murtomaa, H., & Kinnunen, T. H. (2011). Assessing implementation difficulties in tobacco use prevention and cessation counselling among dental providers. *Implementation Science, 6*, 50. doi: 10.1186/1748-5908-6-50

Ammerman, A. S., Lindquist, C. H., Lohr, K. N., & Hersey, J. (2002). The efficacy of behavioural interventions to modify dietary fat and fruit and vegetable intake: a review of the evidence. *Preventive Medicine, 35*(1), 25-41.

An, L. C., Michie, S., Larsen, K. R., & Bickmore, T. W. (2014). *Panel Discussion: Resolving the Tower of Babel Problem in Behavioural Theories: Benefits of and Developments in Behavioural Ontologies to Support Intervention Programs for Behaviour Change* Paper presented at the 35th Annual Meeting & Scientific Sessions of the Society of Behavioural Medicine, Philadelphia.

Armitage, C. J., & Conner, M. (2001). Efficacy of the Theory of Planned Behaviour: a meta-analytic review. *Br J Soc Psychol, 40*(Pt 4), 471-499.

Bandura, A. (1998). Health promotion from the perspective of social cognitive theory. *Psychology & Health, 13*(4), 623-649. doi: 10.1080/08870449808407422

Bhattarai, N., Prevost, A., Wright, A., Charlton, J., Rudisill, C., & Gulliford, M. (2013). Effectiveness of interventions to promote healthy diet in primary care: systematic review and meta-analysis of randomised controlled trials. *BMC Public Health, 13*(1), 1-14. doi: 10.1186/1471-2458-13-1203

Blumer, H. (1986). *Symbolic interactionism: Perspective and method.* Englewood Cliffs, NJ: Prentice-Hall.

Bonell, C., Fletcher, A., Morton, M., Lorenc, T., & Moore, L. (2012). Realist randomised controlled trials: a new approach to evaluating complex public health interventions. *Soc Sci Med, 75*(12), 2299-2306. doi: 10.1016/j.socscimed.2012.08.032

Campbell, M., Fitzpatrick, R., Haines, A., Kinmonth, A. L., Sandercock, P., Spiegelhalter, D., & Tyrer, P. (2000). Framework for design and evaluation of complex interventions to improve health. *BMJ (Clinical Research Ed.), 321*(7262), 694-696.

Campbell, N. C., Murray, E., Darbyshire, J., Emery, J., Farmer, A., Griffiths, F., . . . Kinmonth, A. L. (2007). Designing and evaluating complex interventions to improve health care. [Review]. *BMJ, 334*(7591), 455-459. doi: 10.1136/bmj.39108.379965.BE

Campbell, R., & Bonell, C. (in press). Development and Evaluation of complex multi-component interventions in public health. In B. Detels R, Lansang MA, Gulliford M. (Ed.), *Oxford Textbook of Public Health. (6th edition).* Oxford: OUP.

Cane, J., O'Connor, D., & Michie, S. (2012). Validation of the theoretical domains framework for use in behaviour change and implementation research. *Implementation Science, 7.* doi: 10.1186/1748-5908-7-37

Carlile, P. R., & Christensen, C. M. (2004). *The cycles of theory building in management research. Harvard Business School Working Paper No. 05–057.* Boston: Harvard Business School.

Coleman, T. (2010). Do financial incentives for delivering health promotion counselling work? Analysis of smoking cessation activities stimulated by the quality and outcomes framework. *Bmc Public Health, 10.* doi: 10.1186/1471-2458-10-167

Collins, L. M., Murphy, S. A., Nair, V. N., & Strecher, V. (2005). A strategy for optimizing and evaluating behavioural interventions. *Annals of Behavioural Medicine, 30*(1), 65-73.

Conner, N., & Norman, P. (2005). *Predicting Health Behaviour: Research and Practice with Social Cognition Models* (Second ed.). Buckingham Open University Press

Craig, P., Dieppe, P., Macintyre, S., Michie, S., Nazareth, I., & Petticrew, M. (2008). Developing and evaluating complex interventions: the new Medical Research Council guidance. *BMJ, 337*. doi: 10.1136/bmj.a1655

Cutrona, S. L., Choudhry, N. K., Stedman, M., Servi, A., Liberman, J. N., Brennan, T., . . . Shrank, W. H. (2010). Physician effectiveness in interventions to improve cardiovascular medication adherence: a systematic review. [Research Support, N.I.H., Extramural Review]. *Journal of general internal medicine, 25*(10), 1090-1096. doi: 10.1007/s11606-010-1387-9

Davies, P., Walker, A. E., & Grimshaw, J. M. (2010). A systematic review of the use of theory in the design of guideline dissemination and implementation strategies and interpretation of the results of rigorous evaluations. *Implementation Science, 5*. doi: 10.1186/1748-5908-5-14

Dixon-Woods, M., Bosk, C. L., Aveling, E. L., Goeschel, C. A., & Pronovost, P. J. (2011). Explaining Michigan: developing an ex post theory of a quality improvement program. *Milbank Q, 89*(2), 167-205. doi: 10.1111/j.1468-0009.2011.00625.x

Dyson, J., Lawton, R., Jackson, C., & Cheater, F. (2010). Does the use of a theoretical approach tell us more about hand hygiene behaviour? The barriers and levers to hand hygiene. *Journal of Infection Prevention.* doi: 10.1177/1757177410384300

Ezzati, M., Lopez, A. D., Rodgers, A., Vander Hoorn, S., Murray, C. J. L., & Coll, C. R. A. (2002). Selected major risk factors and global and regional burden of disease. *Lancet, 360*(9343), 1347-1360. doi: 10.1016/S0140-6736(02)11403-6

Francis, J. J., O'Connor, D., & Curran, J. (2012). Theories of behaviour change synthesised into a set of theoretical groupings: introducing a thematic series on the theoretical domains framework. [Editorial, Research Support, Non-U.S. Gov't]. *Implementation Science, 7*, 35. doi: 10.1186/1748-5908-7-35

Fuller, C., Michie, S., Savage, J., McAteer, J., Besser, S., Charlett, A., . . . Stone, S. (2012). The Feedback Intervention Trial (FIT)--improving hand-hygiene compliance in UK healthcare workers: a stepped wedge cluster randomised controlled trial. *PLoS ONE, 7*(10), e41617. doi: 10.1371/journal.pone.0041617

Gardner, B., Wardle, J., Poston, L., & Croker, H. (2011). Changing diet and physical activity to reduce gestational weight gain: a meta-analysis. *Obesity Reviews, 12*(7), e602-620. doi: 10.1111/j.1467-789X.2011.00884.x

Gigerenzer, G. (2010). Personal Reflections on Theory and Psychology. *Theory & Psychology, 20*(6), 733-743. doi: 10.1177/0959354310378184

Glanz, K., & Bishop, D. B. (2010). The Role of Behavioural Science Theory in Development and Implementation of Public Health Interventions. *Annual Review of Public Health, Vol 31, 31,* 399-418. doi: 10.1146/annurev.publhealth.012809.103604

Glanz, K., Rimer, B. K., & Viswanath, K. (2008). *Health behaviour and health education: theory, research, and practice*: John Wiley & Sons.

Grimshaw, J. M., Thomas, R. E., MacLennan, G., Fraser, C., Ramsay, C. R., Vale, L., . . . Donaldson, C. (2004). Effectiveness and efficiency of guideline dissemination and implementation strategies. *Health Technology Assessment, 8*(6), iii-iv, 1-72.

Grol, R. (2001). Successes and failures in the implementation of evidence-based guidelines for clinical practice. *Medical Care, 39*(8 Suppl 2), II46-54.

Grol, R., & Grimshaw, J. (1999). Evidence-based implementation of evidence-based medicine. *The Joint Commission journal on quality improvement, 25*(10), 503-513.

Grol, R., & Wensing, M. (2004). What drives change? Barriers to and incentives for achieving evidence-based practice. *The Medical journal of Australia, 180*(6 Suppl), S57-60.

Guillaumie, L., Godin, G., & Vezina-Im, L. A. (2010). Psychosocial determinants of fruit and vegetable intake in adult population: a systematic review. *International Journal of Behavioural Nutrition and Physical Activity, 7,* 12. doi: 10.1186/1479-5868-7-12

Hardeman, W., Sutton, S., Griffin, S., Johnston, M., White, A., Wareham, N. J., & Kinmonth, A. L. (2005). A causal modelling approach to the development of theory-based behaviour change programmes for trial evaluation. *Health education research, 20*(6), 676-687. doi: 10.1093/Her/Cyh022

Hartmann-Boyce, J., Stead, L. F., Cahill, K., & Lancaster, T. (2013). Efficacy of interventions to combat tobacco addiction: Cochrane update of 2012 reviews. *Addiction, 108*(10), 1711-1721. doi: 10.1111/add.12291

Head, K., Noar, SM. . (2013). Facilitating progress in health behaviour theory development and modification: the reasoned action approach as a case study. *Health Psychology Review.*

House of Lords Science and Technology Select Committee. (2011). *Behaviour Change. 2nd Report for Session 2010-12.* London: The Stationery Office Limited (on authority of the House of Lords).

Johnston, B. C., & Mills, E. (2004). N-of-1 randomized controlled trials: an opportunity for complementary and alternative medicine evaluation. *Journal of Alternative and Complementary Medicine, 10*(6), 979-984. doi: 10.1089/acm.2004.10.979

Judah, G., Aunger, R., Schmidt, W.-P., Michie, S., Granger, S., & Curtis, V. (2009). Experimental pretesting of hand-washing interventions in a natural setting. *American Journal of Public Health, 99*(Suppl 2), S405-S411. doi: 10.2105/AJPH.2009.164160

Kaner, E. F., Dickinson, H. O., Beyer, F., Pienaar, E., Schlesinger, C., Campbell, F., ... Heather, N. (2009). The effectiveness of brief alcohol interventions in primary care settings: a systematic review. *Drug Alcohol Rev, 28*(3), 301-323. doi: 10.1111/j.1465-3362.2009.00071.x

Kelly, M., Morgan, A., Ellis, S., Younger, T., Huntley, J., & Swann, C. (2010). Evidence based public health: A review of the experience of the National Institute of Health and Clinical Excellence (NICE) of developing public health guidance in England. *Social Science and Medicine, 71*(6), 1056-1062. doi: 10.1016/j.socscimed.2010.06.032

Kim, N., Stanton, B., Li, X., Dickersin, K., & Galbraith, J. (1997). Effectiveness of the 40 Adolescent AIDS-Risk Reduction Interventions: A Quantitative Review. *Journal of Adolescent Health, 20*(3), 204-215. doi: 10.1016/s1054-139x(96)00169-3

Kotz, D., Brown, J., & West, R. (2014). "Real-world" effectiveness of smoking cessation treatments: a population study. *Addiction, 109*(3), 491-499. doi: 10.1111/add.12429

Lewin, K. (1951). Field theory in social science. In D. Cartwright (Ed.), *Selected theoretical papers*. New York: Harper & Row.

Lim, S. S., Vos, T., Flaxman, A. D., Danaei, G., Shibuya, K., Adair-Rohani, H., ... Ezzati, M. (2012). A comparative risk assessment of burden of disease and injury attributable to 67 risk factors and risk factor clusters in 21 regions, 1990?2010: a systematic analysis for the Global Burden of Disease Study 2010. *The Lancet, 380*(9859), 2224-2260.

Lipsey, M. W. (2004). Theory as method: Small theories of treatments. *New directions for program evaluation, 1993*(57), 5-38.

Marteau, T., Dieppe, P., Foy, R., Kinmonth, A. L., & Schneiderman, N. (2006). Behavioural medicine: changing our behaviour - A growing body of evidence shows how to make behavioural interventions effective. *British Medical Journal, 332*(7539), 437-438. doi: 10.1136/bmj.332.7539.437

McKenzie, J., O'Connor, D., Page, M., Mortimer, D., French, S., Walker, B., . . . Green, S. (2010). Improving the care for people with acute low-back pain by allied health professionals (the ALIGN trial): A cluster randomised trial protocol. *Implementation Science, 5*(1), 1-17. doi: 10.1186/1748-5908-5-86

Meehl, P. E. (1978). Theoretical risks and tabular asterisks: Sir Karl, Sir Ronald, and the slow progress of soft psychology. *Journal of consulting and clinical Psychology, 46*(4), 806-834.

Michie, S. (2008). Designing and implementing behaviour change interventions to improve population health. *Journal of Health Services Research and Policy, 13*(suppl 3), 64-69. doi: 10.1258/jhsrp.2008.008014

Michie, S., & Abraham, C. (2004). Interventions to change health behaviours: Evidence-based or evidence-inspired? *Psychology & Health, 19*(1), 29-49. doi: 10.1080/0887044031000141199

Michie, S., Atkins, L., & West, R. (2014). *The Behaviour Change Wheel: A Guide to Designing Interventions.* London: Silverback Publishing.

Michie, S., Johnston, M., Abraham, C., Lawton, R., Parker, D., Walker, A., & Grp, P. T. (2005). Making psychological theory useful for implementing evidence based practice: a consensus approach. *Quality & Safety in Health Care, 14*(1), 26-33. doi: 10.1136/qshc.2004.011155

Michie, S., Johnston, M., Francis, J., Hardeman, W., & Eccles, M. (2008). From theory to intervention: Mapping theoretically derived behavioural determinants to behaviour change techniques. *Applied Psychology-an International Review-Psychologie Appliquee-Revue Internationale, 57*(4), 660-680. doi: 10.1111/j.1464-0597.2008.00341.x

Michie, S., Johnston, M., Rothman, A. J., Kelly, M., & de Bruin, M. (2014). Developing methodology for designing and evaluating theory-based complex interventions: an ontology for linking behaviour change techniques to theory: Medical Research Council.

Michie, S., & Prestwich, A. (2010). Are interventions theory-based? Development of a theory coding scheme. *Health Psychology, 29*(1), 1-8. doi: 10.1037/a0016939

Michie, S., Richardson, M., Johnston, M., Abraham, C., Francis, J., Hardeman, W., . . . Wood, C. E. (2013). The behaviour change technique taxonomy (v1) of 93 hierarchically clustered techniques: building an international consensus for the reporting of behaviour change interventions. *Annals of Behavioural Medicine, 46*(1), 81-95. doi: 10.1007/s12160-013-9486-6

Michie, S., van Stralen, M. M., & West, R. (2011). The behaviour change wheel: A new method for characterising and designing behaviour change interventions. *Implementation Science, 6.* doi: 10.1186/1748-5908-6-42

Michie, S., & West, R. (2013). Behaviour change theory and evidence: a presentation to Government. *Health Psychology Review, 7*(1), 1-22. doi: 10.1080/17437199.2011.649445

Moher, D., Schulz, K. F., Simera, I., & Altman, D. G. (2010). Guidance for Developers of Health Research Reporting Guidelines. *PLoS Medicine, 7*(2), e1000217. doi: 10.1371/journal.pmed.1000217

Mokdad, A. H., Marks, J. S., Stroup, D. F., & Gerberding, J. L. (2004). Actual causes of death in the United States, 2000. *Jama-Journal of the American Medical Association, 291*(10), 1238-1245. doi: 10.1001/jama.291.10.1238

Moser, R. P., Hesse, B. W., Shaikh, A. R., Courtney, P., Morgan, G., Augustson, E., . . . Coa, K. (2011). Grid-Enabled Measures: Using Science 2.0 to Standardize Measures and Share Data. American Journal of Preventive Medicine, 40(5, Supplement 2), S134-S143. doi: http://dx.doi.org/10.1016/j.amepre.2011.01.004

National Institute for Health and Care Excellence. (2007). *Behaviour change at population, community and individual levels.* London: National Institute for Health and Care Excellence.

National Institute for Health and Care Excellence. (2014). *Behaviour change: individual approaches.* London: National Institute for Health and Care Excellence.

Nigg, C. R., Allegrante, J. P., & Ory, M. (2002). Theory-comparison and multiple-behaviour research: common themes advancing health behaviour research. *Health education research, 17*(5), 670-679. doi: 10.1093/Her/17.5.670

Noar, S. M., Benac, C. N., & Harris, M. S. (2007). Does tailoring matter? Meta-analytic review of tailored print health behaviour change interventions. *Psychol Bull, 133*(4), 673-693. doi: 10.1037/0033-2909.133.4.673

Noar, S. M., & Zimmerman, R. S. (2005). Health Behaviour Theory and cumulative knowledge regarding health behaviours: are we moving in the right direction? *Health education research, 20*(3), 275-290. doi: 10.1093/Her/Cyg113

Nutbeam, D., Harris, E (Ed.). (2004). *Theory in a Nutshell: A Guide to Health Promotion Theory* . New York: McGraw-Hill Book Company.

Painter, J. E., Borba, C. P. C., Hynes, M., Mays, D., & Glanz, K. (2008). The use of theory in health behaviour research from 2000 to 2005: A systematic review. *Annals of Behavioural Medicine, 35*(3), 358-362. doi: 10.1007/s12160-008-9042-y

Pfoh, E., Dy, S., & Engineer, C. (2013). Interventions To Improve Hand Hygiene Compliance: Brief Update Review. In Agency for Healthcare Research and Quality (Ed.), *Making Health Care Safer II: An Updated Critical Analysis of the Evidence for Patient Safety Practices*. Rockville, MD: AHRQ.

Popper, K. (1959). *The Logic of Scientific Discovery, p.16*: Taylor & Francis e-Library, 2005.

Prestwich, A., Sniehotta, F. F., Whittington, C., Dombrowski, S. U., Rogers, L., & Michie, S. (2013). Does Theory Influence the Effectiveness of Health Behaviour Interventions? Meta-Analysis. *Health Psychology*. doi: 10.1037/a0032853

Rabin, B. A., Purcell, P., Naveed, S., Moser, R. P., Henton, M. D., Proctor, E. K., . . . Glasgow, R. E. (2012). Advancing the application, quality and harmonization of implementation science measures. *Implementation Science, 7*, 119. doi: 10.1186/1748-5908-7-119

Roe, L., Hunt, P., Bradshaw, H., & Rayner, M. (1997). *Health promotion interventions to promote healthy eating in the general population: a review*: Health Education Authority London.

Rothman, A. J. (2004). "Is there nothing more practical than a good theory?": Why innovations and advances in health behaviour change will arise if interventions are used to test and refine theory. *International Journal of Behavioural Nutrition and Physical activity, 1*(11), doi:10.1186/1479-5868-1181-1111.

Rothman, A. J. (2009). Capitalizing on Opportunities to Refine Health Behaviour Theories. *Health Education & Behaviour, 36*, 150s-155s. doi: 10.1177/1090198109340514

Sabaté, E. (2003). *Adherence to long-term therapies: evidence for action*. Geneva: World Health Organisation.

Sabatino, S. A., Lawrence, B., Elder, R., Mercer, S. L., Wilson, K. M., DeVinney, B., . . . Glanz, K. (2012). Effectiveness of interventions to increase screening for breast, cervical, and colorectal cancers: nine updated systematic reviews for the guide to community preventive services. *Am J Prev Med, 43*(1), 97-118. doi: 10.1016/j.amepre.2012.04.009

Schulz, K. F., Altman, D. G., & Moher, D. (2010). CONSORT 2010 Statement: updaterd guidelines for reporting parallel group randomised trials. *BMJ, 340,* c332. doi: http://dx.doi.org/10.1136/bmj.c332

Schuster, M. A., McGlynn, E. A., & Brook, R. H. (1998). How good is the quality of health care in the United States? *Milbank Quarterly, 76*(4), 517-563, 509.

Sheeran, P., Gollwitzer, P. M., & Bargh, J. A. (2013). Nonconscious processes and health. *Health Psychology, 32*(5), 460-473. doi: 10.1037/a0029203

Skinner, E. A. (1996). A guide to constructs of control. *J Pers Soc Psychol, 71*(3), 549-570.

Solomon, S., & Kington, R. (2002). National efforts to promote behaviour-change research: views from the Office of Behavioural and Social Sciences Research. *Health education research, 17*(5), 495-499. doi: 10.1093/Her/17.5.495

Stephenson, J. M., Imrie, J., & Sutton, S. R. (2000). Rigorous trials of sexual behaviour interventions in STD/HIV prevention: what can we learn from them? *AIDS, 14 Suppl 3,* S115-124.

Summerbell, C. D., Waters, E., Edmunds, L. D., Kelly, S., Brown, T., & Campbell, K. J. (2005). Interventions for preventing obesity in children. *Cochrane Database of Systematic Reviews*(3). doi: 10.1002/14651858.CD001871.pub2

Swann, C., Bowe, K., Kosmin, M., & McCormick, G. (2003). *Teenage pregnancy and parenthood: a review of reviews. Evidence briefing*: Health Development Agency London.

Taylor, N., Conner, M., & Lawton, R. (2011). The impact of theory on the effectiveness of worksite physical activity interventions: a meta-analysis and meta-regression. *Health Psychology Review,* 6(1), 33-73. doi: 10.1080/17437199.2010.533441

Taylor, N., Sahota, P., Sargent, J., Barber, S., Loach, J., Louch, G., & Wright, J. (2013). Using intervention mapping to develop a culturally appropriate intervention to prevent childhood obesity: the HAPPY (Healthy and Active Parenting Programme for Early Years) study. *International Journal of Behavioural Nutrition and Physical Activity,* 10(1), 1-16. doi: 10.1186/1479-5868-10-142

US National Institutes of Health. (2014). *Grid Enabled Measures: Constructs.* https://www.gem-beta.org/public/ConstructList.aspx?cat=1 accessed on 13.01.2014.

Webb, L. T., Joseph, J., Yardley, L., & Michie, S. (2010). Using the Internet to Promote Health Behaviour Change: A Systematic Review and Meta-analysis of the Impact of Theoretical Basis, Use of Behaviour Change Techniques, and Mode of Delivery on Efficacy. *J Med Internet Res,* 12(1), e4.

Weinstein, N. D. (2007). Misleading Tests of Health Behaviour Theories. *Annals of Behavioural Medicine,* 33(1), 1-10. doi: 10.1207/s15324796abm3301_1

Weiss, C. H. (1995). Nothing as practical as good theory: exploring theory-based evaluation for comprehensive community initiatives for children and families. In K. A. C. Connell J. P. , Weiss L. B. S., & C. H. (Ed.), *New approaches to evaluating community initiatives: Concepts, methods, and contexts*. Washington DC: Aspen Institute.

West, R., & Brown, J. (2013). *Theory of Addiction (second edition)*. Oxford: Wiley Blackwell.

West, R., & Shahab, L. (2009). Smoking cessation. In A. Killoran & M. Kelly (Eds.), *Effectiveness and efficiency in public health: systematic approaches to evidence and practice*. Oxford: Oxford University Press.

World Health Organisation. (2009). *Interventions on diet and physical activity: what works: summary report*. Geneva: WHO.

About the authors

Susan Michie

Susan Michie is Professor of Health Psychology at University College London, UK, where she is Director of the Centre for Behaviour Change (www.ucl.ac.uk/behaviour-change) and of the Health Psychology Research Group. With a background in experimental and clinical psychology, and Professor Michie has been a key player in advancing behavioural science methods, including the application of theory to developing and evaluating interventions to promote the prevention and management of ill health and the delivery of evidence-based health services. She regularly contributes to national and international policy work, including, including as co-director of the National Centre for Smoking Cessation and Training; member of NICE's Implementation Strategy Group and of its Behaviour Change Programme Guidance Development Group; Chair of the Behaviour and Communications group of the cross-Government Scientific Pandemic Influenza Advisory Group; member of Public Health England and the Department of Health's Behavioural Insights Expert Advisory Group. She is author of over 200 scientific articles and of the Behaviour Change Wheel: Guide to Designing Interventions (2014). For more information, see www.ucl.ac.uk/health-psychology/people/michie/.

Robert West

Robert West is Professor of Health Psychology and Director of Tobacco Studies at the Cancer Research UK Health Behaviour Research Centre, University College London, UK. Professor West is also Editor-in-Chief of the journal *Addiction*. He is founder of the PRIME Theory of motivation and author of Theory of Addiction. He has authored more than 500 scientific articles, books and book chapters. He was co-founder of the NHS stop-smoking services. His research includes evaluations of methods of helping smokers to stop and population surveys of smoking and smoking cessation patterns. He is author of 'The SmokeFree Formula' (Orion) which aims to bring the science of stopping to smokers and of the Behaviour Change Wheel: Guide to Designing Interventions (2014). For more information see www.rjwest.co.uk.

Rona Campbell

Rona Campbell is Professor of Public Health Research and leads the Centre for Public Health Research within the School of Social and Community Medicine at the University of Bristol. She is the Director of the UKCRC DECIPHer (Development and Evaluation of Complex Interventions for Public health Improvements) Centre, and the Bristol lead for the NIHR School for Public Health Research. Rona leads programmes of research concerned with multiple risk behaviour in adolescence and health promotion in schools. She is currently involved in conducting a number of systematic reviews, including Cochrane Reviews of the WHO Health Promoting School Framework and of interventions to prevent multiple risk behaviours in young people. Rona has a strong interest in methodological research, including, how to use qualitative methods alongside quantitative approaches, how to synthesise qualitative research findings and how to make better use of social and behavioural theory in public health research. Rona has published over 150 scientific works. For more information see:

www.bristol.ac.uk/social-community-medicine/people/rona-m-campbell/

Jamie Brown

Jamie Brown is a chartered psychologist and Senior Research Fellow of the Society for the Study of Addiction at University College London. Dr Brown has published widely on the relative effectiveness of different methods for stopping and reducing the harm from smoking, has also written about the operation of learning mechanisms in a number of different contexts, and has co-authored the second edition of the book 'Theory of Addiction' together with Professor West. He is currently involved in the management of a number of national surveillance programmes of smoking behaviour and alcohol consumption, and in developing and evaluating a variety of digital interventions to change different health behaviours. He also teaches on the BSc and MSc Health Psychology courses at UCL and acts as an Assistant Editor at the journal *Addiction*.

Heather Gainforth

Heather Gainforth, PhD is a researcher with the UK's National Centre for Smoking Cessation and Training (NCSCT) and is a member of the Health Psychology Research Group at University College London, UK. She has been awarded a Fellowship from the Canadian Institutes of Health Research. Her research focuses on examining social and psychological factors that foster behaviour change in general and in special populations, developing and evaluating interventions, and understanding the process of implementing evidence-based practice. This includes finding ways of improving the delivery of behavioural support for smoking cessation.

For more information see
www.researchgate.net/profile/Heather_Gainforth